W9-BSZ-298

Publishing Economics

Publishing Economics

Analyses of the Academic Journal Market in Economics

Edited by

Joshua S. Gans
Melbourne Business School, University of Melbourne, Australia

Edward Elgar
Cheltenham, UK • Northampton, MA, USA

Published by
Edward Elgar Publishing Limited
Glensanda House
Montpellier Parade
Cheltenham
Glos GL50 1UA
UK

Edward Elgar Publishing, Inc.
136 West Street
Suite 202
Northampton
Massachusetts 01060
USA

A catalogue record for this book
is available from the British Library

Library of Congress Cataloguing in Publication Data
Publishing economics : analyses of the academic journal market in economics /
edited by Joshua Gans.
    Includes index.
        1. Economics literature—Publishing. 2. Scholarly publishing. I. Gans,
Joshua, 1968–

HB74.5.P83 2000
070.5—dc21   99–089245

ISBN 1 84064 283 1

Printed and bound in Great Britain by MPG Books Ltd, Bodmin, Cornwall

Contents

PART THREE: TO CO-AUTHOR OR NOT TO CO-AUTHOR

PART FOUR: THE INFLUENCE OF ECONOMICS JOURNALS

Introduction

Joshua S. Gans

When I was a PhD student at Stanford University, I had a unique experience that gave me some insight into the demand of the economics profession; at least its academic side. By "demand," I am talking about what academic economists care passionately about; namely, the publication process. What universally captured the attention of some of the profession's most noted contributors were not new ideas on unemployment, inflation, poverty, environmental issues or how close price is to short-run marginal cost. Instead, it was whether our process of identifying the most valuable of these ideas actually worked. It is this issue that appears to capture the attention of academic economists at all levels. As this volume is a collection of papers of economists looking introspectively at the publication process in the profession I thought it would be useful to recount that experience.

It began when George Shepherd, also a Stanford graduate student, and I surveyed leading economists, asking them to reflect on difficulties they faced in publishing their most influential pieces. The idea for this survey came to us during a lecture by Professor Ken Arrow in his History of Economic Thought class. He had mused about the difficulties his teacher, Harold Hotelling, had in publishing his famous paper on exhaustible resources – one of the first papers to formalise an economic problem using the tools of dynamic optimisation. Keynes at the *Economic Journal* had initially rejected that paper. This story caused us to wonder whether this experience of rejection accompanied other influential works.[1]

As it turned out no inquiry into rejection had yet been undertaken and, furthermore, there were plenty of folk legends of such rejection to wet our appetite. So George and I crafted a letter and sent it to 130 leading economists inviting them to tell us any tales of rejection.

The response was immediate and overwhelming. We had clearly struck a nerve. Almost 80 percent replied, many with several pages of tales and their own thoughts about the efficiency of the publication process. It was surprising to have discovered an issue that ignited such fervor. Respondents vividly recounted how their initial work was rejected time and time again.

They recalled precise referee and editor comments. They admitted the misgivings this gave them about their career. And they expressed their concern that little had changed today and how their students faced similar difficulties.

The result of this survey is included as Chapter 3 of this volume.[2] That article, publishing by the *Journal of Economic Perspectives*,[3] reviewed the response to the survey and revealed just how many famous economic papers were initially rejected by some of the leading journals of their time. Hotelling's story was one of many; indeed, the sheer number of important results that faced initial negative reviews was a surprise to many.

The article itself had an intense response after it went to press. It spurred debate as to whether there was a flaw in the way the profession identified important work.[4] Was it part of a conservatism in economics or a natural consequence of the early novelty of such research? Was it something to do with economics and the application of the scientific method or the difficulties associated with separating values inherent in policy goals from pure economic analysis? Did this happen in other disciplines?[5] More than one journal editor indicated to me that the article gave them pause to think carefully about negative reviews and their decision to reject.

The article also influenced how researchers considered their own publication experience. On one level, by highlighting the difficulties of the profession's finest, it comforted many people that their own experience of rejection (and it was very rare to find someone without many) was not unusual. On another level, the article gave some people the impression that their work may have been rejected unreasonably and that it was the system and not the substance of their work that was at fault. Thus, there is a tension between empathy and complacency in the attitudes readers took from the stories of rejection. The former is a positive effect but the latter did concern me somewhat.[6]

Nonetheless, the experience of writing the "rejections" article and observing the reaction to it signaled several things to me. First, economists were extremely interested in the practices of their profession. Second, they applied economic logic to those practices. (It was easy to couch the accept/reject decision in terms of the probabilities of Type I and Type II errors.) And, finally, by looking at their own practices, it was possible to gain some insight about the way economic processes worked. In the case of rejection this involved determining the value and hence, demand for ideas in a world of uncertainty. All of these suggested to me that there was some benefit to agglomerating some of the interesting research that economists have embarked on about the publication process in the profession. Whence, this volume.

SUCCESS AND REJECTION IN ECONOMICS

The papers selected for this volume all involve economists applying economic analysis to uncover truths about the publication process. Most of the papers are empirical but there are some theoretical contributions as well. Some are whimsical while others involve a more serious analytical exercise. All have in common that they were published in some of the discipline's leading journals thereby indicating the general interest of such lines of research.

The volume begins with the less serious of these contributions; the "rejections" paper (Chapter 3) included among them. Chapter 1 reprints Axel Leijonhufvud's classic "Life Among the Econ." This article captured the attention of its generation of economists and, in so many ways, its sentiment still rings true today. Leijonhufvud reviews the economics profession as if it were an isolated tribe (the "Econ") in a less technological sophisticated age. The members of the "Econ" are motivated purely by peer acceptance and achieve this by carving ever more elaborate "modls." Upon reading this chapter, one is challenged to consider what value economic modeling has to society and also how the profession values it. How do we determine whether one piece of economic theory is valuable or not; especially when the distance from basic contribution to real world policy analysis can be so far?

The next paper (Chapter 2) offers friendly advice for new lecturers and assistant professors in economics. Daniel Hamermesh runs the gauntlet of taking a PhD dissertation to the journals, amalgamating the wisdom of those that have traveled that path and in the process cautioning young economists against game playing and warning them about the rocky road ahead. The "Guide to Etiquette" has, in many ways, become the graduation gift of choice for new academics.

Turning to more serious academic exercises, in Chapter 4, Sharon Oster and Daniel Hamermesh conduct an empirical analysis of the determinants of research productivity by academic economists (as measured by the quality of the journal they publish in).[7] They find that research productivity declines with age but that early success does breed later relative success. Moreover, this decline is not because of any difference in rejection rates for older researchers suggesting that the decline is more on the supply-side than any demand-side bias. Like many of the chapters in this volume, when looking for bias and discrimination in the publication process, scant evidence is forthcoming.

REFEREES AND EDITORS

The next set of chapters of this volume deal explicitly with the review process itself; that is, how peer review actually works and what behaviour characterizes editorial decision making. Chapter 5 is a useful starting point in this exercise. There, Daniel Hamermesh again takes a close examination of who referees and what they do. He finds that, in general, referees are more established than those they are refereeing. Moreover, there appears to be no bias in the assignment of "good" referees; that is, such referees are assigned regardless of factors such as age or inexperience. Hamermesh also examines the time lags associated with refereeing. In this regard, there appears to be evidence of "types"; that is, referees either are diligent or they are not. In addition, monetary rewards rarely assist in speeding up the process (an issue we return to in Chapter 9).

Reinforcing Hamermesh's work is an earlier study by David Laband (Chapter 6). That study, using a survey of editors at several journals, examined whether the referee process was merely about screening the quality of papers or whether the process itself assisted in generating higher quality research. Laband found that screening was not the only factor and that referees did "add value" to papers. Editors, in contrast, did not play this role and assisted the process by matching papers to appropriate referees.

In Chapter 7, Rebecca Blank also informed an old debate about refereeing; namely, does author secrecy alter their chances of rejection? Double blind refereeing is argued to minimize bias from elitism and other forms of discrimination. Against this are arguments that referees can utilize identity to assist in reviewing (that is, expressing confidence about complex mathematical proofs) and besides, they can identify authors anyway. Blank utilized a controlled experiment conducted in the late 1980s at the *American Economic Review*. She found that acceptance rates were lower and reviews more critical when the author's identity was unknown. There appeared little bias in acceptance rates but papers from near-top institutions or non-academic institutions were more likely to be accepted when reviewing was double blind. Finally, for double blind refereeing, approximately 55 percent of reviewers claimed to be able to identify the author concerned.

Like Hamermesh and Blank, David Laband and Michael Piette (Chapter 8) also examine potential bias in the review process. They are concerned with common accusations that certain journals associated with certain schools and editors in general treated their own students more favourably than others in accepting papers. They utilize citations as an indicator of paper quality and assess whether accepted papers by economists identified closely with editors are of lower quality than other papers. While there is evidence that these editors accept some poor quality papers, it appears that editor connections (controlling for other determinants of paper quality) improve rather than detract from average paper quality. Laband and Piette conclude that any favouritism that exists may assist in attracting better quality papers with personal connections biasing an economist's decision regarding where to submit their paper. This could be argued to reduce potential transaction costs in the market for economic ideas.

In contrast to the above studies, Maxim Engers and I use economic theory to examine of the question of monetary rewards for referees (Chapter 9). Referees are paid little if at all. With the concerns about reviewing times and referee quality, this was somewhat puzzling. After all, would not journal quality be improved if some money could be spent improving the refereeing process? Against this argument were claims that refereeing activity was conducted out of non-monetary motives such as "service to the profession" and a personal concern for journal quality. However, this did not explain why referees might not be motivated by monetary reward as well. Our theoretical examination took both arguments seriously and found that it was the interaction of the two that explained the almost inelastic supply response of referees to monetary incentives; as alluded to by Hamermesh's (Chapter 5) study. The reason was that while monetary rewards might improve direct incentives for timely review; they do it for all referees. Hence, a referee also concerned about the overall efficiency of the process can rely on the existence of the high monetary reward to participate less often. In equilibrium, the cost of encouraging referees is simply too high given the small improvement in refereeing speed.

The examination of peer review and editorial selection processes is fundamental to the way in which economics ideas are disseminated. These studies indicate the usefulness of economic methods in analysing these but they also suggest the potential fruitfulness of further research using the potential wealth of data in this area.

TO CO-AUTHOR OR NOT TO CO-AUTHOR

Getting papers published is one aspect of the academic reward structure in economics. Another important aspect is the choice of whether to collaborate in your research. Choosing to go it alone means you reap all of the potential glory while collaborating means dividing it up. Of course, collaboration may improve research quality, and hence the chances of publication.

Chapter 10 deals with the division of the rents from co-authored publications. Raymond Sauer looks at how published papers feed into academic salaries. Not surprisingly, he finds that paper quality is important while co-authored papers are "worth" less in monetary terms. Indeed, the monetary value of a paper of given quality is simply divided up among co-authors. To the extent that economists are motivated by monetary concerns this suggests that co-authored papers are of higher quality than had the same research been embarked upon separately.

John Hudson (Chapter 11) reinforces the value of co-authorship by examining changes in the level of collaboration in economics. Since World War II, the percentage of multi-authored papers in top journals has gone from less than 10 to over 50 percent. Hudson demonstrates a consistent trend towards more multi-authored research; attributing it to the greater opportunities afforded by advances in transport and communications. Once again this suggests the value of collaboration in economic research.

Finally, Maxim Engers, Simon Grant, Stephen King and I (Chapter 12) – as if to prove the value of collaboration (!) – investigate the possible theoretical rationales behind the extensive use of the alphabetical ordering of names in multi-authored papers. In this volume, six of the eight multi-authored papers follow that norm. Economics stands in marked contrast to other disciplines in the social and natural sciences in this regard. The alphabetic norm means that co-authors elect to send no signal to the market regarding who contributed what to the paper. But this is in an environment where the both sides of the academic labour market would value such attribution. The ultimate reason postulated for the lack of a signal is the potential harm an alternative signal would have on co-authors with names "lower" in the alphabet; especially when the market places weight on the fact that an alphabetical ordering signals little. This harm is greater than the potential gain to the other co-author from providing such a signal, and hence they agree to follow the alphabetic convention.

Collaboration in research is a fundamental way in which higher quality research is generated. However, the issues raised in each of these studies indicate the tension between collaboration and attribution. The second feature is fundamental to individual motivations and peer acceptance in scientific fields. Once again this line of inquiry offers potential for so much more, utilizing the data that comes from already published work.

THE INFLUENCE OF ECONOMICS JOURNALS

The final part of the volume takes a selection of papers that try to measure the influence of economics journals. The papers selected are representative of that literature and are not exhaustive. However, all such papers (and associated rankings of economists) always attract wide interest and help establish leading general and field journals. As such, it is useful to include a selection here.

The three chapters take three distinct approaches to examining the influence of particular journals. The first study (Chapter 13) was initiated by the Nobel Laureate, George Stigler, and completed after his death. Using the *Social Science Citation Index*, that study looks at patterns of citation among journals. Theoretical research tends to be cited by applied researchers much more than the other way around. Core general journals cite each other more than ones in specialized fields that experience more self-citation. Finally, economics has had an important influence on related fields (such as finance).

The second study by David Laband and John Wells (Chapter 14) looks at changes in the types of papers published in the three oldest US journals. This analysis gives some insight into changes in the nature of economic journal publications over the last century. The final study, also by Laband with Michael Piette (Chapter 15) is the most recent comprehensive ranking of journals using data from the *Social Science Citation Index*. It provides an analysis of which journals have had more citations from their papers using various measure of paper quality. While other studies exist, this is a fine example of such quality rankings that are today used in departmental decision making regarding tenure and promotions. For completeness, no volume like this could be without it.

ACKNOWLEDGEMENTS

My colleagues and collaborators including Maxim Engers, Simon Grant, Stephen King and George Shepherd have stimulated my own interest in how economists have come to analyse the publication process in their own profession. But also to be acknowledged are the many participants in coffee room and conference discussions, in particular Kenneth Arrow and Scott Stern, regarding the above issues. It is their interest that motivated this volume. Finally, I wish to thank Robin Carey for her diligent assistance in formatting this volume.

Every effort has been made to trace all the copyright holders but if any have been inadvertently overlooked the publishers will be pleased to make the necessary arrangements at the first opportunity.

NOTES

1. Moreover, we were fortunate in that we only had to ask Professor Arrow himself whether such a survey had been undertaken to see whether we could fill the gap. After all, if it had been done he would surely have been one of the respondents. This is one case where a sample size of one was enough.

2. George Shepherd has taken our survey responses and put them into a book, *Rejected: Leading Economists Ponder the Publication Process*, Sun Lakes (AZ): Horton, 1995.

3. Somewhat ironically that article had one of the fastest acceptance times ever. George and I walked from class straight to Joe Stiglitz, who was then editor of the *Journal of Economic Perspectives*, who offered to publish the idea. Furthermore, he would do this even if the article were written poorly; offering to rewrite the article if we had trouble delivering a coherent version!

4. At conferences and coffee rooms for many years since I have been party to discussions arising from the article. More times than not, these debates arose in my presence without the parties knowing that I had co-authored the article. (In the words of an old American Express commercial, "Everyone knew my work but nobody knew my name!")

5. From discussions I have had it seems that the level of rejection in economics is an order of magnitude above other disciplines; in particular, natural sciences. However, I am not aware of any study identifying any systematic difference.

6. Of course, for me the article totally destroyed any possibility of sympathy from colleagues if I lament that a paper of mine was rejected. All I get is the response, "well, you should know all about that!"

7. In constructing this productivity measure, Oster and Hamermesh utilize Laband and Piette's (Chapter 15) measures of journal quality and also Sauer's (Chapter 10) finding the co-authored articles are given less weight in peer evaluation than single-authored articles.

PART ONE

Rejection and Success in Economics

1.   Life Among the Econ[*]

Axel Leijonhufvud

The Econ tribe occupies a vast territory in the far North. Their land appears bleak and dismal to the outsider, and travelling through it makes for rough sledding; but the Econ, through a long period of adaptation, have learned to wrest a living of sorts from it. They are not without some genuine and sometimes even fierce attachment to their ancestral grounds, and their young are brought up to feel contempt for the softer living in the warmer lands of their neighbours, such as the Polscis and the Sociogs. Despite a common genetical heritage, relations with these tribes are strained – the distrust and contempt that the average Econ feels for these neighbours being heartily reciprocated by the latter – and social intercourse with them is inhibited by numerous taboos. The extreme clannishness, not to say xenophobia, of the Econ makes life among them difficult and perhaps even somewhat dangerous for the outsider. This probably accounts for the fact that the Econ have so far not been systematically studied. Information about their social structure and ways of life is fragmentary and not well validated. More research on this interesting tribe is badly needed.

---

[*] Reprinted with permission of the copyright holder from the *Western Economic Journal*, Vol.11, No.3, September 1973, pp. 327-37.

University of California, Los Angeles. *(Original) Editor's Note:* Since many our young readers are, with the idealism so characteristic of contemporary youth, planning to launch themselves on a career of good deeds by going to live and work among the Econ, the editor felt that it would be desirable to invite an Econologist of some experience to write an account of this little known tribe. Diligent inquiry eventually turned up the author of the present paper. Dr. Leijonhufvud was deemed an almost perfect candidate for the assignment, for he was exiled nearly a decade ago to one of the outlying Econ villages (Ucla) and since then has not only been continuously resident there but has even managed to get himself named an elder (under what pretenses – other than the growth of a grey beard – the editor has been unable to determine).

CASTE AND STATUS

The information that we do have indicates that, for such a primitive people, the social structure is quite complex. The two main dimensions of their social structure are those of caste and status. The basic division of the tribe is seemingly into castes; within each caste, one finds an elaborate network of status relationships.

An extremely interesting aspect of status among the Econ, if it can be verified, is that status relationships do not seem to form a simple hierarchical "pecking-order," as one is used to expect. Thus, for example, one may find that A pecks B, B pecks C, and *then C pecks A*! This transitivity of status may account for the continual strife among the Econ which makes their social life seem so singularly insufferable to the visitor. Almost all of the travellers' reports that we have comment on the Econ as a 'quarrelsome race' who 'talk in of their fellow behind his back,' and so forth. Social cohesion is apparently maintained chiefly through shared distrust of outsiders. In societies with a transitive pecking-order, on the other hand, we find as a rule that an equilibrium develops in which little actual pecking ever takes place. The uncivilized anomaly that we find among the Econ poses a riddle the resolution of which must be given high priority in Econological research at this time.

What seems at first to be a further complication obstructing our understanding of the situation in the Econ tribe may, in the last analysis, contain the vital clue to this theoretical problem. Pecking between castes is traditionally not supposed to take place, but this rule is not without exceptions either. Members of high castes are not infrequently found to peck those of lower castes. While such behavior is regarded as in questionable taste, it carries no formal sanctions. A member of a low caste who attempts to peck someone in a higher caste runs more concrete risks – at the extreme, he may be ostracized and lose the privilege of being heard at the tribal midwinter councils.

In order to bring out the relevance of this observation, a few more things need to be said about caste and status in the tribe. The Econ word for caste is 'field.' Caste is extremely important to the self-image and sense of identity of the Econ, and the adult male meeting a stranger will always introduce himself with the phrase 'Such-and-such is my field.' The English root of this term is interesting because of the aversion that the Econ normally have to the use of plain English. The English words that have crept into their language are often used in senses that we would not recognize. Thus, in this case, the territorial connotation of 'field' is entirely misleading for the castes do not live apart. The basic social unit is the village, or 'dept.' The depts of the Econ always comprise members of several 'fields.' In some cases, nearly every caste may be represented in a single dept.

A comparison of status relationships in the different 'fields' shows a definite common pattern. The dominant feature, which makes status relations among the Econ of unique interest to the serious student, is the way that status is tied to the manufacture of certain types of implements, called 'modls.' The status of the adult male is determined by his skill at making the 'modl' of his 'field.' The facts (a) that the Econ are highly status-motivated, (b) that status is only to be achieved by making 'modls,' and (c) that most of these 'modls' seem to be of little or no practical use, probably accounts for the backwardness and abject cultural poverty of the tribe. Both the tight linkage between status in the tribe and modl-making and the trend toward making modls more for ceremonial than for practical purposes appear, moreover, to be fairly recent developments, something which has led many observers to express pessimism for the viability of the Econ culture.

Whatever may have been the case in earlier times, the 'fields' of the Econ apparently do not now form a strong rank-ordering. This may be the clue to the problem of the non-transitivity of individual status. First, the ordering of two castes will sometimes be indeterminate. Thus, while the Micro assert their superiority over the Macro, so do the Macro theirs over the Micro, and third parties are found to have no very determined, or at least no unanimous, opinion on the matter. Thus the perceived prestige of one caste relative to another is a non-reflexive relation. In other instances, however, the ranking is quite clear. The priestly caste (the Math-Econ) for example, is a higher 'field' than either Micro or Macro, while the Devlops just as definitely rank lower. Second, we know that these caste-rankings (where they can be made) are not permanent but may change over time. There is evidence, for examine, that both the high rank assigned to the Math-Econ and the low rank of the Devlops are, historically speaking, rather recent phenomena. The rise of the Math-Econ seems to be associated with the previously, noted trend among all the Econ towards more ornate, ceremonial modls, while the low rank of the Devlops is due to the fact that this caste, in recent times, has not strictly enforced the taboos against association with the Polscis, Sociogs, and other tribes. Other Econ look upon this with considerable apprehension as endangering the moral fiber of the tribe and suspect the Devlops even of relinquishing modl-making.

If the non-transitivity of Econ status seems at first anomalous, here at least we have a phenomenon with known parallels.[1]

GRADS, ADULTS, AND ELDERS

The young Econ. or 'grad,' is not admitted to adulthood until he has made a 'modl' exhibiting a degree of workmanship acceptable to the elders of the 'dept' in which he serves his apprenticeship. Adulthood is conferred in an intricate ceremony the village to village. In the more important villages, furthermore, (the practice in some outlying villages is unclear) the young adult must continue to demonstrate his ability at manufacturing these artifacts. If he fails to do so, he is turned out of the 'dept' to perish in the wilderness.

This practice may seem heartless, but the Econ regard it as a manhood rite sanctioned by tradition and defend it as vital to the strength and welfare of the dept. If life is hard on the young, the Econ show their compassion in the way that they take care of the elderly. Once elected an elder, the member need do nothing and will still be well taken care of.

TOTEMS AND SOCIAL STRUCTURE

While in origin the word 'modl' is simply a term for a concrete implement, looking at it only in these terms will blind the student to key aspects of Econ social structure. 'Modl' has evolved into an abstract concept which dominates the Econ's perception of virtually all social relationships-whether these be relations to other tribes, to other castes, or status relations within his caste. Thus, in explaining to a stranger, for example, why he holds the Sociogs or the Polscis in such low regard, the Econ will say that 'they do not make modls' and leave it at that.

The dominant role of 'modl' is perhaps best illustrated by the (unfortunately very incomplete) accounts we have of relationships between the two largest of the Econ castes, the 'Micro' and the 'Macro.' Each caste has a basic modl of simple pattern and the modls made by individual members will be variations on the theme set by the basic modl of the caste. Again, one finds that the Econ define the social relationship, in this instance between two castes, in terms of the respective modl. Thus if a Micro-Econ is asked why the Micro do not intermarry with the Macro, he will answer: 'They make a different modl,' or 'They do not know the Micro modl.' (In this, moreover, he would be perfectly correct, but then neither, of course, would he know the Macro modl.)

Several observers have commented on the seeming impossibility of eliciting from the member of a 'field' a coherent and intelligible account of what distinguishes his caste from another caste which does not, in the final analysis, reduce to the mere assertion that the modls are different. Although more research on this question is certainly needed, this would seem to lend considerable support to those who refer to the basic modl as the *totem* of the caste. It should be noted that the difficulty of settling this controversial question does not arise from any taboo against discussing caste with strangers. Far from being reticent, the Econ will as a rule be quite voluble on the subject. The problem is that what they have to say consists almost entirely of expressions of caste-prejudices of the most elemental sort.[2]

To the untrained eye, the totems of major castes will often look well-nigh identical. It is the great social significance attached to these minor differences by the Econ themselves that have made Econography (the study of Econ arts and handicrafts) the central field of modern Econology. As an illustration, consider the totems of the Micro and the Macro. Both could be roughly described as formed by two carved sticks joined together in the middle somewhat in the form of a pair of scissors (cf. Figure 1.1).

Certain ceremonies connected with these totems are of great interest to us because of the indications that they give about the origin of modl-making among the Econ. Unfortunately, we have only fragmentary accounts by various travellers of these ceremonies and the interpretations of what they have seen that these untrained observers essay are often in conflict. Here, a systematic study is very much needed.

The following sketchy account of the 'prospecting'-ceremony among the Macro brings out several of the riddles that currently perplex Econologists working in this area:

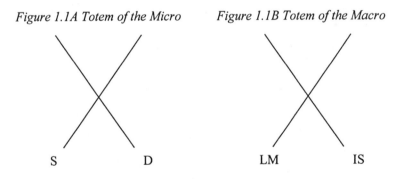

Figure 1.1A Totem of the Micro   *Figure 1.1B Totem of the Macro*

S   D   LM   IS

The elder grasps the LM with his left hand and the IS with his right and, holding the totem out in front of himself with elbows slightly bent, proceeds in a straight line – 'gazing neither left nor right' in the words of their ritual[3] – out over the chosen terrain. The grads of the village skip gaily around him at first, falling silent as the trek grows longer and more wearisome. On this occasion, it was long indeed and the terrain difficult ... the grads were strung out in a long, morose and bedraggled chain behind their leader who, sweat pearling his brow, face cast in grim determination, stumbled onward over the obstacles in his path ... At long last, the totem vibrates, then oscillates more and more; finally, it points, quivering, straight down. The elder waits for the grads to gather round and then pronounces, with great solemnity: 'Behold, the Truth and Power of the Macro.'

It is surely evident from an account such as this why such a major controversy has sprung up around the main thesis of the 'Implementarist' School. This influential Econographic School argues that the art of modl-carving has its historical origin in the making of tools and useful 'implements,' and that ceremonies such as the one described above reflect, in ritual form, the actual uses to which these implements were at one time put.

Fanciful as the 'Implementarist' hypothesis may seem, it would be injudicious to dismiss it out of hand. Whether the Macro-modl can be regarded as originally a 'useful implement' would seem to hinge in the first place on whether the type of 'prospecting' ritualized in the described ceremony produces actual results. The Macro themselves maintain that they strike gold this way. Some travelers and investigators support the contention, others dismiss it as mere folklore. The issues are much the same as those connected with attempts to appraise the divining-rod method of finding water. Numerous people argue that it works – but no scientific explanation of why it would has ever been advanced.

We do have some, apparently reliable, eyewitness' reports of gold actually being struck by the Macro. While not disputing the veracity of all such reports, skeptical critics argue that they must be heavily discounted. It is said, for example, that the Econ word for 'gold' refers to any yellowish mineral however worthless. Some Econologists maintain, moreover, that the prospecting ceremony is seldom, if ever, conducted over unknown ground and that what the eyewitnesses have reported, therefore, is only the 'discovery' of veins that have been known to the Macro for generations.

One might ask how the practice manages to survive if there is nothing to it. The answer is simple and will not be unexpected to those acquainted with earlier studies of the belief-systems of primitive peoples. Instances are known when the ceremony has not produced any concrete results. When this happens, the Macro will take either of two positions. Either he will accuse the member performing the ceremony of having failed to follow ritual in some detail or other, or else defend the man's claim that the gold is there by arguing that the digging for it has not gone deep enough.[4]

It is clear enough that, whichever position is taken, the 'phenomena are saved' in the sense that the role of the totem in the belief-system of the caste remains unassailed.

MYTHS AND MODLS

In recent years, interest in controversies about whether certain Econ modls 'work' or not (or in what sense they may be said to 'work') has dwindled. This is certainly not because the issue has been settled – it is fair to say that we are today less certain than ever of what the answers to the questions raised by the Implementarists would be. It is rather that our methodological perspective has changed so that the Implementarist issue is no longer seen as productive of 'good' questions. The 'New Econology,' as it is known, stresses *Verstehen* and, correspondingly, rejects attempts to appraise Econ belief-systems according to rationalistic criteria purloined from modern natural science.[5]

It has become increasingly clear that the Econ associate certain, to them significant, beliefs with every modl, whether or not they also claim that modl to be a 'useful tool.' That taking 'usefulness' as the point of departure in seeking to understand the totemic culture of this people leads us into a blind alley is particularly clear when we consider the Math-Econ caste.

The Math-Econ are in ways the most fascinating, and certainly, the most colorful, of Econ castes. There is today considerable uncertainty whether the 'priest' label is really appropriate for this caste but it is at least easy to understand why the early travelers came to regard them in this way. In addition to the deeply respectful attitude evidenced by the average Econ towards them, the Math-Econ themselves show many cultural patterns that we are wont to associate with religious orders or sects among other peoples. Thus they affect at poverty that is abject even by Econ standards and it seems clear that this is by choice rattier than necessity. It is told that, to harden themselves, they periodically venture stark naked out into the chill winds of abstraction that prevail in those parts. Among the rest of the Econ, who ordinarily perambulate thickly bundled in wooly clothing, they are much admired for this practice. Furthermore, glossolaila – the ability to say the same thing in several different tongues[6] – is a highly esteemed talent among them.

The Math-Econ make exquisite modls finely carved from bones of walras. Specimens made by their best masters[7] are judged unequalled in both workmanship and raw material by a unanimous Econographic opinion. If some of these are 'useful' – and even Econ testimony is divided on this point – it is clear that this is purely coincidental in the motivation for their manufacture.

There has been a great deal of debate in recent years over whether certain Econ modls and the associated belief-systems are best to be regarded as religious, folklore and mythology, philosophical and 'scientific,' or as sports and games. Each category has its vocal proponents among Econologists of repute but very little headway has been made in the debate.

The ceremonial use of modls (see above) and the richness of the general Econ culture in rituals has long been taken as evidence for the religious interpretation. But, as one commentator puts it, 'If these beliefs are religious, it is a religion seemingly without faith.' This interpretation seems to have stranded on this contradiction in terms and presently is not much in favor. More interesting are the arguments of those who have come to view certain Econ belief-systems as a form of quasi-scientific cosmological speculation. As an illustration, Mrs. Robinson's description of what she terms the 'Doctrine of K,' which is found prevalent among the members of the powerful Charles River villages, inevitably brings to mind the debates of the ancient Ionian philosophers over whether water, air, or fire was the 'basic stuff' of the universe. The Doctrine of K bears, in fact, striking resemblances to the teachings of Anaximander.[8] It is known, moreover, that in some other depts a 'Doctrine of M' is taught but we do not as yet have an understandable account of it and know, in fact, little about it except that it is spurned (as heresy?) by the Charles River Econ. Spokesmen for the cosmology view buttress their arguments by pointing out the similarities between the Math-Econ and the Pythagorean brotherhood. Whether the Math-Econ know it or not, they point out, they do obey the ancient Pythagorean principle that 'philosophy must be pursued in such a way that its inner secrets are reserved for learned men, trained in Math.'

The sports and games interpretation has gained a certain currency due to accounts of the modi-ceremonies of the Intern caste.[9] But even here it is found that, though the ceremony has all the outward manifestations of a game, it has to the participants something of the character of a morality play which in essential respects shapes their basic perception of the world.

THE ECON AND THE FUTURE

It would be to fail in one's responsibility to the Econ people to end this brief sketch of life in their society without a few words about their future. The prospect for the Econ is bleak. Their social structure and culture should be studied now before it is gone forever. Even a superficial account of their immediate and most pressing problems reads like a veritable catalogue of the woes of primitive peoples in the present day and age.

They are poor – except for a tiny minority, miserably poor. Their population growth rate is among the highest in the world. Their land is fairly rich, but much of the natural resources that are their birthright has been sold off to foreign interests for little more than a mess of pottage. Many of their young are turning to pot and message. In their poverty, they are not even saved from the problems of richer nations – travellers tell of villages half-buried in the refuse of unchecked modl-making and of the eye-sores left on the once pastoral landscape by the random strip-mining of the O'Metrs. It is said that even their famous Well Springs of Inspiration are now polluted.

In the midst of their troubles, the Econ remain as of old a proud and warlike race. But they seem entirely incapable of 'creative response' to their problems. It is plain to see what is in store for them if they do not receive outside aid.

One may feel some optimism that the poverty problems *can* be solved. While population growth may slow down in time, one can have little hope that the ongoing disintegration of Econ culture will be halted or could be reversed. Here the sad and familiar story of a primitive people's encounter with 'modern times' is repeating itself once again. The list of symptoms is long and we will touch only on a few.

Econ political organization is weakening. The basic political unit remains the dept and the political power in the dept is lodged in the council of elders. The foundations of this power of the elders has been eroding for some time, however. Respect for one's elders is no more the fashion among the young Econ than among young people anywhere else. Authority based on age and experience has weakened as recognized status has come increasingly to be tied to cleverness in modl-making. (As noted before, many elders will be inactive as modl-makers.) Although dept establishments have responded to these developments by cooptation of often very young modl-makers as 'elders,' the legitimacy of the political structure in the eyes of the Econ people is obviously threatened – and the chances of a constructive political response to the tribe's problems correspondingly lessened.

The Econ adult used to regard himself as a lifelong member of his dept. This is no longer true – migration between depts is nowadays exceedingly common and not even elders of a village necessarily regard themselves as permanent members. While this mobility may help them to cope with the poverty problem, it obviously tends further to weaken political organization. Urbanization should be noted as a related problem – many villages are today three or four times as large as only a generation or two ago. Big conurbations, with large transient populations, and weak and ineffective political machinery – we are all familiar with the social ills that this combination breeds.

Under circumstances such as these, we expect alienation, disorientation, and a general loss of spiritual values. And this is what we find. A typical phenomenon indicative of the break-up of a culture is the loss of a sense of history and growing disrespect for tradition. Contrary to the normal case in primitive societies, the Econ priesthood does not maintain and teach the history of the tribe. In some Econ villages, one can still find the occasional elder who takes care of the modls made by some long-gone hero of the tribe and is eager to tell the legends associated with each. But few of the adults or grads, noting what they regard as the crude workmanship of these dusty old relics, care to listen to such rambling fairytales. Among the younger generations, it is now rare to find an individual with any conception of the history of the Econ. Having lost their past, the Econ are without confidence in the present and without purpose and direction for the future.

Some Econographers disagree with the bleak picture of cultural disintegration just given, pointing to the present as the greatest age of Econ Art. It is true that virtually all Econographers agree that present modl-making has reached aesthetic heights not heretofore attained. But it is doubtful that this gives cause for much optimism. It is not unusual to find some particular art form flowering in the midst of the decay of a culture. It may be that such decay of society induces this kind of cultural 'displacement activity' among talented members who despair of coping with the decline of their civilization. The present burst of sophisticated modl-carving among the Econ should probably be regarded in this light.

NOTES

1. Cf., e.g., the observations concerning the Indian *jajmani*-system in Manning Nash, *Primitive and Peasant Systems*, Scranton, Pa., 1966, pp. 93ff, esp. p. 94: 'For example, goldsmiths give polluting services to potters, and the potters receive pollution from herders, who in turn give polluting services to goldsmiths. In this exchange of ritually crucial interaction the goldsmiths see themselves above the potters and below the herders, but the herders are below the potters, yet above the goldsmith caste.' Precisely.
2. This observation is far from new. One finds it recorded, for example, in Machluyp's *Voyages* in the account of "The Voyage of H.M.S. Semantick to the Coast of Econland."
3. The same wording appears in the corresponding Micro-ritual. It is reported that the Macro belittle the prospecting of the Micro among themselves saying that the Micro 'can't keep from gazing right.' The Micro, on their side, claim the Macro 'gaze left.' No one has offered a sensible hypothesis to account for this particular piece of lithurgical controversy. Chances are that far-fetched explanations are out of place and that this should simply be accepted as just another humdrum example of the continual bickering among the Econ.
4. The latter rationalization is the more palatable since it put blame on a different caste, namely the O'Maitres or O'Metrs (transcriptions vary) who do the digging work of both the Macro and the Micro.
    The 'diggers' caste is of special interest to those concerned with the underdevelopment of the Econ. Traditionally the lowest Econ caste, the O'Metrs, were allowed to perform only the dirtiest manual tasks and – more

significant in Econ eyes – lacked a totem of their own. In more recent times, however, it is through this caste that industrialization has begun to make some inroads among the Econ. Free from the prejudices instilled through an education concentrating on modl-carving and the associated totemic beliefs, the O'Metrs take willingly to modern machinery and have become quite proficient for example, at handling power shovels and power mills. The attitude of the rest as one would expect, one of mingled scorn and envy.

5.   C. Levi-Strauss, *The Savage Mind*, should be mentioned here as essential reading for anyone with a serious interest in the belief-systems of the Econ.

6.   I.e., in several Math tongues – the Indo-European languages, for example, do not count.

7.   The budding collector of Econographica should know that most of the work found on the market today is imitative and done by apprentices. Much of it nonetheless aesthetically superior to, say, the crudely carved totems of the Macro and certainly to the outsized, machine-made modls nowadays exported by the O'Metrs who have no artistic tradition to fall back on.

8.   Arthur Koestler, *The Sleepwalkers*, New York 1968, pp. 22-23, aptly summarizes Anaximander's teachings: "The raw material (of the universe) is none of the familiar forms of matter, but a substance without definite properties except for being indestructible and everlasting. Out of this stuff all things are developed, and into it they return; before this our world, infinite multitudes of other universes have already existed, and been dissolved again into the amorphous mass."

If one were to dignify this primitive doctrine with modern terminology, one would have to put Anaximander in the 'putty-putty, bang-bang' category.

9.   One observer casts his account of this ceremony explicitly in parlour-game terms: 'Each player gets 2 countries, 2 goods, 2 factors, and a so-called Bowley Box...' etc., etc., and also compares the Intern game, in terms of intellectual difficulty, with checkers.

2.   The Young Economist's Guide to Professional Etiquette[*]

Daniel S. Hamermesh

Nearly all advanced graduate students and new assistant professors demonstrate astounding naivete in their non-substantive professional dealings. Graduate programs in economics offer courses that lead to written drafts of important research; they teach little about how to refine those drafts and, more generally, about the personal interactions that cut and polish intellectual diamonds in the rough. I provide here a short course aimed at removing that naivete and helping young economists to avoid *faux pas* that might reduce their success in the profession.

IF I AM NOT FOR MYSELF, WHO IS FOR ME?

With tenure decisions usually made 5½ years after you start your first full-time academic job, a leisurely revision of your thesis and slow submission for publication court disaster. A major reason for denying tenure at most schools is lack of publications resulting from the researcher's slow start. Committee work, lecture preparation and advising students can quickly fill your schedule. At least one manuscript from your thesis should be sent to a journal before you have finished your first year as an assistant professor. Better still, have the entire thesis material submitted by that time, then move

[*] Reprinted with permission of the copyright holder from the *Journal of Economic Perspectives,* Vol.6, No.1, Winter 1992, pp. 169-70.

Michigan State University. Graduate students and many necessarily anonymous faculty at my own and other schools provided helpful suggestions and a wealth of anecdotes. I am especially indebted to Thomas Klier and Michael McPherson. The staff at Gadjah Mada University, Yogyakarta, Indonesia, provided excellent facilities for preparing this guide.

on to other research. Unless you discipline yourself to produce research and try to publish it, it simply will not happen.

Young economists are often extremely diffident about presenting their work. Remember, though, good research is rarely done in solitary confinement; and appearing inexperienced in public leaves you no worse off than obscurity and anonymity. A presentation can improve your work, acquaint senior scholars with it, and raise your visibility with editors and potential employers.

Present your work at seminars, professional meetings and conferences. These last in particular often welcome younger people, and can be broadly attended. If you do so, make sure you get the paper to discussants at least 10 days before the meeting. At least one well-known economist has killed off many relatives in excuses about tardy papers and has a wide reputation for irresponsibility.

Do not be embarrassed to send your work to more senior people (but do not be forlorn if few or none respond). A simple cover note stating that the recipient might be interested is sufficient. Do not write a letter praising your work; and never attempt to enhance the recipient's interest by criticizing others. I received a cover letter that asked, "Are 20 million Americans wrong, or are [the authors' antagonists] wrong?" This appeal generated neither respect nor interest. An advanced graduate student asked if he should mail his revised paper to a senior economist who had already provided comments. Except for very close friends and colleagues, you cannot ask people to read multiple drafts. His only 'hook' was to send the revision as a courtesy, with thanks for the earlier comments but with no expectation of eliciting further aid.

The chief rule in presenting your research orally is to make sure that you convey the paper's main contribution. Too often, a junior lecturer will spend a large fraction of the allotted time reviewing the literature or engaging in needless algebraic pyrotechnics. Stick to your point. You have every right to tell a pesky interlocutor that you will handle a question after the presentation, provided you do so gently. One-and-a-half hours are enough to demonstrate what you have done and why it is important, if you prevent others from wasting time and do not yourself dissipate the time with trivia.

When is a draft ready to send out for comments and presentation? Except for seminars at your own institution (where the participants may be more friendly, or at least more forgiving), I recommend using the draft before the one you plan to submit for publication. By this time the roughest edges are rounded off, yet it is still possible to improve the work greatly. Waiting until the near-final version turns your interactions with other scholars into mere formalities.

How to respond to written and oral comments? *Don't* respond to written comments that you think are foolish or correct, and don't, as one student proposed, write a detailed refutation. Other than offering thanks for the comments when you next see the person, no written response is necessary unless the point is partly correct and would benefit from further discussion. For oral comments (including those offered at seminars), immediate thanks are always in order, for both brilliant insights and complete nonsense. Disputation may be beneficial, but only to advance understanding *by both parties*, not to score debating points.

The deepest expression of gratitude is explicit thanks in the acknowledgement footnote of the paper. Thank people who offered major substantive comments that you incorporated, but avoid the usual callow exculpation of them. If you have borrowed heavily and fairly generally from someone else's work, be sure to include a statement to that effect in the footnote or elsewhere in the paper. A journal editor asked one department chair about a young colleague whom a referee accused of wholesale plagiarism. The young man had not plagiarized; but the problem would have been avoided (and the paper perhaps not summarily rejected) if he had noted his intellectual debt. Beyond these, the footnote should include only your title, affiliation, and thanks for any grants that supported the work.

An editor is unlikely to choose someone whom you have thanked to referee your paper. Thus, some economists strategically fail to thank people, hoping for a friendly referee. Others thank someone who has nor seen the paper, as a talisman against that person being chosen. DON'T PLAY THESE GAMES – the gains are not worth the potential costs of being caught.

You now revise your paper in light of the comments that you thought were useful. Make sure the paper is not overly long, as no editor wants to publish even 50 typescript pages, and few referees wish to read that much. Your writing style may not win you a Pulitzer Prize, but it should not be so horrendous that it masks your ideas. (A good guide is McCloskey, 1987.) Check that the paper is not riddled with typing errors; they may lead a referee to infer that the substance of your work is also careless. Verify that all pages are included; on several occasions I have received papers to referee that were missing pages.

Do not worry about the detailed style instructions that appear in many journals. Those are for the final submission of an accepted paper. Editors are not prejudiced against a legibly-typed submission that is not in the journal's final format. Even if the journal does not request one, it may make sense to enclose a short abstract of the paper.

Most professional communication is in refereed journals (although this journal is *not* one), all of which welcome unsolicited submissions. In choosing among these, avoid underselling your work. Start with a higher-quality outlet than your eventual target. Better journals are more widely read, which increases attention to your subsequent efforts (Siow, 1991). They use higher-quality referees (Hamermesh, 1991), so that you probably receive better comments. Also, most of the 40 departments among the top 25 require publications in leading journals for granting tenure. The professional returns to choosing a better journal are higher. But a strategy of aiming high requires a thick skin; the acceptance rate at major economics journals is around 10 percent. Thus, it pays to have a 'submission tree' in mind, a sequence of alternative outlets for your work.

Choose a journal whose recent offerings suggest the editor might be interested in your work; that published a paper included in your references; or that a senior colleague tells you is appropriate. Some journals specialize in theory, or in empirical work, or by subfield. To acquaint different audiences with your work, avoid journals where you have published within the last year or where you have just had a paper accepted (unless the editor explicitly invites submission). Certainly do not, as a colleague did early in his career, submit a second paper upon receipt of the letter accepting the first. He was kindly told by the editor to withdraw the second paper.

Unlike in some fields (like legal scholarship), submitting a paper to several economics journals is absolutely forbidden. An editor wrote to me stating that a referee had handled my paper elsewhere and wondering if I had submitted it to two places. I had not – it had been rejected at the other journal – but the implied threat in the letter showed the importance attached to this prohibition.

A cover letter for your submitted paper might be: "Please consider the enclosed manuscript, 'Paper Title,' for possible publication in the *Review of Economic Nonsense.* I look forward to your response on this paper." If a submission fee is enclosed, mention it. Nothing else is needed. Do not summarize the paper, ballyhoo it, tell the editor why the journal is appropriate, or discuss your personal or professional problems.

Nearly all journals send an acknowledging postcard when your paper is received. I have never failed to receive a postcard. (I did, though, receive one from a journal to which I had not submitted a paper, but to whose editor I had sent the paper for comments.) If you have not received the postcard within one month, you should call the editorial office.

The real wait is for an editorial response. I have had responses within two weeks (negative) and as long as 13 months (somewhat positive). Colleagues report initial responses taking 24 months (both negative and positive). After four to six months, it is reasonable to call or write the editorial office. In most cases the editor is aware of the problem, but is waiting for a dilatory referee. Occasionally, though, the paper has slipped through the cracks. One colleague waited two years, only to hear that a new editor had discovered his paper in a filing cabinet, and that the referee who had been assigned to it had died. Having read the paper the previous evening, the new editor accepted it without changes.

An editor will not reject a paper solely because of an author's reminder after four to six months of waiting. (One even reprimanded an author for 'letting your comment grow a beard' by waiting four months to inquire.) I sent a birthday card to a journal editor (whom I knew) on the first anniversary of submission (of a paper that was later accepted). A long editorial lag can jeopardize the paper's publication. One junior colleague waited ten months to inquire about a paper's status for fear of offending the editor. The editor responded that he was having trouble deciding, but that he wanted the paper revised. The resubmission several months later was immediately rejected *by a new editor* who was not interested in the topic.

One fine day you will receive an editor's letter and the reports that the editor obtained from referees. By far the most common is a Type 1 letter, outright rejection. Most editors are careful to make clear they do not wish to see the paper again. They include statements like, "... your paper does not contain a contribution sufficient enough to warrant publication." You should view the paper as finished with that journal.

Only if you believe the referee comments are completely misguided (a frequent view of rejected authors) *and* the editor indicates that he or she relied heavily on the referee should you think to ask the editor to reconsider your work. Even then, think twice. An editor's mention of a specific reason for rejection does not invite resubmission; the editor usually has several reasons. Asking for reconsideration may make you look foolish; you may wish to submit future work to the journal; and there are more fish in the sea of journals.

A Type II letter, the next most common, suggests major changes with no strong hope of eventual publication. Examples range from: "I would be willing to consider a major revision of the paper, but ... I can promise you nothing. My judgment is that you have an uphill battle;" to, "The *Journal of Economic Rubbish* will not be able to publish your paper. One of the responses is positive enough that I would not entirely rule out the possibility of resubmission. ... Another possibility would be to submit a revised version elsewhere;" to, "If you are willing to completely redo the paper to take account of the reviewers' criticisms, we would be willing to take another look at it."

Should you bother resubmitting the paper? Only the third letter is encouraging. One young colleague firmly believed that a letter like it was an outright rejection and took substantial convincing before resubmitting her paper. A good rule is that, unless the door has been slammed in your face, or you cannot in good conscience comply with the editorial suggestions, you should resubmit the paper. The vagaries of the refereeing and editorial process make the likelihood of eventual acceptance far greater on a resubmission, even after a tepid response, than on any alternative second journal of equal quality. Also, if you constructed a 'submission tree,' your next alternative will be of lower quality. Only on the first Type II letter should there have been any hesitation to resubmit.

The still less common Type III letter encourages resubmission but asks for substantial revisions, along the lines of: "Please prepare a revision ... that deals with these issues. I will check back with the referees before making a decision."

A Type IV letter states that the journal is happy to publish your paper and asks for none, or only editorial changes. This species is extremely rare.

Before sending the paper to a different journal in response to a Type I or very negative Type II letter, wait at least one week to digest the letters. Then, if the editor or referees made comments *that you think are useful*, incorporate them. In many cases a conscientious editor or helpful referee will indicate other potential outlets for the paper, perhaps better ones than you had in mind. Send the paper off to the next journal, and wait again. Remember that the editorial/refereeing process is sufficiently random that one rejection hardly provides definitive information about the quality of the paper. Several colleagues report that after they had become discouraged by initial rejection, other authors published papers that an objective observer would agree were substantively identical to the rejected works.

If the paper is rejected by a second journal, what do you do with a two-time loser? Two rejections do not a bad paper indicate; but three, and certainly four rejections suggest something is seriously wrong with the work. At least rethink the paper completely. You may also realize that your time is better spent on new projects. Euthanasia – permanent commitment of the paper to the filing cabinet – is recommended for papers that are terminally ill; and most experienced economists have buried papers after repeated rejections. The problem diminishes with experience, not because one writes fewer bad papers, but because one gains increasing access to non-refereed outlets. (Those outlets are often indistinguishable from the filing cabinet.)

Assume your work was good enough (or you were fortunate enough), and you did not receive an outright rejection. Take a few weeks to mull over the referee(s') and editor's comments. Remember that waiting too long can result in your confronting a new, less sympathetic editor when you resubmit, or the same editor may reject your resubmission on the grounds that the result is now well-known. One journal editor states that a resubmission will not be considered if the delay exceeds one year.

The resubmitted paper should include all major changes that the referees and editor suggested, unless you are convinced that they are mistaken. In that case, a detailed explanation should accompany the resubmission (on which more below). For minor suggestions, appease the editor or referee if the change does not lower the quality of the paper. This is what produces the accretion of footnotes as drafts progress toward publication. If two referees make suggestions that conflict directly, you must sort out which (if any) is correct. The resubmission letter should clarify what you did and why.

The editor may indicate that the paper can be shortened, and may be explicit about the desired length. The ceiling should be strictly adhered to. Playing games with longer paper, single spacing, narrower margins, and so on, is transparent to the editor.

Between initial submission and resubmission you may have had some brilliant new insights on the topic. Isn't an invitation to resubmit also a chance to display the fruit of your additional labor? Don't succumb to this temptation. Minor changes can be included, with a justification in the resubmission letter. But if the new work is sufficiently different or extensive, it merits another paper. Editors and referees react adversely to attempts to lengthen a publication by sneaking in additional material.

The resubmission letter should summarize and justify all the major changes you have made. Specific references to individual referees' comments help the editor reach a decision. One journal even suggests numbering each part of the referee reports and keying your letter to these numbers. Other than a final sentence like, "I look forward to hearing from you on this revised paper," nothing else is required. The letter need not exceed two pages, though I have seen longer ones that essentially restate the paper.

Do not make gratuitous comments about the referees, both because such comments are never justified, and because the editor may send your letter to the same referees along with the revised manuscript. On some Type II and III resubmissions none or not all the referees will be contacted; in rare cases new referees will be sought on Type II resubmissions.

Your second wait will end when you receive another editorial letter and perhaps additional referees' reports. If the editor and referees were satisfied with your revision, the letter will accept the paper. Most commonly it will request yet another resubmission. Or the letter may be a rejection, giving you the choice between euthanasia for the paper and submission elsewhere.

The same etiquette applies on the second resubmission, and usually the changes suggested are more minor. But what if the process seems nonconvergent? One editor invited a colleague to resubmit and enclosed two favorable referees' reports. The resubmission generated an unfavorable report from a third referee and another invitation to resubmit. A second resubmission produced a glowing report from a fourth referee. A third invited resubmission was rejected curtly with a negative report from a fifth referee! In the very rare case where the paper does not seem to be converging to publication, you should ask whether they will eventually publish your piece. If an explicit commitment is not received after the second resubmission, it may indicate the editor does not have the heart to deliver the *coup de grace*. You may be better off submitting the paper elsewhere.

Your paper is 'accepted' when the editor writes that it will be published in some agreed-upon form. At that point or earlier the editor may suggest style changes and request that you rewrite your paper in accordance with the style of the journal. (Instructions are usually enclosed with the letter.) Always abide explicitly by the style requirements. The ease of making these changes on word processors gives no excuse for shirking, and you have the chance to build up capital with the journal's editorial staff.

The cover letter that transmits the final version to the journal should state that you have made the small changes requested. You might also ask when the editor expects the article to appear, and when you will receive galley or page proofs. Publication can be as quick as two months after final acceptance, or as long as two years (Yohe, 1980). (The economics profession is regrettably slow in this area compared to the so-called hard sciences.) After that, your next contact with the journal (except with the few journals that ask you to check the copy-edited manuscript) is to examine proofs. All journals request an immediate turnaround on these; failure to honor the request does not (usually) jeopardize publication, but it does type you as irresponsible.

READ THE GALLEYS CAREFULLY! One press recommends, "Another person should read the manuscript aloud slowly while you read the proof. If this is not possible, you should proofread by reading word for word from the manuscript to proof." One colleague had a reference to the New York *Jets* and ignored the error in the galleys that identified the New York *Jests*. Be especially careful checking mathematics, and watch out for transposed numbers, rows or columns in tables.

Checking galleys is not the time to amend the article; most journals threaten dire consequences for any changes, and some actually charge you for changes. Also, don't buy the reprints the journal offers. They are an expensive throwback in an era of high quality photocopying. Having checked the galleys and filled out whatever forms are required, send the package back immediately and look forward to seeing your paper in print some months later. When the paper appears, make enough photocopies to supply people who gave you useful comments and others in the profession who might be interested in or benefit from seeing the published work.

IF I AM FOR MYSELF ALONE, WHAT AM I?

Even as a junior person, you will receive drafts of papers from colleagues and graduate school friends. There is no obligation to comment on papers you receive, especially if you have nothing to say. If you have nothing to say on any paper you receive, though, you might question whether you have sufficient interest to justify remaining in the profession. Unless your comments are absolutely trivial, it is worth taking the time to write a letter, telephone or talk face-to-face with the author. Major comments are received all too infrequently by most authors, but even minor ones are rare.

Unless you are convinced that your research will generate a deluge of helpful suggestions, aiding others is the only way to build up the capital that will prevent you from doing your own work in an intellectual vacuum. No one has any obligation to pay attention to your research, not even your dissertation advisor, after you have headed out into the cold cruel world. This activity should not detract from your own research. Surely, though, there are times when your work is not progressing. A 'morning person' like me can set aside evenings for this type of professional service. Pick times that fit your own diurnal or hebdomadal comparative advantage.

This sort of mutual intellectual aid society can be a lasting relationship. One individual and I have been commenting on each other's work for over 20 years, though we have never been classmates or colleagues. Neither of us remembers who made the initial step; but I at least continue to benefit immensely from his comments.

Attending seminars is another aspect of reciprocity. You cannot expect people to attend your presentations unless you attend theirs. Seminars are good places to absorb research results, generate your own new ideas, and learn how to present your own work. In addition, economists are a verbal lot; the disputation in the best seminar situations has an almost Talmudic cast that sharpens the economic thinking of all participants. Some economists have gained reputations for brilliance from their comments at seminars, and a concomitant professional recognition, that far exceeds the impact of their written work.

How talkative should a young economist be at seminars? Save corrections of minor algebraic or statistical errors for a private talk with the lecturer after the presentation. Repeated silly interruptions will gain you the reputation of a fool; wait a few seconds before opening your mouth. One brilliant young colleague comments frequently but only occasionally sensibly at seminars; however, his useful comments are among the best any lecturer could get. The fraction of incorrect or idiotic remarks that is tolerated is directly proportional to the brilliance of the correct ones.

Refereeing is a more formal service to the research of others. As you become known, you will receive an increasing stream of requests to referee.

(One editor explicitly states in acceptance letters that he will send you papers to referee and asks you to respond immediately if you do not wish to do so. The implicit threat of revoking the acceptance creates a powerful disincentive to decline!) Most editors ask that you respond within one or two months, and a few journals provide a small monetary incentive for compliance. Many editors request a referee's report that will be sent to the author and a cover letter with your recommendation about publication.

No junior person should ever decline a request to referee because of pressing commitments, as none can claim to be swamped with other professional service. At most schools this sort of service is expected, desired and even rewarded. However, if the paper is far removed from your own work, send it back to the editor *by return mail* stating this fact. Offer to referee a paper more in your area, lest the editor infer that you are shirking your professional responsibility.

If you have already refereed the manuscript for another journal, also return the request to the editor immediately. Double jeopardy should not be part of refereeing, even if the paper has been amended in response to your comments. If no one else is as capable as you of refereeing the piece, perhaps the editor should reject it as being of very limited interest.

Having decided to referee the paper, do it expeditiously. A delay exceeding two months is unconscionable, though regrettably common. Only the most brilliant young person should risk developing a reputation for slacking, and being responsible ingratiates you with editors and editorial staff. It probably has no effect on whether they will publish your work, since editors strive to publish high-quality research regardless of the authors' peccadilloes; but it can affect their desire to push your paper through the refereeing process. Refereeing the paper should hardly be all-consuming, nor should it be broad-brush. The amount of time devoted to a paper depends on your interest in it and its difficulty. If your report is not at least one tightly written page, though, you probably did not give the paper enough attention.

In writing your report (to be seen by the author), lead off with a succinct summary of the paper, or move immediately to your major comments, criticisms and suggestions. Then deal with specific, less important problems and arguments. Do point out mathematical and econometric errors; but unless the central result of the paper depends on such an error, finding one is not by itself cause for a negative view of the work. If you recommend rejecting the paper, informing the author of a more appropriate outlet (if you believe the paper is publishable somewhere) is helpful. The proper tone of the report is conveyed well by one editor's admonition to referees: "The reports should ... be no more abrasive than absolutely necessary. Especially if the manuscript is to be declined, insert a kind remark if you can. It will shine like a good deed in a naughty world." A major purpose of refereeing is to improve research. Your constructive comments may be ignored if they are couched in a negative tone.

Never make your report part of a vendetta against another researcher. The temptation is often great, as you will be asked to referee papers by scholars who have criticized your own work, who have sharply conflicting views, or who have been patently nasty to you. Resist temptation. Do not make gratuitous comments about the author's morality. In one case, such comments led to legal action by the author against the referee. Never go beyond the refereeing process, as numbers of economists have done, by writing an unsolicited letter to an editor seeking to stifle publication of an article.

Your letter to the editor should mention briefly (not repeat) the major problems, strengths and contributions of the paper. It should also assess whether even a greatly revised version of the paper merits publication in that particular journal. A large fraction of rejections should result partly from cover letters that state something like: "Though there is nothing wrong with the paper, the original point is fairly minor and of insufficiently general interest to appear in a major journal." Keep this in mind when you receive a Type I letter despite what appear to be moderately favorable referees' reports.

Frankness is crucial in the cover letter, as the editor may lack the expertise to place the paper in the context of other research. If you recommend rejection, make it as clear as the colleague who wrote, 'Let me state plainly that this is a very bad paper.' Do not, though, base your recommendation on strategic considerations involving your own research, such as speculation that publication of the paper might diminish interest in your work.

In many cases, you will receive a resubmitted manuscript for further refereeing. Unless the author added new material or made a truly fundamental mistake that you failed to catch in the original, your comments and criticisms should be limited to follow-ups. Otherwise, you are encouraging a nonconvergent refereeing process and being unfair to the author.

A FEW GENERAL RULES

First, do not be hostile. People pay attention to correct and interesting ideas they read or hear. Hostility only reduces the attention your ideas receive by concentrating listeners on your style instead of your substance.

Second, be forthcoming and speak up; be assertive without being pushy. Each year roughly 800 new PhDs in economics are minted. Unless you advertise your ideas, your work will be ignored.

Finally, and most important, the Golden Rule (biblical, not growth-theoretic) is a good guide for professional etiquette for young economists.

REFERENCES

Hamermesh, Daniel (1991), "The Appointment-Book Problem and Commitment, with an Application to Refereeing?" unpublished paper, Michigan State University.

McCloskey, Donald (1987), *The Writing of Economics*, New York: Macmillan.

Siow, Aloysius (1991), "First Impressions in Academe," *Journal of Human Resources*, **26**, 236-55.

Yohe, Gary (1980), "Current Publication Lags in Economics Journals," *Journal of Economic Literature*, **18**, 1050-55.

3.   How are the Mighty Fallen: Rejected Classic Articles by Leading Economists[*]

Joshua S. Gans and George B. Shepherd

Do elite economists suffer publication setbacks? Are the economists who produce the important articles content with the refereeing process? We asked over 140 leading economists, including all living winners of the Nobel Prize and John Bates Clark Medal, to describe instances in which journals rejected their papers. We hit a nerve. More than 60 percent responded, many with several blistering pages.[1] Paul Krugman expressed the tone of many letters: "Thanks for the opportunity to let off a bit of steam."[2]

A few economists indicate that no journal has rejected their work. Most of these authors publish mainly in books, and submit few papers to journals. John Kenneth Galbraith explains that his unblemished record "is not entirely the result of the excellence of my writing, much as I would like to believe it so. The deeper truth is that not for many years now have I submitted more than a very few papers to our, as they are called, learned journals. Consequently there has not been a great deal to reject." Robert Solow's experience is similar: "The fact is that I have never had a paper rejected by a journal. Probably this is because I hate writing articles."

[*] Reprinted with permission of the copyright holder from the *Journal of Economic Perspectives*, Vol.8, No.1, Winter 1994, pp. 165-80.

Stanford University. We thank William Shepherd, Joseph Stiglitz, Timothy Taylor, and Gavin Wright for their thoughtful comments and advice, and Kenneth J. Arrow for inspiring the project. Most of all, we are grateful to the leading economists who contributed anecdotes and analysis, and we regret that this article's shortness forces us to save much of their wit and insight for the forthcoming book, *Rejected: Leading Economists Ponder the Publication Process* (Shepherd, forthcoming 1994).

In contrast, almost all leading economists who regularly submit to journals have suffered rejection, often frequently. In the big leagues, even the best hitters regularly strike out. For example, Paul Samuelson states: "Yes, journals have rejected papers of mine, some of them later regarded as 'classics.' I used to say, with only moderate exaggeration, that the quality of papers of mine at first rejected is not less than the quality of papers accepted at once." Our survey demonstrates that many papers that have become classics were rejected initially by at least one journal – and often by more than one. A publisher rejected George Orwell's *Animal Farm* because "[i]t's impossible to sell animal stories in the U.S.A." (Bernard, 1990). Similarly, economics journals can overlook excellence.

This paper presents a selection of dispatches from the publication battle-front. We begin by discussing rejections that winners of the Nobel Prize and John Bates Clark Medal have endured, and some other notable cases. We then turn to the record of John Maynard Keynes' quirky refusals, when he was the *Economics Journal*'s editor, of several important articles and authors. Finally, we offer some thoughts about the implications of these findings.[3]

THE GRIM REAPER KNOCKS ON ALL DOORS: NOBEL LAUREATES AND CLARK MEDALISTS

Most winners of the Nobel Prize and John Bates Clark Medal have had papers rejected: only three of the 20 winners who responded in our survey did not admit at least one rejection. The spurned stars were diverse: conservatives, mathematical economists, non-mathematical progressives, Keynesians, monetarists, neo-classicists, young, old, authors of papers on a broad range of subjects.

James Tobin remembers vividly the rejection of a paper that he prepared as the inaugural Cowles Foundation Discussion Paper (CFDP), after the Foundation moved to Yale. "It was a great coup for Yale University and its Economics Department when in 1955 the Cowles Commission moved from Chicago to Yale. It was for me too, because I became the Director of this world-renowned research group. ... I had by fortunate chance a paper all ready to be CFDP 1. What could be better than to have the first paper distributed in Cowles's new life authored by the new director, recruited from the Yale faculty, not imported from Chicago." Tobin's paper for the first time extended probit (0,1) regression analysis to applications with multiple regressors.

Tobin submitted the paper to the *Journal of the American Statistical Association*. The journal rejected it, twice. "The referees for the *Journal of the American Statistical Association* were not impressed, not even after I re-submitted with many of their specific complaints treated." The paper died until Tobin's 1975 volume of collected essays resurrected it.[4]

Tobin recalls that "[t]he rejection, anticlimactic as it happened to be, was disappointing. But all was not lost." Tobin soon developed a theory for handling $(0,x)$ variables with any number of regressors. "This analysis was baptized "Tobit" by Arthur Goldberger. The name obviously echoed "probit." Maybe Goldberger was also evoking my chief claim to fame in those days, my one-paragraph appearance, thinly disguised as Tobit, in *The Caine Mutiny*, the popular novel by my 1942 naval reserve classmate Herman Wouk."

Last autumn marked the 50th birthday of Wolfgang Stolper's and Paul Samuelson's "Protection and Real Wages." The article addressed the impact of tariffs on the distribution of income, and introduced general-equilibrium models as analytic tools. The authors submitted it to the *American Economic Review*, which rejected it bluntly. According to Samuelson, the referee "thought it would prejudice the noble cause of free trade; and, besides, it was primarily a theoretical curiosum." The *Review of Economic Studies* later published the paper.[5]

Econometrica rejected what Franco Modigliani describes as "one of the best known and widely cited of my early papers": his paper that introduced the Duesenberry-Modigliani consumption function. He explains: "In 1948-49 I had been working on a paper developing a theory of aggregate saving behavior which has since been known as the Duesenberry-Modigliani consumption function. ... I presented my paper at a 1949 Conference on Income and Wealth, and then submitted it for publication to *Econometrica*. The paper was returned with a letter from Trygve Haavelmo, who I believe was the Editor of *Econometrica*, rejecting my paper with no offer to revise and resubmit. As I recall, the only reason for rejecting the paper was that in his view these were no times for formulating ingenious new hypotheses, the important issue of the time being to pursue better estimation methods recognizing problems of simultaneity. By contrast, my paper used single equation methods." The paper later appeared in *Studies of Income and Wealth*.

In 1962, William Sharpe submitted his paper, "Capital Asset Prices: A Theory of Equilibrium Under Conditions of Risk," to *the Journal of Finance*. The paper, which was to have over 2,000 citations, introduced the capital asset pricing model. The Journal editor, on the advice of a referee, rejected the paper, although Sharpe remembers the rejection as "equivocal." The editor indicated that Sharpe's assumption that all investors made the same predictions was so "preposterous" that it made his conclusions "uninteresting" (Bernstein, 1992, pp. 194-95). Sharpe kept trying with the

Journal, and succeeded only after new editors arrived. "[T]he editorship was in the process of being changed. Eventually other referees were brought in and the new editor agreed to publication, which took place in 1964."[6]

Gary Becker, who sits atop several citations rankings, feels that he too has suffered the slings and arrows of outrageous referee reports. "Like most economists, I have had a number of manuscripts rejected by journals and other publishers." He singles out one example. Early in his career, he submitted what became "Competition and Democracy" to the *Journal of Political Economy*. The then editor Earl Hamilton agreed to publish it. He eventually withdrew the commitment because of negative comments by Frank Knight, who was one of the people who refereed the paper. "I still have a copy of Knight's referee report, and I cannot say that I am any more impressed by it now than at that time." Becker "became discouraged by the report and put the article away" until he finally published it in the *Journal of Law and Economics* several years later. However, by that time, other articles had been published that employed the same approach.[7]

Franklin Fisher reports: "'The costs of automobile model changes since 1949' (written with Zvi Griliches and Carl Kaysen) is probably the best-known paper in which I ever had a hand." When the authors submitted the paper to the *AER*, "The paper received an enthusiastic referee's report but was nevertheless rejected by the *AER*." The editor indicated "that the automobile-model-change paper 'was not of sufficient independent interest to warrant publication in the *American Economic Review*.'" Fisher's story ends happily. "We easily published the study in the *Journal of Political Economy*, and it has gone on to be anthologized so many times that long ago I lost count" (Monz, 1992).

Although Paul Krugman has published several influential papers, journals reject most of his work. "This is in response to your letter of April 3 requesting stories about paper rejections – if any, you say!! As it happened, your letter arrived in the same day's mail as the second rejection of a paper that 1 thought (and still think) is one of my better ones. I don't know what other peoples' experience is, but I would estimate that 60% of my papers sent to refereed journals have been rejected on the first try." Despite his publication troubles, Krugman recently received the John Bates Clark Medal.

One of Krugman's examples: "I guess the biggest rejection I have had was of my first paper on monopolistic competition and trade. I sent 'Increasing Returns, Monopolistic Competition, and International Trade' to the *QJE* sometime in mid-1978. It took eight months to get a reply: a rejection based on a single referee report, which I now wish I had saved. The referee agreed that increasing returns and imperfect competition were

Table 3.1 Some Rejected Papers, Listed by Place of Eventual Publication

Akerlof, George, "The Market for 'Lemons': Quality, Uncertainty and the Market Mechanism," *Quarterly Journal of Economics*, August 1970, 84:3, 488-500.

Arthur, W. Brian, "Competing Technologies, Increasing Returns, and Lock-In by Historical Events," *Economic Journal*, March 1989, 99, 116-31.

Becker, Gary S., "Competition and Democracy," *Journal of Law and Economics*, 1958, 1, 105-09.

Becker, Gary S., "A Theory of the Allocation of Time," *Economic Journal*, September 1965, 75, 493-517.

Bhagwati, Jagdish, "Immiserizing Growth: A Geometrical Note," *Review of Economic Studies*, June 1958, 25, 201-05.

Black, Fisher, and Myron Scholes, "The Pricing of Options and Corporate Liabilities," *Journal of Political Economy*, May/June 1973, 81:3, 637-54.

Buchanan, James M., "External and Internal Public Debt," *American Economic Review*, December 1957, 47:6, 995-1000.

Chichilnisky, Graciela, "Basic Goods, Commodity Transfers and the New International Economic Order," *Journal of Development Economics*, December 1980, 7:4, 505-19.

Corden, W. Max, "The Structure of a Tariff System and the Effective Protective Rate," *Journal of Political Economy*, June 1966, 74:3, 221-37.

Debreu, Gerard, "Numerical Representations of Technological Change," *Metroeconomica*, August 1954, 6:2, 46-68.

Fisher, Franklin M., Zvi Griliches, and Carl Kaysen, "The Costs of Automobile Model Changes Since 1949," *Journal of Political Economy*, October 1962, 70:5, 433-51.

Friedman, Milton, "Professor Pigou's Method for Measuring Elasticities of Demand from Budgetary Data," *Quarterly Journal of Economics*, November 1935, 50:1, 151-63.

Harrod, Roy, "The Law of Decreasing Costs," *Economic Journal*, December 1931, 41, 566-76.

Hotelling, Harold, "The Economics of Exhaustible Resources," *Journal of Political Economy*, April 1931, 39:2, 137-75.

Jonung, Lars, "Ricardo on Machinery and the Present Unemployment: An Unpublished Manuscript by Knut Wicksell," *Economic Journal*, March 1981, 91:361, 195-205.

Kalecki, Michal, "A Theorem on Technical Progress," *Review of Economic Studies*, May 1941, 7:1, 178-84.

Krugman, Paul R., "Increasing Returns, Monopolistic Competition, and International Trade," *Journal of International Economics*, November 1979, 9:4, 469-79.

Krugman, Paul R., "Target Zones and Exchange Rate Dynamics," *Quarterly Journal of Economics*, August 1991, 106:3, 669-82.

Lazear, Edward P., and Sherwin Rosen, "Rank-Order Tournaments as Optimal Labor Contracts," *Journal of Political Economy*, October 1981, 89:5, 841-64.

Lucas, Robert E., "Expectations and the Neutrality of Money," *Journal of Economic Theory*, April 1972, 4:2, 103-24.

May, Robert, and John Beddington, "Nonlinear Difference Equations: Stable Points, Stable Cycles, Chaos," *mimeo.*, Princeton University, Department of Biology, 1975.

May, Robert, "Simple Mathematical Models with Very Complicated Dynamics," *Nature*, June 10, 1976, 261, 459-67.

Modigliani, Franco, "Fluctuations in the Savings-Income Ratio: A Problem in Economic Forecasting," *Studies of Income and Wealth*, Vol. 11. York: National Bureau of Economic Research, 1949, 371-440.

Ohlin, Bertil, *Interregional and International Trade*, Cambridge: Harvard University Press, 1933, Chapters 1-3, Appendix I.

Scitovsky, Tibor, "A Reconsideration of the Theory of Tariffs," *Review of Economic Studies*, 1942, 9:2, 89-110.

Sharpe, William, "Capital Asset Prices: A Theory of Equilibrium Under Conditions of Risk," *Journal of Finance*, 1964, 19:3, 425-42.

Stolper, Wolfgang, and Paul A. Samuelson, "Protection and Real Wages," *Review of Economic Studies*, November 1941, 9, 58-73.

Tobin, James, "Multiple Probit Regression of Dichotomous Variables," *Collected Essays of James Tobin*, Vol. 2. Chicago: Markham, 1975, Chapter 43.

very important in the international economy, but did not feel that our understanding of these issues would be helped by writing down formal models."

The paper eventually appeared in the *Journal of International Economics*, but only over two *JIE* referees' objections. Jagdish Bhagwati was the *JIE*'s editor at the time: "I published it myself despite two adverse referee reports by very distinguished experts on the theory of increasing returns! It did take some courage and also a strong sense of the importance of the paper for me to do so, since Krugman had been my student and normally I would lean over backwards not to publish my own students' work."

Our respondents indicate that most of their articles that endure initial rejection appear later in other journals. However, like Becker, Krugman notes that, even if another journal eventually prints a paper, the delay that initial rejection causes may permit others to beat the paper into the intellectual market. Krugman sent his "Target Zones and Exchange Rate Dynamics" to the *Journal of Political Economy*. "This time I got two favorable referee reports. The paper was nonetheless rejected ... by [the referee] who thought that the paper was of 'insufficient general interest' for the *JPE*. The paper didn't come out (in the *QJE*) until August 1991. By that time the target zone literature, all of which made use of the techniques first introduced in my paper, had exploded, and consisted of at least a hundred published and unpublished pieces; in fact, I had to add a postscript to the *QJE* version referring to subsequent literature."

Journals have declined several of James Buchanan's papers. For example, he notes that "my first piece on public debt theory, 'External and Internal Public Debt,' which was finally published in *AER*, was curtly and rudely rejected by E.H. Chamberlin at *QJE*, saying simply "We cannot accept the article." There was no reason, no referee report, anything. That was the shortest rejection I ever got."

Gerard Debreu has dents in his publication record. "[A]round 1951 I submitted an article entitled 'Numerical Representations of Technological Change' to the *Journal of Political Economy* which rejected it. I believe that one of the reasons, maybe the main reason, given for that rejection was that the paper was too mathematical for the *J.P.E.*, and indeed it was." *Metroeconomica* later published the paper.

Harry Markowitz has "had my share of rejections." For example, he indicates that a paper on a new database "was rejected because it presented a 'sexist language.' In particular, it referred to 'workman-like ....'"

Finally, *Econometrica* refused a Kenneth Arrow paper on inventories – although, at the time, he was President of the Econometric Society,

Econometrica's parent organization. He remarks diplomatically that the incident demonstrated the Society's impartial integrity.

MORE REMARKABLE REJECTIONS

George Akerlof's seminal contribution to the economics of information, "The Market for 'Lemons': Quality, Uncertainty and the Market Mechanism," considered whether markets would exist if product quality were unobservable. Before the *Quarterly Journal of Economics* finally accepted Akerlof's paper four years after he first sought to publish it, three journals called it a lemon. "I submitted it in June, 1967 to the *American Economic Review*. I got a reply from the editor which said that the article was interesting but the *American Economic Review* did not publish such trivial stuff."

The article next went to the *Journal of Political Economy*. Again it was rejected. Although the *AER* editor had refused the article because it was trivial, the *JPE* referee's report asserted the opposite: that the paper was too general to be true. "It seemed to give a universality to my paper that was never intended. It said amongst other things that eggs came in different qualities, but they were graded and then traded. Didn't "The Market for 'Lemons'" predict that no markets would occur at all if there were quality differences? Thus, in the view of this referee my paper predicted too much. Perhaps he forgot that the paper predicted the nonexistence of many markets which do not, in fact, exist."

Akerlof kept trying. "I next sent the article to the *Review of Economic Studies*. I had been urged by one of its co-editors to do that. Instead it went to another editor whose view of "The Market for 'Lemons'" was decidedly less favorable. It was rejected on the grounds again that it was 'trivial.' Finally I sent it to the *QJE* which accepted it with some degree of enthusiasm."

The rejections discouraged Akerlof. "I do think its early rocky reception did have an effect on my own work. It was not until 1973, when I spent 6 months on sabbatical in England, that I realized that quite a few people had read the paper, and even liked it. I believe I would have done follow-up work on 'The Market for "Lemons"' sooner, if I had not been made to feel lucky just to have it published at all. (I must say I still feel very lucky that it was published.)"

Akerlof believes that journal editors refused the article both because they feared the introduction into economics of informational considerations and because they disliked the article's readable style. "The editors probably objected most to two things. They were afraid that if 'information' was brought into economics, it would lose all rigor, since in that case almost anything could be said – there being so many ways that information can affect an equilibrium. They also almost surely objected to the style of the article which did not reflect the usual solemnity of economic journals."

Robert May is a distinguished biologist who has produced important and influential work on chaos theory. Encouraged by several mathematical economists, May and John Beddington submitted an economically-oriented paper on endogenous instability in simple dynamic models to *Econometrica*. The journal's editor rejected the paper with a fill-the-blanks form letter:

Dear <u>Mr. May</u>,

Enclosed is/are the report(s) of a/two referee(s) on your paper.
I regret it is not suitable for publication in *Econometrica*.

Yours sincerely,
[signature]

According to May, the lone, two-paragraph referee report indicated that the paper's findings "were well-known and not interesting. I wrote a cross reply to the editor, who said that his reviewer was expert and who was I anyway."

May gave up on economists. "At this point, back then, I simply decided that economists were not worth bothering with (life being very busy), and that generally the ends I wish to serve outside biology would be adequately handled by the review I was then writing for Nature. This was the 1976 Nature review (which remains, I believe, the most cited paper in the field of 'chaos,' which currently is going on for 2,000 citations)."

Robert Lucas' 1972 paper, "Expectations and the Neutrality of Money," introduced rational expectations concepts into monetary theory and macro-economics. However, the *American Economic Review* rejected the paper. The editor, writing in 1970 before the explosion in economics journals' mathematical complexity, objected to the paper's technical style. "If it has a clear result, it is hidden by the exposition." The referee concurred: "I find the paper exceedingly formal and I am not sure I fully understand the economics of the theorems Lucas presents. ... I have been following fairly closely the format of the articles published in the *AER*, and in comparison, Lucas' exposition is pitched at what I think is a distressingly arid level. The exposition is much more formal, for example, than either that of the original Samuelson paper or that of the Cass-Yaari paper – both of which took pains to get at the economic content of their theorems." Lucas eventually published the paper in the *Journal of Economic Theory*.

The *Quarterly Journal of Economics* missed its chance for "Immiserizing Growth," Jagdish Bhagwati's first professional paper. He notes, "The *QJE* turndown of the paper, influential as it became soon after publication, was perhaps due to the luck of the draw which all of us face as authors, sometimes driving us to distraction when the referees appear to be tendentious and capricious."

It appears that some authors' relationships with journal editors may have permitted the authors to avoid the risk of rejection: editors at several journals apparently permit certain authors sometimes to bypass the journals' normal refereeing processes. Richard Posner explains: "I am afraid I have no interesting anecdotes for you. I have had papers turned down, all right, but very few economics papers. Most of my economics papers have been published by journals edited by close friends (such as Ronald Coase and Bill Landes, when they edited the *Journal of Law and Economics*, or George Stigler and Sam Peltzman when they edited the *JPE*, or the *Bell Journal* when it was edited by Paul MacAvoy), and in many of these cases there weren't even formal submissions."

Similarly, Ronald Coase notes, "I have never found any difficulty in getting my articles published. I have either published in house journals (e.g. *Economica*) or the article was written as a result of a request (e.g. for a conference) and publication was assured."

Others suggest that an editor who exempts the papers of intellectual allies from the regular selection process may tend unfairly to reject work that disagrees with the editor's views. One economist submitted a paper on entry barriers to a Chicago journal. The rejection was "a 13-page essay citing every Chicago deity as to why there could be no such thing as entry barriers; the referee's essay made no reference to the paper at hand."

Only after years of rejections by four journals did Brian Arthur's "Competing Technologies, Increasing Returns, and Lock-In by Historical Events" appear in the *Economic Journal*. Arthur had employed a simple writing style. "I was at pains to keep the ideas in the forefront and not buried under a lot of theorems and pseudo-mathematical verbiage. I greatly admired Akerlof's Lemons paper as a piece of exposition and decided to write the paper in a similar, accessible, informative style. Given the current economics editorial process, this proved to be disastrous."

The paper began a six-year odyssey. "First it was dismissed at *AER* in desultory fashion. Then I submitted it to *QJE*, and it was turned down there. Then because Clower had left *AER* I resubmitted it to *AER*. It underwent one refereeing go-round, followed by two appeals. Finally, two years after this second submission, *AER* turned it down again. ... I then submitted it to

EJ; and it got turned down. I appealed; and finally, in 1989, *EJ* published it. ... The problem was consistently that the ideas were 'already known' somehow, not formulated in a sophisticated format, as an i-o game problem, or the discussion was too 'chatty' and therefore naive. I put the paper through eight rewrites in this process; each time it became stiffer, more formal, less informative, and possibly as a result more publishable."

Like other authors, Arthur suggests that delay from the rejections threatened his ideas' currency. "Because papers based on mine had started to appear in the literature," referees told him that "the idea ... is already recognized in the literature."[8]

Two journals rejected the paper by Fischer Black and Myron Scholes that contained their widely-used option-pricing formula. They first sent what would become "The Pricing of Options and Corporate Liabilities" to the *Journal of Political Economy*. The editor rejected it, without even sending it to referees. Too much finance, too little economics. They then tried the *Review of Economics and Statistics*. Again they received a rejection without even a referee report. The *JPE* published the piece only after Chicagoans Eugene Fama and Merton Miller spoke with the *JPE*'s Chicago editor. Because of the delay, the *Journal of Finance* printed Black's and Scholes' empirical tests of their formula before the *JPE* printed the formula itself (Bernstein, 1992, pp. 220-221 supplies this anecdote).

"I have, of course, had articles turned down," says Oliver Williamson. Brookings rejected his book *Markets and Hierarchies: Analysis and Antitrust Implications*. "The referees were of orthodox persuasions and did not see much merit in the exercise. The approach, the author, or both were believed to be so beyond redemption that no revision was invited. ... The Free Press later published it, in 1975. The 1990 citations exceed those to *The General Theory* and to the *Wealth of Nations*, though not those to Marx (*Capital*)."

James March takes his lumps in good humor. "I have certainly had articles rejected, even on occasion for good reasons. ... I recall on one occasion a referee filing a two paragraph commentary on a paper I co-authored suggesting (in the first paragraph) that the key theorem involved was trivially obvious and (in the second) that it was wrong. I thought on the whole that he ought to choose."[9]

THE VISIBLE HAND OF JOHN MAYNARD KEYNES

Through much of the first half of this century, John Maynard Keynes edited the *Economic Journal*, the period's premier economics publication. Our respondents provided a striking number of comments about Keynes as editor. Kenneth Boulding submitted his first article to Keynes, "and received a delightful conditional acceptance with some very valuable suggestions for improving the article, which I followed." Keynes then published Boulding's revised paper. However, other encounters with Keynes – who was often advised by his student Frank Ramsey – produced less delight.[10]

In 1923, Bertil Ohlin submitted to the *Economic Journal* a paper that introduced the factor proportions theorem in international economics. The theorem eventually earned Ohlin a Nobel Prize. Keynes returned the manuscript with a blunt rejection note: "This amounts to nothing and should be refused, J.M.K." Ohlin explained, "Probably by mistake [the note] was included in the package, when I got my manuscript back. I still have the note, and regard it as a valuable document. The paper Keynes rejected was never published" (Patinkin and Leith, 1977, pp. 161-2).

Similarly, Keynes rejected Harold Hotelling's "The Economics of Exhaustible Resources." The paper stated what is now known as Hotelling's Law: that the price of an exhaustible resource rises with the interest rate. Hotelling proved the result using the calculus of variations. However, the *Economic Journal* had earlier published Frank Ramsey's "The Mathematics of Saving," which also used calculus of variations.

Although the two papers addressed different topics, Keynes rejected Hotelling's piece on the basis that the calculus of variations technique was overly complex, and, in any event, the *Economic Journal* had already published Ramsey's article that used the same technique. Kenneth Arrow recalls: "When I spoke to Hotelling along these lines, he gravely informed me that he had originally submitted the paper to the *Economic Journal*. Although it had, he said, some motto which implied that it was open to economic analysis of all viewpoints, the paper was rejected as being too difficult for its readers. It was then published by the *Journal of Political Economy*, which was certainly not noted as an organ for mathematical economics."

Keynes rejected Roy Harrod's article that first sketched the marginal revenue curve. Although the *Economic Journal* finally published the article years later, Harrod felt that the delay in publication cost him credit for the new concept. Harrod writes in his biography of Keynes (1951, p. 159n) that he was "injured by Keynes' zeal": "During 1928 I submitted a short article, setting out what I called the 'increment of aggregate demand curve.' Keynes showed this to F.P. Ramsey who raised objections. Being in poor health at the time, and heavily burdened with college duties, I was discouraged and put the article away in a drawer for eighteen months. I then took the matter up with Ramsey, who was an old friend, and he recanted. The article was re-submitted and appeared in June 1930. ... [I]f Keynes had not listened so readily to Ramsey's criticisms and the article had appeared in 1928, any claim to have 'invented' this well-known tool in economics would be without challenge."

Paul Samuelson remembers, "Roy Harrod went to his grave bitter because Maynard Keynes, absolute monarch at the *Economic Journal*, turned down his early breakthroughs in the economics of imperfect competition. Thus, Harrod was robbed of credit for the 'marginal revenue' nomenclature. All this was on the advice of Frank Ramsey, genius in logic and mathematics. To genius every new idea is indeed 'obvious' and besides all that was already in 1838 Cournot. Hard cheese for Harrod, or for any of us, if the trace of our new brainchild can be found in 1750 Hume or 1826 von Thunen."

Keynes drew first blood with Milton Friedman. "The first professional paper that I published was entitled "Professor Pigou's Method for Measuring Elasticities of Demand from Budgetary Data." It was initially submitted to the *Economic Journal*. It consisted of a criticism of some work by the famous British economist A. C. Pigou. I received a reply from John Maynard Keynes, who was then editor of the *Economic Journal*, saying that he had shown it to Professor Pigou and Professor Pigou did not believe the criticism was correct, and therefore he was not inclined to publish it."

Friedman then sent the piece on to the *QJE*. "After having it refereed – I believe by Wassily Leontief since the paper was highly mathematical – Professor Taussig accepted it and the paper was published in the November 1935 issue of the *Quarterly Journal of Economics*."

Keynes also refused to publish what became one of Tibor Scitovsky's best-known papers. "One of my earliest, most quoted and reprinted papers, "A Reconsideration of the Theory of Tariffs," was turned down by Keynes as unsuitable for publication in the *Economic Journal* and was published soon thereafter in the 1942 Feb. issue of the *Review of Economic Studies*. Curiously enough, Keynes' closest friend and collaborator, R. F. (later Lord) Kahn, was the first person to quote from and draw attention to the main points of that paper in a short note in the first 1947-48 issue of the same Review."[11]

LESSONS AND IMPLICATIONS

The refereeing process displays a Dr. Jekyll and Mr. Hyde personality. Many respondents praised the positive side: that the refereeing process guides the best work to the best journals, matches unusual papers with appropriate publications, induces improvements in the papers themselves – and preserves the reputations of famous economists by keeping their bad work unpublished. For example, Edward Lazear and Sherwin Rosen indicate that their three-year ordeal with the *Journal of Political Economy* over "Rank-Order Tournaments as Optimal Labor Contracts" was worthwhile: Lazear thanks the referee "for the pain and suffering that he put a young professor through. It was time well spent."[12] Jean Tirole notes, "One of my best papers was rejected once, but it was entirely my fault." Takashi Negishi's experience was similar. "As far as my own papers are concerned, in most cases I thought editors and referees were right for rejected papers, so that I did not try other journals." Amartya Sen agrees: "I was on the whole lucky with submissions but those that were rejected were deservedly chucked!"

However, our project also revealed much dissatisfaction with the process. Many respondents deplored bored, careless editors and referees. "We have all had rejections that infuriated us because the reviewers always seem not to have read our work with the care and understanding that it merits," wrote William Baumol. Similarly, Graciela Chichilnisky notes, "The more innovative and interesting the paper, the more likely it is to be rejected, in my experience. Editors seldom read papers, and referees don't read them carefully either." Richard Freeman describes the "relief one normally gets from a rejection: the certain knowledge that the editor and referees are blind baseball umpires, members of The Three Stooges, or incompetents in even more drastic ways."

Many respondents indicated special difficulty in obtaining fair journal evaluations of unorthodox papers. The evolving attitudes of journals toward mathematical complexity present the issue starkly. Until the 1970s, editors regularly rejected articles because they contained technical mathematics.[13] The dominant editorial orthodoxy emphasized intuition, and viewed sophisticated mathematics as arid and irrelevant. Early papers by Tinbergen, Friedman, Hotelling, Debreu, and Lucas were all rejected for excess mathematics.[14]

In the 1970s, the technical tide rolled in. Leading journals filled with theorems and equations. Articles that contained only clear ideas in clear prose began to be rejected because they contained insufficient mathematics. Examples include the Akerlof and Arthur articles.

A rejection usually does not kill a paper; among our examples, a rejected paper usually finds life at another journal, even if the paper is unorthodox. Richard Nelson explains "that while, if one is writing something that is not quite orthodox one must expect some rejections, if one keeps on searching out other journals, one finally will get published in a good place. Indeed, I think that is significantly more true today than it was, say, fifteen years ago.

A whole collection of new journals has opened up since that time signalling welcomes to somewhat unorthodox approaches."[15]

However, even if a paper eventually is published, delay from earlier rejections can permit competing papers to be published first, or can reduce the paper's impact. For example, the *American Economic Review, Review of Economics and Statistics*, and *Economic Journal* all rejected one of F.M. Scherer's papers. The journal that eventually published the piece had, at the time, only 55 United States subscribers.

Responses from several journal editors seek to hearten authors by noting that an article's rejection may constitute neither a personal rebuke nor disparagement of the article's ideas. However, the following rejection letter from a Chinese economics journal inflicts the same damage as a blunt, two-sentence refusal: "We have read your manuscript with boundless delight. If we were to publish your paper, it would be impossible for us to publish any work of lower standard. And as it is unthinkable that in the next thousand years we shall see its equal, we are, to our regret, compelled to return your divine composition, and to beg you a thousand times to overlook our short sight and timidity (Bernard, 1990, p. 44)."

The risk of rejection that even leading economists confront causes not only anxiety and anger, but also Job-like reflection. Every economist at some point ponders: "Why me?" Paul Krugman's conclusion: "The self-serving answer is that my stuff is so incredibly innovative that people don't get the point. More likely, I somehow rub referees and editors the wrong way, maybe by claiming more originality than I really have. Whatever the cause, I still open return letters from journals with fear and trembling, and more often than not get bad news. I am having a terrible time with my current work on economic geography: referees tell me that it's obvious, it's wrong, and anyway they said it years ago."

Whether rejection is gentle or rough, baseless or correct, it arouses passion. Richard Freeman remarks, "Everyone has a 'good' paper rejected at one time because of a vicious unfair stupid referee, and everyone has a 'bad' paper rejected at one time because it deserves to be buried. Neither are quite as devastating as a teenager being rejected in some passionate one-sided romance, but still you can't forget them."[16]

Are the tales of publishing woe merely frictions of a healthy reviewing process? Or are they major injustices in a fundamentally rotten system? Thomas Schelling bravely acknowledges what most other referees know: even the most fair and conscientious referees and editors err. "I do remember recommending to the Harvard University Press that it not publish a manuscript that, when they published against my advice, did go on to become important. I don't dare let anybody know what manuscript it was." Nonetheless, the outpouring of irritation and anger at the publication process that our project provoked – by the famous economists whom the process has benefited most – creates concern about whether the process functions adequately.

NOTES

1. A forthcoming book – *Rejected: Leading Economists Ponder the Publication Process* – presents all of the responses in full, with additional commentary by leading journal editors and further analysis and publication guidance (see Shepherd, forthcoming 1994).
2. One response expressed incomplete enthusiasm: "I consider your project to be basically derisive, and not worth my attention."
3. Unless we indicate otherwise, all of the rejections that we report were unconditional, with no leave to revise and resubmit.
4. Table 3.1 presents the eventual citations for many of the papers that we discuss.
5. Important articles in the international economics field have been rejected with regularity. For example, Samuelson had difficulty publishing his paper that first exposed the transfer problem in trade theory. After Samuelson's results themselves became conventional, the *American Economic Review* rejected Graciela Chichilnisky's paper that both generalized and contradicted Samuelson's results. The *Journal of Development Economics* published Chichilnisky's paper instead, and later devoted a complete issue to the paper's ideas.
6. The worst publishing experience that Theodore Schultz relates is a bad book review: "a review of one of my best books that appeared in the *Economic Journal*, UK. The reviewer, late Lord Ballard, wrote the most conceivable, devastating review. The consequences were that it condemned the book so severely that the readers of the review could not believe what they had read and promptly bought the book! The sales and translations could not have been better."
7. Becker clashed with an editor regarding his article on the allocation of time. "It was originally submitted to the *Review of Economics and Statistics*. Although the editor, Otto Eckstein, agreed to publish it, he wanted me to cut it down by a huge amount. I became miffed at this suggestion, so I then submitted it to the *Economic Journal*."
8. Waldrop (1992) provides a more complete story of Arthur's difficulties.
9. Gordon Tullock refuses to permit rejection to discourage him. He is preparing a book made up solely of his papers that journals have refused. We hope that he finds a publisher.
10. Jan Tinbergen describes Keynes' confidence. "In 1946 I had the privilege to meet personally John Maynard Keynes, I informed him that I had estimated the price elasticity of the demand for export goods of a number of countries and found figures around -2, the figure he had used intuitively in his famous 'The Economic Consequences of the Peace' (1920). I thought he would be happy that his intuition had been 'proved to be correct'; typically an econometrician's

attitude. His reaction was different: 'how pleasant for you to have found the correct figure.' For him his intuition was the truth, rather than results of econometrics. He may have been right! This may have been a lesson for me."

11. Similarly, in 1924, Keynes rejected an article by Knut Wicksell that later was published as "Ricardo on Machinery and the Present Unemployment: An Unpublished Manuscript by Knut Wicksell," *Economic Journal*, see Jonung (1981). Keynes also refused Michal Kalecki's "A Theorem on Technical Progress." It later appeared in the *Review of Economic Studies* (1941).

12. Similarly, Max Corden suggests that one journal's rejection of what became an important paper proved fortunate; it permitted another journal's editor to improve the paper greatly. "The article of mine which has had the biggest influence, as judged by citations, on the subsequent literature and on empirical work, is 'The Structure of a Tariff System and the Effective Protective Rate,' [which appeared in the *Journal of Political Economy* in 1966]. The first version was rejected by the *EJ*. The criticisms were technical and dealt with rather minor points, and the referee clearly did not perceive the significance of the main idea. But I then revised it and sent it to Harry Johnson for advice. He suggested I submit it to the *JPE* (of which he was the editor). He then made numerous constructive suggestions for improvements, all of which I accepted. The original *EJ* referees had done me a service in leading me to publish a far better paper."

13. Indeed, even the major journals were unable to print mathematical notation. When Franco Modigliani and Merton Miller submitted their 1958 paper that set forth the Modigliani-Miller theorem to the *American Economic Review*, the editor refused to permit the paper to include $\bar{x}$; the *American Economic Review*'s type fonts contained no mathematical symbols. The authors put up a fuss and finally obtained their $\bar{x}$.

14. Back in 1948, Charles Roos (1948, pp. 127-28) reported a case that suggested the difficulties of combining mathematics, statistics, and economics. A young economist sought to extend static economic theory into a testable dynamic structure. His paper used technical mathematics and statistics. A leading American economics journal refused to publish the paper unless he removed the mathematics and statistics. A mathematics journal would publish it only without the statistics and economic theory. A statistics journal demanded that he eliminate the mathematics and the economics.

15. Several respondents find it easier to publish in some fields than in others. For example, Vernon Smith has had relative difficulty in publishing his experimental economics papers. "This is the way we (experimentalists) live! A far cry from the days when I did only theory. Then I could publish my toilet paper."

16. In addition to the stories that we have told in detail, respondents complained of discrimination on the basis of sex and politics, and of promising young researchers' being discouraged by publication frustration, to the point of leaving economics. However, Blank (1991) suggests that sex discrimination does not exist at one major economics journal.

REFERENCES

Bernard, Andre (ed.) (1990), *Rotten Rejections*, London: Penguin Books.

Bernstein, Peter (1992), *Capital Ideas: The Improbable Origins of Modern Wall Street*, New York: Free Press.

Blank, Rebecca M. (1991), "The Effects of Double-Blind versus Single-Blind Reviewing: Experimental Evidence from the *American Economic Review*," *American Economic Review*, **81**, 1041-67; Chapter 7 of this volume.

Harrod, Roy (1951), *The Life of John Maynard Keynes*, New York: Norton.

Moggridge, D.E. (1992), *Maynard Keynes: An Economist's Biography*, London: Routledge.

Monz, John (ed.) (1992), *Econometrics: Essays in Theory and Applications: Collected Papers of Franklin M. Fisher*, Cambridge: MIT Press.

Patinkin, Don, and J. Clark Leith (eds) (1977), *Keynes, Cambridge and the General Theory*, London: Macmillan.

Roos, Charles F. (1948), "A Future Role for the Econometric Society in International Statistics," *Econometrica*, **16**, 127-34.

Shepherd, George B. (forthcoming 1994), *Rejected: Leading Economists Ponder the Publication Process*, Arizona: Thomas Horton and Daughters.

Waldrop, M. Mitchell (1992), *Complexity: The Emerging Science at the Edge of Order and Chaos*, New York: Simon & Schuster.

4.   Aging and Productivity Among Economists[*]

Sharon M. Oster and Daniel S. Hamermesh

Abstract: Economists' productivity over their careers and as measured by publication in leading journals declines very sharply with age. There is no difference by age in the probability that an article submitted to a leading journal will be accepted. Rates of declining productivity are no greater among the very top publishers than among others, and the probability of acceptance is increasingly related to the author's quality rather than the author's age.

It is well known that productivity declines with age in a wide range of activities. Lehman (1953) suggests an early peak in productivity in a variety of scientific and artistic endeavors, and Diamond (1986) documents the pattern for several scholarly pursuits. Levin and Stephan (1992) provide clear evidence that this decline exists even after careful attempts to account for individual and cohort differences. Fair (1994) finds declines in physical ability among elite runners, as does Lydall (1968, pp.113 passim) in physical abilities of the population generally. In this study we examine productivity declines in our own field. The main new results arise from our use of two different types of information, the equivalent of household and establishment data, to study the stone field over essentially the same period of time. Section I discusses the general results on aging and productivity, whereas section II presents evidence of the importance of heterogeneity.

[*] Reprinted with permission of the copyright holder from the *Review of Economics and Statistics*, Vol.80, No.1, 1998, pp. 154-7.

Yale University and University of Texas, respectively. We thank all of those who provided data, and Steve Allen, Jeff Biddie, Richard Blundell, Ray Fair, Martin Feldstein, Zvi Griliches, Preston McAfee, participants at brown-bag seminars at several universities, and two referees for helpful comments. The authors are 49 and 54 years old, respectively.

I.   DECLINING PRODUCTIVITY WITH AGE

Using the American Economic Association (AEA) Directory of Members, we identified tenured economics faculty at 17 top research institutions and obtained the years of their Ph.D. degrees.[1] With the citation index of the *Journal of Economic Literature* we replicated portions of the curricala vitae of each of the 208 economists currently in the economics departments of those institutions who received Ph.D. degrees between 1959 and 1983.[2]

To measure productivity we construct three indexes, combining papers published in refereed journals. Prior research suggests that, at least in terms of salary determination, the returns from nonrefereed publications are quite low Sauer (1988), so that we ignore such publications in calculating these measures. I_1 weights an article by the journal where it appears based on citations to that journal, using values generated by Laband and Piette (1994). This index distinguishes strongly among journals. For example, the *Journal of Political Economy* has a weight of 59.1, whereas *Economic Inquiry* has a weight of 7.9. In constructing I_1 we use the weights associated with the decade in which the articles were published. I_2 distinguishes somewhat less among journals by assigning all articles in the nine "core" journals identified by Laband and Piette a value of 1, whereas all other journals are valued at 0.5.[3] Finally, I_3 gives all papers a weight of 1. Coauthored articles were given half credit, consistent with Sauer's (1988) findings on the economic returns to coauthorship.[4]

We measure the change in productivity over the life cycle by the percentage change in the number of publications from 9-10 years past the Ph.D. to the periods 14-15 years and then 19-20 years after. For most of the elite economists the base period is equivalent (accounting for publication lags) to the time of tenure, when one might expect that incentives to produce are at a peak. Using two-year publication records at each point reduces the effects of noise in the performance measures. One might argue that still other scientific life-cycle mileposts (e.g., attaining a full professorship) should be accounted for too (and to some extent the 14-15-year point does this). But our main purpose is simply to provide detailed evidence on the relationship to age, and our data are not sufficient to infer the impact of every possible milepost.

Table 4.1 contains data on productivity loss by Ph.D. vintage measured by each of the three indexes. If we consider I_1 and I_2, the two indexes that take journal quality into account, the decline appears to be quite substantial. Between years 9-10 and 14-15 elite economists as a group lose 29 to 32% of their output. From years 9-10 to 19-20 they lose 54 to 60%. In other words,

Table 4.1 Percentage Loss in Productivity by Age and Ph.D. Cohort

| Ph.D. Cohort | Productivity Decline Over: | | | | | |
| | Years 10-15 after Ph.D. | | | Years 10-20 after Ph.D. | | |
	I_1	I_2	I_3	I_1	I_2	I_3
1959-1964	32	36	25	58	54	36
1965-1969	30	17	21	61	46	28
1970-1973	32	42	8	51	56	11
1974-1978	16	25	12	–	–	–
All cohorts	29	32	17	54	60	26

productivity losses are on the order of 5% per year from the time of peak productivity. However, the losses do not appear to accelerate over these 10 years of the economists' work lives. The loss from year 10 to year 20 is approximately twice that from year 10 to year 15.

Another way to study the age-productivity relationship is to examine journals rather than individuals. The first row in each pair of years in Table 4.2 shows the ages of authors of full-length refereed articles in several leading journals (*American Economic Review, Journal of Political Economy*, and *Quarterly Journal of Economics*).[5] The median age of authors in the 1980s and 1990s was 36. Scholars over age 50 when their studies are published are a minute fraction of all authors in these journals. Creative economics at the highest levels is mainly for the young. That is as true in the 1990s as it was in the 1960s, although the age distribution of authors does seem to have shifted slightly rightward in the late 1970s.

The second row in each pair in Table 4.2 shows the age distributions of random samples of the membership of the American Economic Association in years near those for which the authors' ages were tabulated.[6] The distributions are heavily concentrated between 36 and 50. Decadal variations reflect rapid expansion of American universities in the middle and late 1960s, stagnation in the 1970s and much of the 1980s, and a possible fragmentation of the profession in the 1980s as specialized associations expanded. A substantial percentage of AEA members is over age 50 implying that older economists are greatly underrepresented among authors in major journals relative to their presence among those who view themselves as part of the economics profession.[7]

Among the several groups of physical scientists analyzed by Levin and Stephan (1992) the decline of productivity (high-quality publishing) with

Table 4.2 Percentage Distributions of Major-Journal Authors and of AEA
*   Members By Age*

Year	Age (years)			Number of Authors
	Less than 36	36-50	Over 50	
1963 Authors	51.3	46.0	2.7	111
1964 Members	32.4	41.0	26.6	
1973 Authors	61.4	32.7	5.9	153
1974 Members	43.0	33.4	23.6	
1983 Authors	46.3	50.0	3.7	188
1985 Members	25.2	52.5	22.3	
1993 Authors	46.6	47.4	6.0	234
1993 Members	19.2	51.3	29.5	
All years Authors	50.6	44.6	4.8	686
Members	29.9	44.6	25.5	

Notes: Full-length refereed articles. Authors whose ages were identifiable are 96.5% of the total in 1963, 99.4% in 1973, 98.9% in 1983, 100% in 1993, and 99.0% over the four decades.

age was very pronounced. McDowell's (1982) small samples of scholars in a variety of disciplines suggest less rapid declines in productivity with age (in publications unweighted by quality), with the sharpest declines and earliest peaks in the "hard" sciences, and later peaks among English professors and historians. The evidence from our two very different types of samples of economists and economics publishing that account for the quality of publications suggests that, for whatever reason, economics is at least as much a "young person's game" as are the physical sciences.

II.   HETEROGENEITY IN DECLINING PRODUCTIVITY

The evidence in section I documents the decline in productivity at the sample means. Information on the age-productivity relationship at the extremes of the sample is interesting in its own right and might help shed some light on the possible causes of the apparent decline in productivity with age. The simplest test compares productivity losses among the top early performers with that of the entire sample of economists at elite

Table 4.3 Productivity in Year 20 as a Function of Productivity in Year 10 (N = 121)

Independent Variables	Dependent Variables		
	$I_{1,20}$	$I_{2,20}$	$I_{3,20}$
$I_{j,10}$	0.41	0.44	0.72
	(0.08)	(0.11)	(0.08)
$I^2_{j,10}$	-0.0004	-0.001	-0.02
	(0.0003)	(0.05)	(0.009)
R^2	0.12	0.19	0.23

Note: Standard errors are in parentheses.

institutions. Among the top 10% of early producers the mean values of I_1, I_2, and I_3 at year 20 were 64, 50, and 22%, respectively. These means are quite close to those listed for the entire sample in Table 4.1. Thus on average early promise seems to be sustained in this sample. Of the 12 top researchers on whom we have 20 years of data, five were still among the top dozen producers at year 20.

These conclusions are confirmed when we examine the entire sample. For each index $I_j, j = 1, 2, 3$, we estimate b_0 and b_1 in

$$I_{j,20} = b_0 I_{j,10} + b_1 I^2_{j,10} \qquad (4.1)$$

Table 4.3 reports the parameter estimates. For all three indexes productivity in year 20 is positively and significantly related to productivity in year 10. There is also substantial productivity loss. The joint hypothesis that $b_0 = 1$ and $b_1 = 0$ (i.e., no productivity loss) is rejected (*F*-statistics of 134, 152, and 39, respectively). Productivity loss is least severe in I_3, which weights all journals equally, regardless of quality.

If productivity losses were less among economists with high early productivity (high), b_1 would be negative. In fact, for two of the three indexes the estimated b_1 is effectively zero. We cannot reject the hypothesis of a linear relationship between late and early productivity. Only for I_3 does it appear that productivity loss is higher for top early producers, and even here the effect is quite small. An economist in the top 10% of this sample at year 10 loses only an additional 0.5 (unweighted) paper compared to an average researcher in this sample at year 10. The very top producers in this elite sample keep on producing high-quality research, but at a slower rate. Those who were not at the top early in their careers slow down as rapidly as the top people, but their slowdown leads them to publish increasingly in lower quality outlets.

Another way of examining heterogeneity is to look at how authors of different quality fare in the publication process conditional on their efforts. We obtained data on a random sample of initial submissions to a major general journal during a four-month period in 1991. (Some of the data were initially supplied by the journal's office for use in Hamermesh (1994).) Refereeing at this journal is double-blind, so that the chance that referees (though possibly not the editors) were affected by authors' reputations is reduced. The ages of the authors of these 313 papers are measured as of 1993 to account for the probable two-year average lag between the submission of a paper and its publication.

The simple fact in these additional data is that acceptance rates at this journal are remarkably constant by author's age. The probabilities of an article being accepted are 0.122, 0.114, and 0.123 in the three age groups ≤35, 36-50, and >50, respectively.[8] On average there is no decline with age in the acceptance rate of papers submitted to this journal.[9] Probits on the acceptance of a submission that also included variables indicating whether the author was a member of the AEA, was in a top 20 department (as listed in Blank, 1991), was resident in North America, or was female, and the author's prior citation record yield an identical conclusion. The declining presence of older authors in top economics journals does not occur because older authors who keep submitting papers suffer higher rejection rates.

The probits included interaction terms between indicator variables for age and the extent of citations. (Low-cited economists were defined as those with fewer than 10 citations per year, well-cited with at least 10.) As Figure 4.1 clearly shows, acceptance rates for each age group differ sharply by citation status. Comparing authors age 36-50 to those over 50, it is quite clear that the degree of heterogeneity increases with age. This appears to be less true in comparing the oldest to the youngest group, but that inference is due mainly to a very small sample. (Only six authors under age 36, the future superstars of the profession, were well cited.) The general tenor of the combined results from this sample is that the profession signals to less able scholars that their work no longer meets the profession's highest standards, and most of them respond by reducing their submissions to the highest quality journals.

Figure 4.1 Probability of Acceptance by Author's Age and Citations

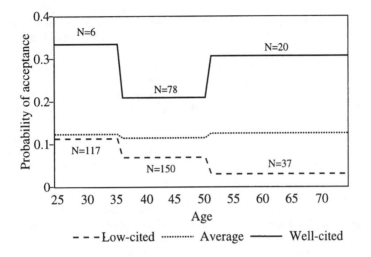

III.   CONCLUSIONS

We have followed the careers of economists and measured the demographic characteristics of publishers in leading journals. The evidence seems quite clear that publishing diminishes with age, especially publishing in leading journals, at rates as rapid as in the physical sciences. Indeed, remarkably few older people publish successfully in the scholarly outlets on which the profession places the highest value. As economists age, those who were the most productive early in their careers are among the few "survivors" still contributing to scholarship through the leading scholarly outlets.

Whether this relationship is due to natural declines in capacity or decreased incentives to produce is extremely difficult to discern. Unlike athletes, where it is likely that pure physical deterioration causes the reduction in productivity with age, among scholars even the fairly subtle facts that we have uncovered can be marshaled as support for each of these competing hypotheses. Without direct observation on how scholars' use of time changes as they age, we are unlikely to be able to distinguish between explanations of the declining age-productivity relationship in science.

NOTES

1. The schools are Berkeley, Carnegie-Mellon, Chicago, Columbia, Harvard, Michigan, Minnesota, Northwestern, Pennsylvania, Princeton, Rochester, San Diego, Stanford, UCLA, Wisconsin, and Yale. They were chosen based on the rankings by Berger and Scott (1990).

2. The on-line index to the *Journal of Economic Literature* begins tracking in 1969. Since we take productivity at 10 years from the Ph.D. as a measure of peak performance, 1959 was the earliest starting dale possible. Similarly, this procedure constrained us to end this sample with economists whose Ph.D.s were from 1983.

3. The core journals are *American Economic Review, Econometrica, Economic Journal, Journal of Economic Theory, Journal of Monetary Economics, Journal of Political Economy, Quarterly Journal of Economics, Review of Economics and Statistics,* and *Review of Economic Studies.*

4. A citations measure could also be used to account for differences in the quality of refereed publications. This would be quite acceptable, although it would generate different difficulties from the quality-weighted publication count I[sub 1], particularly because of differences in citation practices across subfields.

5. These are the three general journals in Noah America that have the biggest impact on the profession Stigler et al. (1995). Included in the table are all full-length articles except Nobel Prize and AEA Presidential addresses. Comments, replies, notes, etc., are also excluded.

6. These data are based on 1000 randomly selected members of the American Economic Association in the particular year. From each issue of the AEA Handbook (or its successor) the first 200 names fisted under the letters A, D, L, R, and W were sampled. Throughout we use chronological age rather than years since receipt of the Ph.D., because not all authors have doctorates.

7. One might object to defining economists as the AEA membership. Very old members might hardly be expected to be active publishers, nor might second-year graduate students, business economists, or those in line government agencies. To avoid making arbitrary distinctions we define potential publishers as those who are interested enough to subscribe to the most widely read scholarly journal in the field.

8. Disaggregating into finer age categories, the acceptance rates (and numbers of submitters) are: age ≤30, 0.130 (23); 31-35, 0.120 (100); 36-40, 0.115 (104); 41-45, 0.147 (68); 46-50, 0.071 (56); 51-55, 0.100 (30); above 55, 0.148 (27). The acceptance rates are nowhere near being significantly different from each other as a group; and the largest *t*-statistic describing the 21 pairwise differences is only 1.33.

9. A large fraction of the papers were coauthored. If we weight the data by the number of coauthors instead of assigning each author the same weight, the results change only minutely. It is also not true that successful young authors' work represents Ph.D. theses or collaborations with senior colleagues. Only two papers by the 15 such authors were parts of dissertations; and only three of the other young authors' papers were with senior economists.

REFERENCES

Berger, Mark, and Frank Scott (1990), "Changes in U.S. and Southern Economics Department Rankings over Time," *Growth and Change*, **21**, 21-31.

Blank, Rebecca (1991), "The Effects of Double-Blind versus Single-Blind Reviewing," *American Economic Review*, **81**, 1041-67; Chapter 7 of this volume.

Diamond, Arthur (1986), "The Life-Cycle Research Productivity of Mathematicians and Scientists," *Journal of Gerontology*, **41**, 520-25.

Fair, Ray (1994), "How Fast Do Old Men Slow Down?" *Review of Economics and Statistics*, **76**, 103-18.

Hamermesh, Daniel (1994), "Facts and Myths about Refereeing," *Journal of Economic Perspectives*, **8**, 153-64; Chapter 5 of this volume

Laband, David, and Michael Piette (1994), "The Relative Impacts of Economics Journals: 1970-90," *Journal of Economic Literature,* **32**, 640-66; Chapter 15 of this volume.

Lehman, Harvey (1953), *Age and Achievement*, Princeton, NJ: Princeton University Press.

Levin, Sharon, and Paula Stephan (1992), *Striking the Mother Lode in Science*, New York: Oxford.

Lydall, Harold (1968), *The Structure of Earnings,* Oxford, UK: Oxford.

McDowell, John (1982), "Obsolescence of Knowledge and Career Publication Profiles," *American Economic Review*, **72**, 752-68.

Sauer, Raymond (1988), "Estimates of the Returns to Quality and Coauthorship in Economic Academia," *Journal of Political Economy*, **96**, 855-66; Chapter 10 of this volume.

Stigler, George, Stephen Stigler, and Claire Friedland (1995), "The Journals of Economics," *Journal of Political Economy*, **103**, 331-59; Chapter 13 of this volume.

PART TWO

Referees and Editors

5.   Facts and Myths about Refereeing[*]

Daniel S. Hamermesh

Substantial mystery surrounds the process of refereeing scholarly articles in economics, particularly about the choice of referees, how they are assigned, and, perhaps most important, why they seem to take so very long. By describing the process using the first broad-based sample of referees, I hope to remove some of the mystery, and also to dispel some widely-held myths about refereeing.

There has been a huge amount of research on refereeing, mostly on the fairness and quality of the reviews. Studies involving correlations between referees' opinions on the same article or proposal and the re-refereeing of articles and proposals (Cole et al., 1978; Peters and Ceci, 1982) have been designed to determine whether the process can distinguish quality among submissions. Blank (1991) and many earlier studies (like Crane, 1967) have examined whether refereeing ou1tcomes differ between single- and double-blind trials; and Laband (1990) studied the productivity of refereeing. But we know nothing about what referees do with their time, and very little about who they are and how they are matched to articles.

A NEW SOURCE OF DATA ON REFEREES

Some journals publish occasional tables showing the length of time from submission to acceptance or rejection of a paper. Others present information

[*] Reprinted with permission of the copyright holder from the *Journal of Economic Perspectives,* Vol.8, No.1, Winter 1994, pp. 153-64.

University of Texas at Austin, Texas, and Research Associate, National Bureau of Economic Research, Cambridge, Massachusetts. I thank Jeff Biddle, George Borjas, the editors, and participants at seminars at several institutions for helpful comments on an earlier draft. I am deeply grateful to the editors and administrative assistants who kept and provided the records that made the empirical work possible. The data are available from me on diskette in a LOTUS work file.

with each published article on the dates of initial submission, and/or revision and/or final acceptance. However, there are no secondary data on who referees are, how they are chosen, or how long they take. I therefore asked editors of eleven journals to participate in the following exercise. The editorial office was to keep records resulting from the editor's next 50 requests for reports on initial submissions of articles. These records generated information for each refereeing request on whether the task was accomplished and the length of time it took.[1] The length of the paper was also obtained, as was the referee's name.

Seven editors agreed to keep these records, beginning in November 1989. Their journals include four general journals, designated G1 through G4, and three that publish in only one subspecialty each, S1 through S3. I rank them in descending order according to the rate at which articles in them are cited, as calculated by Liebowitz and Palmer (1984).[2] All six that were ranked by Liebowitz and Palmer were in the top half of the quality distribution of journals, and two were in the top five. By November 1990 all seven editors had returned the recording forms. Of the 350 possible data points, 343 were usable.[3] Given the sampling procedure and response, the data set is a random sample of refereeing at these seven journals.

These editorial records were linked to indicators describing the referees. These included the number of years since receipt of the Ph.D., based in most cases on self-reported information in the *American Economic Association Membership Directory*, 1989.[4] This is a standard measure of productivity used to study earnings generally and those of academic economists particularly (Johnson and Stafford, 1974). The names were also linked to the *Social Science Citation Index* for 1989, and each referee's citations by other scholars in 1989 were included in the data set. This measure of quality seems to be a more important determinant of one outcome of quality differences among economists – dispersion in salaries – than either counts of publications or the status of the outlets of one's research (Hamermesh et al., 1982) and is a standard, albeit imperfect, bibliometric measure of scholarly impact. Because citations are highly skewed, I divided referees into those who were lightly cited (less than 10 times in 1989), well cited (10 through 49 times), and heavily cited (50 or more citations).

Other variables reflect the referee's ties to the particular journal. These include whether the referee is at the same school as the journal's editor, and whether the referee published in that journal during the quinquennium 1986-1990. Also available is information on the gender of referees.

WHO REFEREES?

The first column of Table 5.1 shows sample means describing the characteristics of the economists who submitted the 343 reports in the new sample. Over 50 percent of the referees are cited at least 10 times per year; one-eighth are cited at least 50 times. This is a very high rate of citation. For example, only 85 American economists were cited on average at least 50 times per year from 1971-85 (Medoff, 1989). The mean annual citation rate in the sample, 23, equals that among full professors in economics departments ranked among the second 15 in North America (Hamermesh, 1989).

Referees are neither neophytes nor gray-beards. The mean Ph.D. experience is 16 years, implying that the average referee is roughly 45. Not surprisingly, people are asked to referee increasingly as they near the peak of their careers. Past that peak, they are called on at a diminishing rate.[5]

Ninety percent of referees are men, remarkably close to the 91 percent male faculty in Ph.D-granting economics departments.[6] The extent of journals' reliance on their own authors for refereeing services is surprising. Nearly one-third of referees published recently in the journal, and others presumably had articles under review or forthcoming at the time they refereed. Also, with an entire profession to choose from – there are economists in over 2000 institutions of higher education in the United States alone – the extent that editors rely on colleagues in their own departments attests to the role of propinquity in the choice of referees.

The rest of Table 5.1 demonstrates the differences in refereeing practices among journals. Most important, except that G4 is out of place, the percentage of well- or heavily-cited people declines steadily as one moves down the quality ranking of journals. Papers sent to better journals are refereed by higher-quality scholars, and, one would hope, obtain more useful comments from them. This evidence suggests that among initially identical articles the one sent to a better journal will end up being a better paper. That fact should enhance the incentives to begin publishing attempts by aiming at as high-level a journal as possible (Hamermesh, 1992).

The diversity in journals' practices in choosing referees is noteworthy. Half the referees at G2 are its own authors, while only 6 percent of G4's are. Obversely, the editor at G4 relies heavily on his colleagues, while the extent to which colleagues are pestered to referee varies greatly among the other journals. That the specialized journals S1 and S2 use so many women is a reflection mainly of the high proportion of women in the specialty that those publications represent.

The best answer to the question of this section is that referees are disproportionately the top people in their specialty. But editors also rely heavily on scholars to whom they have easy access.

Table 5.1 Means of Variables, by Journal

Variable	All	G1	G2	G3	G4	S1	S2	S3
				Journal Designation				
CITS1049	0.396	0.500	0.429	0.208	0.449	0.367	0.340	0.480
CITS50	0.122	0.292	0.122	0.021	0.143	0.122	0.100	0.060
Ph.D. Experience	16.49	18.54	14.74	15.77	18.16	10.37	19.80	18.00
Male	0.898	0.938	0.939	0.896	0.939	0.816	0.820	0.940
Same School as Editor	0.116	0.042	0.143	0.042	0.306	0.122	0.140	0.020
Published in Journal	0.318	0.250	0.490	0.271	0.061	0.184	0.420	0.540
Pages	26.74	27.58	25.45	22.29	22.26	33.43	32.78	23.26
$N =$	343	48	49	48	49	49	50	50

ARE REFEREES ASSIGNED FAIRLY?

Many younger economists argue that articles submitted by better-known scholars are assigned to higher-quality referees. The myth is that editors screen out papers by unknowns by assigning them to referees on whose opinions they are unlikely to rely. Coupled with the belief that editors themselves favor well-known researchers, this myth implies that the unknown author faces a double hurdle in getting a paper accepted for publication.

Is this myth correct? In one deeper sense it clearly is. To the extent that well-known people submit their work to higher-quality journals, they will obtain comments from higher-quality referees. With better journals using better referees, sorting of articles at the submission stage guarantees that author quality and referee quality are at least partly matched by the market among journals.

To examine whether editors assign papers to referees nonrandomly, I obtained another set of data from journal G1, listing all the referee-author matches that the editors made over a roughly one-month period in 1991. Table 5.2 presents a contingency table. The rows classify the submissions according to the number of times the author's work was cited in 1990; the columns classify the referees according to their citations that year.[7]

If citations measure quality, and if authors are being matched to referees

Table 5.2 Author-Referee Matches by Citation Count

Referee	Author					
	0-4	5-9	10-49	50-99	100+	Total
0-4	21	3	37	12	6	79
5-9	2	3	4	4	2	15
10-49	3	2	14	4	2	25
50-99	2	0	1	1	0	4
100+	0	1	0	2	3	6
TOTAL	28	9	56	23	13	129

Notes: χ^2-statistics:
1. $\chi^2(9) = 17.58$; all observations, categories 0-4, 5-9, 10-49, 50+; $p = .04$.
2. $\chi^2(4) = 8.32$; all observations, categories 0-9, 10-49, 50 +; $p = .08$.
3. $\chi^2(4) = 2.47$; excludes 6 matches on authors with CITES$\geq$ 100, categories 0-9, 10-49, 50+; $p > .25$.
4. $\chi^2(2) = 1.49$; excludes 10 matches on authors with CITES$\geq$ 50, categories 0-9, 10-49, 50+; $p > .25$.

of the same quality, most of the matches should be along the diagonal of Table 5.2. This evidence does not offer a conclusion at a glance, though there clearly are many matches off the diagonal. To examine whether authors and referees are matched randomly along this dimension of quality I list under Table 5.2 χ^2-tests on various parts of the table. Over the entire table, tests using three or four ranges of citations reject the hypothesis that the author-referee matches are random. The rejections are based, though, solely on the six extremely heavily-cited (more than 100 citations per year) authors. When these few matches are deleted, the matching process appears random.

Whether evidence from other journals would yield the same conclusion is unclear. But the relatively high quality of referees at GI suggests that the scope for matching at most other journals is far less than at G1. If other editors behave as do the editors at G1, matching is even less important than the data in Table 5.2 indicate. At the level of the individual journal, the answer to the titular question of this section is yes: except for a very few superstar authors, editors do not match authors with referees of similar quality.

HOW LONG DOES REFEREEING TAKE, AND WHY?

Of the 343 referees whose opinions were solicited, 269 (78 percent) completed the refereeing task by submitting a report to the editor. Most of these "doers," as I call them, accomplished their task rapidly. Figure 5.1

Referees and Editors

Figure 5.1 Survivor Function, Papers Eventually Refereed

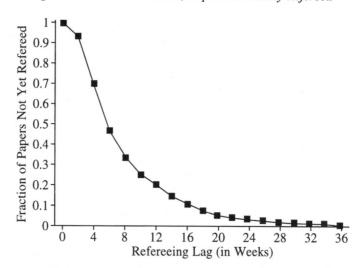

shows the "survivor function" for refereeing requests among those for which reports were eventually received. This function is the fraction of papers that remain unrefereed each week after being mailed to the referee. Half the reports that would be received arrived back at the editorial office within six weeks, and 75 percent did so within 10 weeks. Only 10 percent of doers took more than four months to comply. The overwhelming majority of referees who are doers are in no way responsible for the slow editorial process.

However, 57 potential referees (17 percent of the sample) are "refusers" – they sent the paper back to the editor without a report. (Except for one person they all formally declined the task.) The median time to refusal in this group is 17 days, the 75th percentile is 27 days, and only 10 percent refused after eight weeks. The third group of referees consists of "losers" – they seemingly lose the papers they are sent. Seventeen referees (5 percent of the sample) never submitted a report and never informed the editor that they could not handle the paper. A few were eventually told by the editor not to bother. Most, though, repeatedly promised a report but had not complied by November 1990, when I ceased collecting data. The median time that this small group of losers held papers was eight months.

Most doers respond expeditiously, and refusers, though they are unproductive, respond so quickly that they hardly delay the editorial process. However, the 5 percent of referees who are delinquent account for half of the 10 percent of papers that are held for more than five months. The other half are held by referees in the very thin right tail of the distribution of doers. These few dawdlers cause much of the slowness in the editorial process.

With this division of referees into doers, refusers and losers, and with the evidence on how each group behaves and a few auxiliary assumptions, one can calculate the patterns of how papers will percolate through the refereeing system. For example, if an editor relies on average-quality referees, as measured by experience and citations, one report can be obtained on the median paper in less than two months. For only 10 percent of articles does it take longer than four months to obtain one report. (If editors seek two reports at the start, the median waiting time to receive both rises only to 80 days, and the 90th percentile rises to 6.5 months.) If editors are efficient they can reach a decision on most papers within a few months. In a few cases, though, because of the (small) probability that the paper is sent to a loser or one of the few unusually dilatory doers, the referees' behavior will cause the author a long wait.

Editors might seek to alter this pattern either by using higher-quality or lower-quality referees, again as measured by citations and experience. To address these possibilities, I first estimated a multinomial logit model relating the probabilities of doing, refusing and losing the paper to the measures of quality, experience and citations. I then estimated a proportional-hazard model indicating how the quality measures affect the rate at which doers complete the refereeing assignment.[8] The results show that reliance on heavily-cited, experienced referees increases the expected time to obtain a report by three weeks over a strategy that relies on the average referee. The increase is 3½ weeks compared to a strategy that relies on the most junior and lightly-cited referees. Accounting for a one-week round-trip by mail between the editorial office and referees, these results imply that using highest- instead of lowest-quality referees generates 38 percent additional time costs. This is the implicit price of quality in the market for referees' services.[9]

The short average response time of low-quality referees is made up of a high number of rapid doers and a small, but above-average proportion of losers. Relying on inexperienced referees lowers the mean response time but increases the risk that the referee will be a loser and will be responsible for keeping the paper in editorial limbo.

The statistical analysis also permits calculating the effect of prolixity on refereeing delays in this sample of papers that ranged from 4 to 81 pages. Referees are more likely to refuse to handle longer papers (though no more likely to lose them). Each additional 10 pages slows a typical doer's completion of the refereeing task by one week.

The refereeing process may be slow; but most individual referees do their jobs quickly. In a few cases the process is slowed by the very few dilatory referees who simply fail to respond or who respond very tardily.

Authors should also realize that some of the slowness in the process is the price they pay for the services of higher-quality referees who generally respond more slowly.

CAN REFEREEING BE SPEEDED UP?

One obvious method to prod referees (at least obvious to economists) is to offer them a monetary reward for prompt service. Currently payments of this sort are offered by only a scattering of economics journals. In most cases a small dollar amount is paid if a referee's report is completed in a month or six weeks (though one journal offers a sliding scale, with a larger fee if the job is completed within one month, a smaller payment in the second month, and no payment thereafter). Small payments have no effect on the behavior of very prompt referees. Obversely, referees who would either refuse, lose the paper, or take a very long time to do the job without the monetary bribe are also unlikely to alter their behavior in response to any small incentive. The biggest impact should be on those referees who would otherwise complete the task within a few weeks after the date that would qualify them for the bribe.

With only a few journals offering bribes for prompt service, those that do so take advantage of a potentially high elasticity of supply to a narrowly-defined activity. However, if more journals were to offer bribes, their impact would be reduced. With this caveat in mind, do the existing bribes seem to work? Journal G1 pays for completion within a nominal one month (in actuality, if the report is received within six weeks – 42 days – of the date it was requested). This allows us to infer the relative effect of monetary incentives on waiting time.

Figure 5.2 shows Kaplan-Meier estimates of the "daily hazard rate," the daily probability that a paper in the queue of unrefereed papers is refereed. The boxes (*) show the hazard rates for journal G1; the plusses (+) show the hazards for the aggregate of the other six journals, which do not offer bribes.[10] (With only three manuscripts outstanding at journal G1, the hazard beyond 98 days is uninteresting.)

Remarkably, the hazard rates are nearly identical in the first two-week interval, and essentially the same in the three intervals containing weeks 9 through 14. However, the hazard rate at G1 is higher in the second and third intervals (days 15-42) and lower in the fourth interval (days 43-56). These three hazards (and these alone) are more than one standard error apart, even with the very small sample size at G1. The bribe pays off by inducing faster refereeing by those people who would otherwise take somewhat, but not very greatly longer than the time allowed to qualify for the bribe. The

Figure 5.2 Hazard Rates of Journal G1 and Other Journals

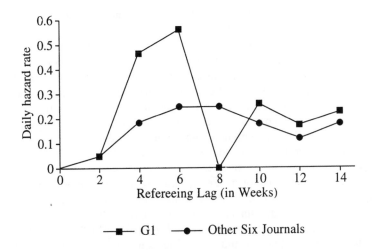

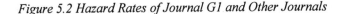

payoff to the journal is substantial: holding constant referees' quality, the mean completion time by doers at G1 is two weeks faster than at the average of the other six journals.

An interesting question is why some doers at G1 fail to complete the task within six weeks. Assuming that the average paper takes six hours to referee, it is true the hourly pay is only $6, far below the value of most economists' time. But if the paper will be refereed later anyway, the alternative to postponing the task is shifting it forward in time by on average two months. Unless the referee has a very high rate of time preference, values his or her time at an unusually high rate, or expects the task to be unusually arduous, it is foolish to postpone refereeing beyond the date that would generate payment of the bribe.[11] Finding that some economists referee articles but fail to qualify for offered bribes demonstrates that not all of us are pure income-maximizers.

Refereeing will be speeded up if bribes are offered (though the impact will be reduced as bribing becomes more widespread). But while bribes speed referees, they fail to discipline the main culprits in slow refereeing – losers of papers and very slow doers. Is there anything editors can do about these miscreants? Journal editors could automatically truncate the long thin tail of waiting times by assuming that any referee who holds a paper for five months is a loser and sending the paper to another referee. For the editorial offices, such a step would obviate the serious headaches of dealing with losers. Authors would gain to the extent that the chance of a very long wait would be reduced, though they would lose the services of a few sluggish but high-quality referees. My guess is that most authors would happily risk the small chance of losing a high-quality referee in exchange for a large gain of time.

It is very likely that the person refereeing a paper is better-known than the author. Referees tend to be economists whose work is cited widely and who are near the peak of their career. Most of these high-quality referees either accomplish the task or refuse the assignment very rapidly. Only a small fraction of refereeing requests are handled slowly.

Despite this there are undeniably very long publication lags in economics. Clearly, part of the problem arises from those few referees who lose papers or take more than five months to complete their task, a difficulty for which I outlined a solution above. Another serious problem is the delay between submission of the final version of an article and its publication, with lags greater than one year being quite common. Their relative infrequency of publication makes it unlikely that economics journals can improve upon this enough to approximate the speed of publication in the physical sciences. But with submissions through electronic media and better scheduling practices in editorial offices, it is difficult to believe that this lag needs to be so long. A third possible cause of problems is editorial malfeasance, as editors change or simply let things slide as they lose interest. Barring palace coups or genuine revolutions, this difficulty is not likely to be removed.

NOTES

1. This is calculated as the days elapsed from the time the manuscript left the editorial office to its receipt back, minus seven days if the Christmas-New Year's holiday intervened.
2. I have designated the one journal that was too new to be rated in that study as S1, based on its immediate success in attracting attention from the profession generally.
3. On three others the editor did not seek a report; one paper was withdrawn by its author; one form was blank; and on one no page-length was recorded. I was unable to calculate Ph.D. experience on one other request.
4. Indexes of other organizations were consulted or the editors were telephoned to supply the information for the few individuals not listed in the Directory.
5. A slightly different perspective on the issue comes from direct evidence on a sample of 41 economists in one department in the academic year 1987-88. The following regression was estimated:
   Referee tasks =
   $$2.08 + .31X - .0095X^2 + 1.76CITS1049 + 16.98CITS50,$$
   $$(1.34) \quad (.20) \quad (.0052) \quad (1.43) \quad\quad (2.92)$$
   where X is years since Ph.D., and the citations variables correspond to the description in the text. Standard errors for the regression are in parentheses; the

R^2 is equal to .52. The mean number of articles refereed was five; the (two) heavily-cited faculty refereed four times the department's average, while the (eleven) widely-cited faculty members referred two more articles than their typical colleague. There is a significant inverse U-shape in experience, with the peak refereeing at 16 years.

6. From American Economic Association, Universal Academic Questionnaire, cited in *CSWEP Newsletter*, Winter 1993, p.8.
7. In the case of multiple-authored papers I use citations to the first author listed. The 129 author-referee matches were based on 80 separate papers.
8. Details of the process are available on request from the author. Also included in the multinomial logit and the proportional-hazard model are dummy variables indicating whether the referee had published in the journal, was at the editor's school, was male, lived in North America, and a continuous variable measuring the length of the paper.
9. Referees with 15 years of experience and those who are heavily cited are the slowest doers and are most likely to refuse the refereeing assignment, all else equal, in the proportional-hazard model and the multinomial logit.
10. The hazards for the other six journals in Figure 5.2 are based on a sample that includes losers as censored observations. The hazard rate lies even closer to that of G1 if only doers are included. (There were no losers at G1.)
11. For example, with a value of time of $200 per hour and an annual rate of time preference of 20 percent it just barely pays to postpone the refereeing job ($200 × 6 hours × $(1.2^{1/6}-1)$ = $37).

REFERENCES

Blank, Rebecca (1991), "The Effects of Double-Blind versus Single-Blind Reviewing: Experimental Evidence from the *American Economic Review*," *American Economic Review*, December, **81**, 1041-67; Chapter 7 of this volume.

Cole, Stephen, Leonard Rubin, and Jonathan Cole (1978), *Peer Review in the National Science Foundation*. Washington, DC: National Academy of Sciences.

Crane, Diane (1967), "Gatekeepers of Science: Some Factors Affecting the Selection of Articles for Scientific Journals," *American Sociologist*, November, **2**, 195-201.

Hamermesh, Daniel (1989) "Why Do Individual-Effects Models Perform So Poorly? The Case of Academic Salaries," *Southern Economic Journal*, July, **56**, 39-45.

Hamermesh, Daniel (1992), "The Young Economist's Guide to Professional Etiquette," *Journal of Economic Perspectives*, **6**, 169-79; Chapter 2 of this volume.

Hamermesh, Daniel, George Johnson and Burton Weisbrod (1982), "Scholarship, Citations and Salaries: Economic Rewards in Economics," *Southern Economic Journal*, **49**, 472-81.

Johnson, George, and Frank Stafford (1974), "Lifetime Earnings in a Professional Labor Market: Academic Economists," *Journal of Political Economy*, **82**, 549-69.

Laband, David (1990), "Is There Value-Added from the Review Process in Economics?: Preliminary Evidence from Authors," *Quarterly Journal of Economics*, **105**, 341-53; Chapter 6 of this volume.

Liebowitz, Stanley, and John Palmer (1984), "Assessing the Relative Impacts of Economics Journals," *Journal of Economic Literature*, **22**, 77-88.

Medoff, Marshall (1989), "The Rankings of Economists," *Journal of Economic Education*, **20**, 405-15.

Peters, Douglas, and Stephen Ceci (1982), "Peer-Review Practices of Psychological Journals: The Fate of Published Articles, Submitted Again," In Harnad, Stevan (ed.), *Peer Commentary on Peer Review*, Cambridge: Cambridge University Press, 3-11.

6. Is there Value-Added from the Review Process in Economics?: Preliminary Evidence from Authors[*]

David N. Laband

Abstract: Do referees employed by journals merely screen acceptable from unacceptable manuscripts or are they charged with an additional value-adding responsibility, vis-à-vis the papers they review? Drawing from editorial correspondence provided by survey respondents, I address this question by examining the relationship between citations of published papers and comments provided by reviewers and editors. Referees' comments demonstrate a positive impact on subsequent citation of papers, while comments made by editors show no such impact. Value-adding by editors appears to derive principally from efficient matching of papers with reviewers.

I. INTRODUCTION

My strong impression is that in the case of the ... article, the two reviewers provided me with detailed comments that were extremely helpful in the revisions that I made, resulting in a much improved final product.

[*] Reprinted with permission of the copyright holder from the *Quarterly Journal of Economics*, Vol.103, No.2, May 1990, pp. 341-52.

Clemson University. I am indebted to a number of individuals for their assistance on this study. First and foremost, I wish to thank the many individuals who were willing and able to provide me with their editorial correspondence on papers published so many years ago. I have benefited greatly from comments by and discussions with Dale Heien, Earl Grinols, Robert D. Tollison, John Pencavel, Terry L. Anderson, and my colleagues, Mason Gerety, Michael T. Maloney, Robert E. McCormick, and T. Bruce Yandle. The usual disclaimer applies.

... the referee comments did not lead to much in the way of revision.

In my opinion the editors and referees for journals are really excellent

... the whole editorial process works much less well than we pretend, not only the lags, but the objectivity and quality of the refereeing. Almost everyone complains simultaneously about (1) the stupidity of the papers they referee, and (2) the stupidity of the comments made by the referees of their papers. Since everyone is refereeing each other's papers, there is obviously an inconsistency here.

I think you find great value added by this journal.

There is *negative* value-added by the review process.

The value-added by the reviewing process is negligible in substance, even though diction and style may have improved to some extent. This is not to say that the refereeing system is unwarranted. I think it is important as a screening device. ... But I also think that the system as a screening device is not functioning very well. One reason is the time cost involved, which seems to be excessive.

There are at least two, not necessarily mutually exclusive views of the function of the peer review process in economics. One is that it functions primarily as a screening mechanism, to identify those manuscripts worthy of publication and separate them from those that are not. From this perspective peer review clearly offers no value-added to submitters, but may provide value-added to editors. Presumably, in this world, peer review is the most cost-effective means of conducting such screening, as determined by editors (and the competition among them for good papers).

An alternative view is that the review process materially assists authors in the production of publishable papers. That is, editors, reviewers, and authors are complementary inputs in the production of (published) scientific knowledge. To the extent that this is an apt characterization of the function of the review process in economics, gains to authors in exchange for the time costs borne are implied.[1]

The purpose of this paper is to analyze empirically the impact of the peer review process on the market-revealed quality of economic research. In brief, I attempt to estimate a knowledge production function, one element of which is the editorial/referee input. Quality of knowledge produced is measured by subsequent citations on each paper. A number of alternative measures of the editorial/referee input are examined, based on information provided by authors of papers published in several of the top economics journals during 1976-1980. The results indicate that reviewers' comments enhance the quality of published papers and that editorial value-added apparently derives from efficient matching of manuscripts and reviewers. While these results do not rule out a screening function for the review process in economics, they clearly demonstrate that screening is not the sole function of the review process.[2]

II.   TESTING FOR VALUE-ADDED FROM THE REVIEW PROCESS IN ECONOMICS

There are solid grounds for expecting to be able to measure empirically value-added from the review process in economics. The mere fact that such a large percentage of accepted papers are revised argues in favor of the theory that authors work jointly with reviewers and editors to produce scientific knowledge. Yet, as the quotations (provided by survey respondents) cited at the beginning of this paper suggest, opinions vary widely within the profession with respect to whether referees actually do add value to the papers they review.

The editorial input arguably is more universally respected by authors, for two reasons. First, editors have proven credentials in most cases, whereas referees do not necessarily, or even probably, come from that end of the talent distribution in economics. Second, editors are, in part, residual claimants to the product that appears in their journals. Thus, they have a certain incentive to perform their quality control services conscientiously. Reviewers, on the other hand, are residual claimants to little of value in exchange for their efforts. True, they may benefit from early reading of high quality research findings, but, in general, there is no quid pro quo for their reviewing services. They have no property rights to their input-share of the final published product and, with strikingly few exceptions, receive no monetary compensation. The few journals that do pay reviewers pay them precious little, certainly less than the opportunity cost of their time spent reviewing. Yet there is the implicit quid pro quo of rendering reviewing services in exchange for reviewing services, in a club context. Moreover, heavier demanders of reviewer services generally are at least asked to pay appropriate prices, since they are undoubtedly requested by editors to undertake more reviews than light demanders.

Editors of several top economics journals were included in my survey; the comments of one editor in particular were illuminating. He admitted that available page space exceeds the space taken up by the supply of inherently high quality papers. Since he cannot easily reduce the number of issues per year, he must devote considerable resources to upgrading the quality of "marginally acceptable" manuscripts (my words, not his) in order to render them viable inclusions in the journal. While this may strike readers as a fantastic admission from a journal editor, he merely voices what the data argue for the other economics journals. The fact is, *every* economics journal publishes papers that never get cited.[3] This suggests either that not enough high-caliber papers are submitted to fill up available page space, or else that the review process, as a screening mechanism, is inefficient. Again, the data support the former interpretation. The vast majority of published papers in

the major economics journals have been revised at least one time, perhaps
several times. Indeed, 98 percent of the full-length papers published in the
Review of Economics and Statistics during 1976-1980 were revised by the
authors in accordance with suggestions made by the reviewers or editor or
both. This kind of statistic simply cannot be explained by a review process
that acts merely to screen acceptable from unacceptable papers. Reviewers
are relied upon to be contributing inputs in a production of knowledge
function that includes authors and editors also. Since editors' time is scarce,
the most important function they perform may well be to efficiently match
referees with submitted manuscripts. The issue of whether reviewers create
positive value-added through their efforts, regardless of what individual
authors may believe, is purely an empirical question.

How can each of the inputs (author, editor, reviewers) in the knowledge
production function be measured? For a specific manuscript this is not an
easy task. Author(s) effort and quality is variable from one research effort to
the next. Thus, the quality of any given first-draft manuscript (Q_i) is perhaps
best described as being equal to the average quality of work that the
researcher produces plus some variance term:

$$Q_i = \overline{Q} + \sigma \qquad (6.1)$$

The quality of a published paper (Q_{pi}) is a function of the quality of the
original manuscript, and the further collaborative efforts of the author(s),
editor, and reviewer(s):

$$Q_{pi} = F(Q_i E_i R_i) \qquad (6.2)$$

Substituting (6.1) into (6.2), we obtain

$$Q_{pi} = F(\overline{Q} + \sigma, E_i, R_i) \qquad (6.2')$$

Editorial correspondence (including referees' reports) with authors is
considered highly confidential by journal editors and is accordingly
extremely difficult to obtain. For that matter, if one had such
correspondence, it is not clear how one would measure the referee or
editorial input. Can one measure the impact of a request that the author(s)
attempt alternative model specifications? How about the impact of a request
to delete certain material?

Let us assume that a journal editor is concerned about the quality of the papers he publishes in his journal. At the present time, postpublication citations appear to provide the most unbiased estimate of the impact/quality of a published paper, at relatively low cost.[4] The average quality of an author's work can be proxied by either the stock of citations (s)he has accumulated during some time period for everything published, or by dividing that stock of citations by the number of articles published during an equivalent time period to the citation stock, as a measure of citations per article published.

Data

The data were obtained via a survey of all traceable authors of full papers published during 1976-1980, inclusive, in the *American Economic Review, Journal of Political Economy, Quarterly Journal of Economics, Journal of Law and Economics, Review of Economics and Statistics,* and *Economic Inquiry.*[5] Requests for information regarding the review process were sent to 731 authors, covering 1,062 papers published in the sample journals (a copy of the requested information appears as Appendix A). For those who responded positively, I subsequently inquired whether each paper had been submitted to any other journals prior to submission to the publishing journal. Of the 731 requests, usable responses were received from 87 authors, covering 98 published papers, including 14 papers that bypassed the normal "peer" review process.[6] Missing data on critical variables reduced the sample of usable papers depending on the model specification run. Sample characteristics of these papers are detailed in Table 6.1.

Most of the variables are self-explanatory. The length of time a manuscript spends in the review process, exclusive of revision time, is measured in days and includes time spent in transit to/from the author. Similarly, the period of time an author spent revising his/her manuscript is measured in days. The referees' input is measured by the number of typed characters in the referee reports returned to the authors. There is an obvious presumption here that the relationship between value-added by the referee and the length of his report is positive. Similarly, editorial input is measured by the number of typed characters in the editor's letter that recommend substantive changes in the manuscript. Author reputation/quality is proxied by the total stock of citations reported in the *Social Sciences Citation Index* for that author during the five years prior to the year in which his/her article appeared in print.[7] Length of paper as text and in total was measured in typed characters. *CITES* refers to the number of times each paper was cited starting in the second year after publication and running for a period of six years.

Table 6.1 Sample Means and Standard Errors

Variable	Noncommissioned papers $n = 75$		Commissioned papers $n = 14$		All papers $n = 89$	
# reviewers	1.39	0.73	0.0	0.0	1.19	0.83
# revisions	1.29	0.75	0.0	0.0	1.10	0.83
Time spent by editor/referees	253.25	139.80	0.0	0.0	216.14	157.13
Revision time	76.05	68.93	0.0	0.0	64.96	69.13
Referee comments (# typed char.)	3,925.01	3,768.02	0.0	0.0	3,340.44	3,746.25
Editor comments (# typed char.)	1,032.27	1,172.82	0.0	0.0	881.73	1,143.21
Author stock of cites-5 years	39.32	77.43	552.21	746.43	112.59	335.18
4 authors	1.32	0.58	1.21	0.43	1.31	0.56
Submitted elsewhere	0.31	0.47	0.0	0.0	0.27	0.45
Referees thanked	0.38	0.49	0.0	0.0	0.34	0.48
Length-text (# typed char.)	27,405	9,844	45,389	28,803	29,974	15,301
Length-everything	46,923	14,474	61,872	34,270	49,059	19,086
Cites-6 years	11.44	17.07	29.86	39.02	14.11	22.25
# informal readers	3.29	3.04	4.71	5.82	3.49	3.56
Readers' stock of cites-5 years	459.17	822.97	1,295.14	1,891.78	578.59	1,070.34
Empirical	0.62	0.49	0.07	0.27	0.54	0.50
Appendix	0.48	0.75	0.0	0.0	0.41	0.72
Tables	2.56	2.61	0.79	1.42	2.31	2.55
Figures	1.37	1.82	1.57	1.70	1.40	1.79
Equations	15.19	13.70	6.93	12.78	14.01	13.82
Footnotes	14.96	9.07	27.50	42.10	16.76	18.12

To test for value-added from the review process in economics, I estimated the straightforward knowledge production function described in equation (6.3):

$$CITES = \alpha_0 + \alpha_1 AUTHQUAL + \alpha_2 REFQUAL$$
$$+ \alpha_3 EDITOR + \alpha_4 SUBELSEWHERE$$
$$+ \alpha_5 LENGTH + \alpha_6 LEADARTICLE + \alpha_7 JOURNAL + E \quad (6.3).$$

Subsequent citations of the article are the dependent variable. Author input is measured as the individual's prior five-year stock of citations divided by the number of articles published by the author in the preceding five years (*AUTHQUAL*). As one measure of reviewer input, I used the number of typed characters in the referee reports (*RCOMMENT*). A possible objection to this measure is that some reviewers may be more verbose than others. It seemed reasonable to suppose that the quality of the reviewers' remarks would be reflected in how long it took the author(s) to revise and resubmit, ceteris paribus. More detailed and higher quality comments arguably take longer to incorporate in a revision than lower quality comments. To control simultaneously for verbosity and quality of reviewers' comments, I divided the length of time taken by the author(s) to revise their paper by the number of typed characters in the referees' report (*REFQUAL*). This provides, in essence, a measure of the impact (on the authors) per typed character of the referees' reports. Finally, a number of authors provided additional comments about their experience, from which I was able to categorize the referees' contributions as major (*HELPFUL* = 1) or minor. The editorial input was proxied by the number of typed characters in the editor's letter(s). The submitted elsewhere dummy variable represents a gross control for the possibility that value-added was received from referees at other journals that rejected the paper prior to its being submitted to the publishing journal. The length variable was included for reasons discussed in Laband (1986). Lead articles in economics journals arguably are positioned so because they constitute abnormally high contributions to the literature, at least in comparison with everything else the journal has accepted at that precise moment in time.[8] Dummy variables for each journal control for inherent differences in citations across journals (see Stigler and Friedland, 1975). The *American Economic Review* is the omitted control journal.

The estimation procedure is ordinary least squares (OLS) regression. Numerous alternative specifications of the basic model described in equation (6.3) were estimated; results of several of these specifications are reported in Table 6.2 and discussed below.

Table 6.2 OLS Regression Results For Equation (6.3)
(Dependent Variable = Citations)

Variable	(1)	(2)	(3)	(4)	(5)	(6)
CONSTANT	8.472	18.685[a]	9.290	20.060[a]	-2.536	6.114
	(11.047)	(5.192)	(9.933)	(6.720)	(8.796)	(5.573)
AUTHQUAL	- 0.076	0.129	0.051	0.355[b]	-0.051	-0.030
	(0.385)	(0.332)	(0.181)	(0.159)	(0.131)	(0.121)
REFQUAL	63.938[a]	69.069[a]				
	(18.418)	(17.369)				
RCOMMENT			$1.7E\text{-}3$	$2.3E\text{-}3^{b}$		
			$(1.2E\text{-}3)$	$(1.2E\text{-}3)$		
HELPFUL					6.547	5.254
					(5.342)	(4.730)
LENGTH	$2.6E\text{-}4$		$2.8E\text{-}4$		$1.9E\text{-}4$	
	$(1.8E\text{-}4)$		$(1.3E\text{-}4)$		$(1.2E\text{-}4)$	
LEADART	9.021		14.171		6.901	
	(7.332)		(7.041)		(4.998)	
SUBELSE	- 4.774		- 7.625		- 5.660	
	(5.646)		(6.232)		(4.528)	
JPE	- 6.079	-4.545	-11.864	- 12.698[c]	4.417	6.388
	(7.640)	(6.586)	(8.127)	(7.663)	(8.308)	(6.664)
QJE	- 15.094	-14.115	-17.833	- 18.208[c]	0.677	-1.069
	(10.159)	(8.751)	(11.894)	(10.698)	(9.559)	(7.903)
JLE	-6.143	-10.948	- 26.691[b]	-22.121[c]	3.023	0.966
	(21.625)	(20.032)	(11.447)	(11.421)	(10.644)	(9.653)
RESTAT	- 16.062[b]	- 16.877[a]	- 18.243[b]	- 20.545[a]	-1.852	-3.001
	(7.930)	(6.343)	(8.610)	(7.822)	(7.691)	(6.103)
EI	- 15.635[c]	- 17.652[a]	- 13.227	- 14.979[b]	-4.384	-4.334
	(8.325)	(6.798)	(8.051)	(7.393)	(8.010)	(6.523)
N_2	50	56	74	81	36	40
R^2	0.4592	0.3969	0.3482	0.2300	0.3655	0.2368
F_{reg}	3.397[a]	4.607[a]	3.419[a]	3.157[a]	1.498	1.463

Notes: a. Significant at 0.01 level.
   b. Significant at 0.05 level.
   c. Significant at 0.10 level.

Counter to Laband (1986), the author quality variable demonstrates little predictive ability. One explanation of this nonfinding is that these top journals are able to select from material that is of sufficiently uniform (high) quality as to overwhelm the between author variation that would be apparent in a wider spectrum of journals.

REFQUAL consistently exerts a positive and statistically significant influence on subsequent citations of papers, in both the reported and numerous unreported estimations. Length of referee reports, as a proxy for value-added, demonstrates a marginally significant, positive impact on subsequent citations of a paper. There also appears to be a positive relationship between referee comments that are self-reported as being helpful and subsequent citations of a paper, although the evidence must be considered tentative at this stage. These results conform nicely to the argument that referees in economics are responsible (in part) for adding value to the manuscripts they review. Again, however, this is not to downplay the role of reviewers in screening "good" from "bad" manuscripts. Since I have no data on submissions, much less quality of submissions, it is impossible to shed any light on this issue. My results, tentative though they may be, do indicate that screening is not the *only* function of reviewers; that the production of scientific knowledge in economics is, to some extent, characterized as a joint production process involving researchers, reviewers, and editors.[9]

Although not reported in Table 6.2, comments by the editors showed no significant influence on the market-revealed quality of papers in any model specification. Neither did a composite variable measuring both the editorial and the referee input as one.[10] This nonresult with respect to the editorial comment may be an artifact of the sample. Editors are highly idiosyncratic vis-à-vis their performance. The sample included editors who rarely send substantive comments to authors, and editors who rarely publish a paper without providing considerable editorial input. The implied high variance around the estimates of *EDQUAL* showed up consistently in regressions that included this variable. Moreover, if this finding is indeed empirically accurate, it does not imply that there is no value-added from editors. As indicated previously, the most valuable function performed by an editor may be efficient matching of manuscripts with reviewers.[11]

Longer articles receive more citations than shorter ones, and lead articles are cited more heavily than all other articles. Coefficient estimates for both variables are positive in all regressions run, and border consistently on statistical significance at the 0.10 level.

Although it seems obvious that an author may receive comments of value from referees for journals that reject his/her manuscript, the data do not reveal the anticipated value-added, in any estimation. This may result, in part, from the fact that the large majority of papers sampled were accepted at the first journal submitted to. Moreover, the submitted elsewhere variable is imprecise in the sense that no distinction is made between referee reports that authors found useful and those that were less-than-useful.

III.   SUMMARY AND CONCLUSIONS

Review lags and quality of reviews received are issues that editors are acutely sensitive to. Evidence supporting this proposition is not difficult to come by. Many editors take pains to publish detailed information about review lags, policies, and other data relating to the editorial/review process at their journals. In a recent issue of the *Journal of Macroeconomics* (Vol. 9, Winter 1987), the editor apologizes for the fact that during a transition period the average decision time on new submissions rose to "an unacceptable length." The editors of the *Journal of Finance* make no bones about their concern for timely, high-quality reviewing and have explicitly made referees partial residual claimants to the quality of their review services: "We keep detailed records of ad hoc reviewers. We record both the time the reviewer took and the quality of the review. The quality of the author as a reviewer is a strong influence on our decision of to whom we will send a manuscript. Once again, the best way to ensure a good review is to be a good reviewer when called upon." (Vol.13, July 1987, p. 805).

The evidence presented in this paper suggests that editors' concern with respect to quality of reviews may be well-founded. Not only do editors depend on reviewers to minimize type I and type II errors, comments by referees have a measurably positive impact on subsequent citation of a paper. Given that citations are the currently accepted standard by which individual (and journal) contributions to economic science are judged, the influence of a journal may depend greatly on both the efficiency with which editors match submissions to reviewers and the caliber of their reviewers.

APPENDIX A. INFORMATION REQUESTED FROM AUTHORS

- For each manuscript:
- # reviewers.
- date letter from editor sent to author(s) with an initial decision, date revision sent to journal, etc., covering the process from start to

the date final notification was sent to the author that the paper was accepted or rejected.

- length of original MS in typed characters (number of character spaces per line in the manuscript times the number of lines per page times the number of pages should serve as a close proxy).

- # references in original MS; # references in final revised MS.

- length of reviewers' comments (number of typed characters).

- length of editor's comments when a revision was requested (number of typed characters).\

NOTES

1. For evidence regarding the lengthiness of the review process in economics, see Coe and Weinstock (1967), Yohe (1980), and Laband, McCormick, and Maloney (1990).
2. The search for value-added necessarily is grounded in the assumption that the review process in economics is intended to add value to manuscripts, not just function as a screening mechanism. For a more detailed elaboration of the theoretical argument, see Laband (1989).
3. Evidence in support of this proposition is provided by Laband, McCormick and Maloney (1990).
4. The pros and cons of using citations as a measure of quality have been aired extensively in the economics literature. See, for example, Lovell (1973), Stigler and Friedland (1975), Gerrity and McKenzie (1978), Davis and Papanek (1984), and Laband (1986).
5. My method of tracing authors of eight-twelve-year-old papers was to consult the AEA membership list (December 1985). Of course, not all authors are members of the AEA. Fifty-nine authors of papers were not contacted since I had no reliable address for them. Respondents were promised anonymity; I therefore must reserve the right to limit access to the data.
6. To check for possible selectivity bias with respect to sample respondents, I compared the mean age and citation stock of respondents and nonrespondents. With respect to age, the means (and standard errors) are 46.456 (8.874) and 45.455 (7.418), respectively. With respect to their stock of citations, the means (and standard errors) are 67.073 (121.101) and 51.123 (173.064), respectively. Neither characteristic reveals significant differences between respondents and nonrespondents. Papers that bypassed the normal peer review process generally fell into one of two categories. Nobel lectures and presidential addresses of the American Economic Association and Western Economic Association were generally published as lead articles in the *AER* or *JPE* for the former and *Economic Inquiry* for the latter. The second category of papers included those actively competed for by editors. In some manner they had heard of the

research in progress and requested the author(s) to submit a manuscript to their journal.

7.   Following the premise that what an entrepreneur thinks of his/her own product bears little relation to the market reception of that product, self-citations were excluded from the totals. Citations were summed for coauthored articles.

8.   Evidence with respect to the market-revealed quality of first versus last articles is provided by Tollison and Carlson (1986). Their evidence is suggestive only, as the truly illuminating comparison is between the lead article and all others published.

9.   An anonymous reviewer suggested that the refereeing effort may be endogenous; that is, that good papers may induce more and better refereeing. To check this possibility, I estimated models in which the three refereeing variables (*REFQUAL, RCOMMENT, HELPFUL*) as well as the length of time taken by the referee to submit his/her report were regressed against *CITES* (as a measure of manuscript quality), *MSLENGTH, AUTHQUAL,* and the journal dummies. Plausible relationships are suggested by the estimates. For example, the volume of referee comments on a manuscript appears to be related negatively to paper quality (referees do not need to say much about good papers). However, in no cases did the estimated coefficient on *CITES* pass the standard significance (0.10) level criterion. This may, in part, be due to the nature of my sample, which selects for papers published only in top journals. There is a quality judgment inherent in the sample that may preclude the kind of finding suggested by the referee.

10. *EDQUAL* is defined as the length of time the author(s) took to revise their paper divided by the number of typed characters in the editor's letter to the author(s) of a substantive nature. Similarly, *REVQUAL* is defined as the length of time the author(s) took to revise their paper divided by the sum of the typed characters in the referees' reports and the typed characters of substance in the editor's letter.

11. In response to my survey, one long-running editor wrote: "...I regard the choice of referees as perhaps the most important decision that editors make." The fact that certain editors normally do not comment substantively on authors' manuscripts should not reflect negatively on their abilities. Editors undoubtedly differ with respect to their ability to efficiently match authors and referees as well as with respect to their constrained ability to offer comments on manuscripts.

REFERENCES

Coe, R.K., and I. Weinstock (1967), "Editorial Policies of Major Economic Journals," *Quarterly Journal of Economics and Business,* **8**, 37-43.

Davis, P., and G. Papanek (1984), "Faculty Rankings of Major Economics Departments by Citations," *American Economic Review,* **74**, 225-30.

Gerritv, D.M., and R.B. McKenzie (1978), "The Ranking of Southern Economics Departments: New Criterion and Further Evidence," *Southern Economic Journal*, **45**, 608-14.

Journal of Finance (1987), "Report of the Managing Editors of the Journal of Finance for 1986," **42**, 805.

Laband, D.N. (1986), "Article Popularity," *Economic Inquiry*, **24**, 173-80.

Laband, D.N. (1989), "Is There Value-Added from the Review Process in Economics?: Theory and Interdisciplinary Evidence," *mimeo.*, Clemson University.

Laband, D N., R.E. McCormick, and M.T. Maloney (1990), "The Review Process in Economics: Some Empirical Findings," *Review of Economics and Statistics*, forthcoming.

Lovell, M.C. (1973), "The Production of Economic Literature: An Interpretation," *Journal of Economic Literature*, **11**, 27-55.

Social Sciences Citation Index, Philadelphia: Institute for Scientific Information, Inc., 1971-87.

Stigler, G.J., and C. Friedland (1975), "The Citation Practices of Economists," *Journal of Political Economy*, **83**, 477-507.

Tollison, R.D., and D.M. Carlson (1986), "The Table of Contents of Economics Journals as Forecasts of Scientific Relevance," *History of Economic Society Bulletin*, **8**, 42-43.

Yohe, G.W. (1980), "Current Publication Lags in Economics Journals," *Journal of Economic Literature*, **18**, 1050-55.

7. The Effects of Double-Blind versus Single-Blind Reviewing: Experimental Evidence from the *American Economic Review*[*]

Rebecca M. Blank

Abstract: The results from a randomized experiment conducted at *The American Economic Review* on the effects of double-blind versus single-blind peer reviewing on acceptance rates and referee ratings indicate that acceptance rates are lower and referees are more critical when the reviewer is unaware of the author's identity. These patterns are not significantly different between female and male authors. Authors at top-ranked universities and at colleges and low-ranked universities are largely unaffected by the different reviewing practices, but authors at near-top-ranked universities and at nonacademic institutions have lower acceptance rates under double-blind reviewing.

Scholars have long been divided regarding the advantages and disadvantages of single-blind versus double-blind reviewing in their scholarly journals. Among 38 well-known journals in chemistry, biology, physics, mathematics, history, psychology, political science, sociology, and

[*] Reprinted with permission of the copyright holder from the *American Economic Review*, Vol.81, No.5, Dec. 1991, pp. 1041-68.

Northwestern University. The author thanks the editors and staff of the *American Economic Review* for their cooperation in gathering data. Particular thanks are due to Orley Ashenfelter, Shirley Griesbaum, and Sandra Grant. Christy Bonner provided excellent assistance during two years of data collection and coding. Additional assistance was provided by Leslie McCafferty and Sandee Smith. The author has benefited from useful conversations with far more people than she can thank by name. Particular thanks go to David Card, Claudia Goldin, and participants in the Labor Economics Seminars at Princeton, Northwestern, Chicago, and MIT. The financial support of the Center for Urban Affairs and Policy Research at Northwestern University is gratefully acknowledged.

anthropology, 11 send submitted papers for outside peer review with the author's name and affiliation removed from the front of the paper (double-blind), while the remainder send submitted papers to referees with the author's name and affiliation visible on the first page (single-blind).[1] Scholars in economics are no different: Among 38 well-known economics journals, 16 have double-blind reviewing policies, while the remainder are single-blind (see Table 7.1). Despite extensive discussion of this issue among editors and authors for many years, no reliable evidence exists comparing the actual differences in outcome and referee behavior under a single-blind versus a double-blind reviewing system.

This paper investigates the impact of single-blind reviewing using data from a unique randomized experiment recently conducted over several years at *The American Economic Review* (*AER*). In this experiment, approximately one-half of the submitted papers were assigned to double-blind reviewing, while the other half were assigned to single-blind reviewing. These data provide information on three areas for which no comparable studies are available. First, the data permit an experimental comparison of the effect of single-blind versus double-blind reviewing on the acceptance rates and referee ratings of papers. Particular attention is given to acceptance and rating differences between the single- and double-blind samples by gender of author, institutional rank of author, referee gender, and referee institutional rank. Second, the data also contain information on how many authors of ostensibly blind papers can actually be identified by the referee. Third, exclusive of the question of refereeing practice, the data provide a wealth of information regarding the determinants of publication at a major economics journal.

The primary conclusion of this study is that there are significant differences in acceptance rates and referee ratings between single-blind and double-blind papers. Most strikingly, double-blind papers have a lower acceptance rate and lower referee evaluations. In addition, double-blind reviewing results in different patterns of acceptance rates and referee ratings by institutional rank of author. While the data are consistent with an argument that women fare better under a double-blind reviewing system, the estimated effects are small and show no statistical significance.

Approximately 55 percent of the referees of double-blind papers cannot identify the author. Referee ratings are generally highly correlated with acceptance rates of papers and show the same patterns, indicating that co-editors largely follow referee advice. Referees of different gender appear to respond differently to double-blind reviewing; female referees rate single-blind papers less favorably, while male referees rate double-blind papers less favorably.

Table 7.1 Refereeing Practices in Economics Journals

Journal name	Double-blind	Single-blind
American Journal of Agricultural Economics	X	
Canadian Journal of Economics		X
Eastern Economic Journal	X	
Econometrica		X
Economic Development and Cultural Change		X
Economic Inquiry		X
Economic Journal		X
Economica		X
Industrial and Labor Relations Review	X	
International Economic Review		X
Journal of Comparative Economics	X	
Journal of Development Economics		X
Journal of Econometrics		X
Journal of Economic Behavior and Organization	X	
Journal of Economic Education	X	
Journal of Economic History	X	
Journal of Economics and Business	X	
Journal of Finance	X	
Journal of Financial Economics	X	
Journal of Health Economics		X
Journal of Human Resources	X	
Journal of Industrial Economics		X
Journal of Labor Economics		X
Journal of Mathematical Economics		X
Journal of Monetary Economics		X
Journal of Policy Analysis and Management	X	
Journal of Political Economy		X
Journal of Post-Keynesian Economics		X
Journal of Public Economics		X
Journal of Urban Economics		X
National Tax Journal	X	
Quarterly Journal of Economics	X	
Rand Journal of Economics		X
Review of Economics Studies		X
Review of Economics and Statistics		X
Review of Income and Wealth		X
Review of Radical Political Economics	X	
Southern Economic Journal	X	

Source: Carolyn A. Miller and Victoria J. Punsalan (1988), except for the *Journal of Economic Education*, which is listed as double-blind after communication with editor.

I.   EXISTING EVIDENCE AND ARGUMENTS
        REGARDING REFEREEING PRACTICES

The primary argument used by proponents of double-blind reviewing is that it minimizes undesirable referee bias. Two particular concerns are typically mentioned. First, referees may be more likely to reject lesser-known authors or authors at lesser-ranked schools, regardless of paper quality. Second, if there is discrimination against women, this may lead to negative reviews when a woman's name is on a paper.

Supporters of single-blind reviewing typically make at least three arguments. First, they argue that referees can almost always identify the author of a paper from the text or the citations, so that double-blind systems are actually rarely double-blind. Second, they argue that there is useful information for the referee in the name and institution of the author that should affect how the paper is read. For instance, the author's identity might signal to a referee whether it is necessary to double-check technical details in a paper with a great deal of mathematical analysis. Third, editors often claim that there are administrative costs associated with double-blind reviewing, because it requires more careful procedures in the editorial office.[2]

It is clear that neither of the two sides in this argument about single-blind versus double-blind reviewing has won a decisive victory within the economics profession. Table 7.1 indicates the refereeing policies of 38 economics journals in 1988.[3] Sixteen of these journals use double-blind reviewing, and the remaining 22 are single-blind. Evidence from earlier published articles indicates that this split has been present for at least the past 25 years.[4]

A few articles have attempted to investigate the effect of single-blind versus double-blind reviewing in economics. Diane Crane (1967) and Cletus C. Coughlin and Anthony O'Brien (1985) compare a journal that maintains consistent refereeing practices over time with a journal that switches between single-and double-blind reviewing. Neither study shows significant changes in the composition of published articles in the journal that switches. Ferber and Teiman (1980) compare acceptance rates for women between single-blind and double-blind journals and find that women have higher acceptance rates in double-blind journals. The problem with these studies is that they do not control for other differences among the journals that they are comparing (e.g., in terms of field, readership, and article submission pool). The causality of the results is therefore difficult to interpret,

Outside economics, the use of single-blind versus double-blind reviewing varies by discipline. The results of a survey conducted in the winter of 1989 among selected top journals in nine disciplines are presented in Table 7.2.[5] In chemistry, physics, math, and psychology, the responding journals uniformly indicate that they use a single-blind reviewing system. It is interesting to note, however, that one physics journal and three psychology journals allow the option of anonymity upon request of the author. Biology appears to have both single-blind and double-blind journals, as does history and anthropology. Political-science and sociology journals report uniformly using double-blind reviewing methods.[6]

While the results of this survey should not be overinterpreted,[7] they do indicate that the debate over single-versus double-blind reviewing is not limited to economics. In fact, almost every discipline has at least a few published articles (mostly editorial) discussing the issue of refereeing practices.

Douglas P. Peters and Stephen J. Ceci (1980; Ceci and Peters, 1982) have conducted the best-known experiment on reviewing practices. They resubmitted 13 previously published articles to top (single-blind) psychology journals, with minor changes to the abstract and first page of the article and an unfamiliar (fake) author and institution.[8] Only three of the 13 papers were detected as duplications; nine of the papers were overwhelmingly rejected for publication. Ceci and Peters conclude that peer review is, at best, a very random procedure and, at worst, is subject to substantial institutional biases. Other empirical analysis includes work by Michael J. Mahoney (1977), who found that correlations between the ratings of different reviewers on the same article were strikingly low; Michael Gordon (1979), who found that physicists rated papers more highly if they were written by authors from similar schools; Harriet Zuckerman and Robert K. Merton (1971), who found little evidence of institutional bias on the part of reviewers; and Ceci and Peters (1984), who found that few referees can identify the authors of double-blind papers.

In summary, the literature on single-blind versus double-blind reviewing spans a wide variety of disciplines and provides rather mixed results. Few of the empirical tabulations provide convincing evidence on the effects or non-effects of refereeing practices, largely because of their inability to control for other factors in the data. If not fully convincing, however, there is at least a disturbing amount of evidence in these studies that is consistent with the hypothesis of referee bias in single-blind reviewing. The data described in the next section of this paper provide an opportunity to analyze that hypothesis in a more convincing way.

Table 7.2 Refereeing Practices Outside Economics

Journal name	Double-blind	Single blind
Chemistry:		
Journal of the American Chemical Society		X
Journal of Chemical Research		X
Angewandte Chemie		X
Journal of Molecular Biology		X
Biology:		
Cell	X	
Molecular and Cellular Biology		X
Journal of Cell Biology		X
Developmental Biology		X
Evolution		X
Genetics		X
Physics:		
Physical Review (A, B, C, and D)		X[a]
Journal of Physics (A, B, D, E, and G)		X
Physics Letters A		X
Mathematics:		
Acta Mathematica		X
Annals of Mathematics		X
Bulletin of the American Mathematical Society		X
History:		
American Historical Review	X	
Journal of American History	X	
Speculum: A Journal of Medieval Studies		X
English Historical Review		X
(Anonymous[b])		X
Psychology:		
Journal of Personality and Social Psychology		X[a]
Psychological Review		X[a]
Psychological Reports		X[a]
Brain Research		X
Journal of Experimental Social Psychology		X
Journal of Behavioral Medicine		X
Political Science:		
American Political Science Review	X	
Political Science Quarterly	X	
International Affairs	X	
Sociology:		
American Journal of Sociology	X	
American Sociology Review	X	
Sociological Inquiry	X	
Social Forces	X	
Anthropology:		
American Anthropologist	X	
American Journal of Physical Anthropology		X
Journal of Anthropological Research		X
Man: The Journal of the Royal Anthropological Institute		X

Notes: [a]Anonymous at author's request. [b]Journal responded to the survey but requested anonymity.
Source: Author's survey, winter 1989; see text for details.

II.   THE EXPERIMENT

The *American Economic Review* has employed single-blind reviewing over most of its recent history.[9] In the mid-1980's, the American Economic Association's Committee on the Status of Women in the Economics Profession formally expressed concern about the potential negative effect on women's acceptance rates of a single-blind system. As a result of this concern and others, the current editor of the *AER* asked the author of this paper to design and propose a randomized experiment for the *AER* that would investigate the effects of single-blind versus double-blind reviewing. The proposal was accepted by the Board of Editors in the spring of 1987, and the experiment began in May 1987, with data collection continuing through the end of May 1989.

When a paper arrives in the *AER*'s main office, it is immediately assigned an identifying number, and a "record card" is typed up, on which the date and substance of all actions regarding this paper will be noted (referees contacted, referee reports received, letters to the author, etc.) Because the *AER* has a co-editor system, the editor merely screens the paper for general field before assigning it to one of four co-editors (including himself). The entire adjudication of the paper is then handled from the co-editor's office. The co-editors select referees, make publication decisions, and communicate with authors. The completed record card for the paper is returned to the main *AER* office only when the paper has been rejected or a final version for publication has been received.

With the initiation of this experiment, every other paper that arrived at the *AER* was designated as double-blind, so that all papers assigned an odd number were double-blind. The editorial assistant who logged in papers immediately removed the name and affiliation of the author from the title page of all copies of the designated double-blind papers and typically scanned the first page for additional titles or notes that would identify the author. In this form, the papers were then sent to the assigned co-editor. Thus, all odd-numbered papers were sent out for refereeing without the author's name or affiliation on the front of the paper, while the even-numbered papers were sent in the same form in which they were submitted to the *AER*.[10]

The co-editor, of course, had immediate access to each paper's record card. While co-editors in some situations may not have checked authors' names until they actually had to write letters communicating their decision, there was no intention of making these papers "blind" with regard to the *AER* co-editors.[11]

In addition, an anonymous referee survey (see Appendix A) was sent to all referees as part of the original referee request from the co-editor. The number of the paper was written on the survey before it was mailed, so that surveys and papers could be matched. This survey asked referees to rate papers from 1 to 5 (1 = first-rate; 5 = seriously deficient) with regard to the paper's theoretical contribution, empirical contribution, contribution to the field, and overall quality. It also asked referees of double-blind papers whether they could identify the author, and if so, who they thought the author was. The referees were clearly informed that their responses to this survey would not be seen by the editors or authors.

Data collection on this project could take place only with time lags. If initial referees are divided, the co-editor may solicit another round of referee reports. In addition, authors of papers that co-editors and referees think might be publishable are typically asked to revise and resubmit their manuscripts. Since analysis of the experimental results required information on final publication decisions, it was not until well after the end of the experiment, in May 1989, that the final round of data collection could actually occur. In fact, even by October 1990, there were still 27 papers on which final publication decisions had not been made: two from 1987, 14 from 1988, and 11 from 1989. These papers are referred to as "not rejected," as distinguished from "accepted."[12]

The primary data set resulting from this experiment contains information on the papers received by the *AER* during the experimental time period, including the gender and institutional rank of the author or authors, whether the paper was part of the single-blind or double-blind sample, the co-editor handling the paper, the weeks to disposition, the number of referees used, and whether the paper was finally accepted or rejected. The secondary data set from this experiment is the collection of referee survey results, which can be matched with the papers. This data set includes referee ratings for four dimensions of each paper, whether the referee can correctly identify the author of double-blind papers, and the gender and institutional rank of the referee.[13]

Note that the referee surveys are particularly useful because they provide information on referee evaluations independent of co-editor judgments. Co-editors' accept/reject decisions may have been unavoidably influenced by the knowledge that someone was evaluating differences in acceptance and rejection rates between the double-blind and single-blind papers, and they may have been particularly sensitive to the fact that attention was being focused on papers written by women.[14] It is because of concern about the role of co-editors as an unavoidable intermediary between referee recommendations and acceptance decisions that the referee survey was implemented.

III.   THE DATA

A. Characteristics of the Overall Sample

Summary characteristics of the data from the experiment are presented in Table 7.3. In discussing these results, I will also discuss the primary coding and definitional questions in the data. Column 1 of Table 7.3 provides information on the total sample of papers and will be discussed first.

In all, 1,498 papers were included in the experiment. Excluded from the sample were any special submissions (such as the President's Address to the American Economic Association) which did not follow the normal reviewing process, as well as all papers submitted as comments on previously published articles.

The gender of authors could be determined in most but not all cases. An effort was made to identify the gender of authors who used only their first initials, authors with names that could be either male or female, and authors with unfamiliar foreign names,[15] but 52 names of unknown gender remain. All tabulations with the data that include the gender variable exclude these observations.

In the case of single-author papers, it is obvious how to code the gender of the author, but 43.7 percent of the sample were multiple-author papers. Three codings of these papers are possible, as indicated in Table 7.3: papers can be identified as "female" if at least one female name is on the paper, if the primary author (first author listed) is female, or if only female names are on the paper. Clearly, the first definition is the most inclusive. Because the sample sizes for women's papers are so small, this first definition (at least one female author) is used to define "female" papers throughout the rest of this analysis.[16]

Authors' institutional rank was coded into one of 10 categories, as listed in Table 7.3. (In cases of multiple authors, the highest institutional rank among them was used.) These 10 categories are defined using the most recent (1982) rankings of economics departments done by the National Academy of Science (Lyle V. Jones et al., 1982).[17] The schools included in each category are listed in Appendix B. Table 7.3 indicates that several of these categories do not have many sample observations. As a result, for the remainder of this analysis, I merge these ten categories into six, combining university departments ranked 6-10 with those ranked 11-20, university departments ranked below 50 with college departments, U.S. government with U.S. private research institutions, and foreign academic with foreign nonacademic institutions.[18]

Approximately 28 percent of *AER* submissions come from economists at schools whose economics departments are ranked among the top 20, 16

Table 7.3 Data from the AER Experiment
  A.   *Data on Papers:*

Statistic	(1) Total sample	(2) Double-blind sample	(3) Single-blind sample
Number of papers	1,498	832 (28)	666 (28)
Percentage of sample		55.5 (1.3)	44.5 (1.3)
Percentage of papers with:			
Author's gender identifiable	96.5 (0.5)	97.6 (0.5)	95.2 (0.8)
At least one female author	12.4 (0.9)	12.3 (1.2)	12.6 (1.3)
Female primary author	8.0 (0.7)	8.1 (1.0)	7.7 (1.1)
Only female authors	6.0 (0.6)	5.9 (0.8)	6.1 (1.0)
One author on paper	56.3 (1.3)	55.4 (1.7)	57.5 (1.9)
Multiple authors on paper	43.7 (1.3)	44.6 (1.7)	42.5 (1.9)
Percentage of papers from:			
University ranked 1-5	9.9 (0.8)	9.4 (1.0)	10.7 (1.2)
University ranked 6-10	6.4 (0.6)	6.9 (0.9)	5.9 (0.9)
University ranked 11-20	11.9 (0.8)	12.9 (1.2)	10.7 (1.2)
University ranked 21-50	16.0 (0.9)	16.7 (1.3)	15.0 (1.4)
University, ranked above 50	25.2 (1.1)	26.0 (1.5)	24.3 (1.7)
College	3.3 (0.5)	3.4 (0.6)	3.2 (0.7)
U.S. government	3.6 (0.5)	3.6 (0.6)	3.6 (0.7)
U.S. private firm/research institution	5.3 (0.6)	5.3 (0.8)	5.4 (0.9)
Foreign academic	17.0 (1.0)	14.7 (1.2)	19.8 (1.5)
Foreign nonacademic	1.4 (0.3)	1.3 (0.4)	1.5 (0.5)
Mean number of weeks to final decision	21.9 (0.5)	20.9 (0.6)	23.3 (0.8)
Mean number of weeks to acceptance	54.0 (2.1)	51.0 (2.7)	56.9 (3.1)
Mean number of weeks to rejection	18.2 (0.4)	17.8 (0.5)	18.7 (0.6)
Mean number of referees used per paper	1.7 (2.0)	1.7 (2.7)	1.7 (3.1)
Percentage of papers with:			
No referees	5.7 (0.6)	5.3 (0.8)	6.3 (0.9)
One referee	31.6 (1.2)	32.2 (1.6)	30.9 (1.8)
Two referees	52.3 (1.3)	52.2 (1.7)	52.6 (1.9)
More than two referees	10.3 (0.8)	10.3 (1.1)	10.2 (1.2)
Referee surveys returned per paper	1.3 (2.2)	1.4 (2.7)	1.2 (3.4)
Percentage of papers with:			
No referee surveys returned	18.4 (1.0)	11.7 (1.1)	26.7 (1.7)
One referee survey returned	39.8 (1.3)	42.7 (1.7)	36.2 (1.9)
Two referee surveys returned	37.0 (1.2)	40.4 (1.7)	32.9 (1.8)
More than two referee surveys returned	4.8 (0.6)	5.3 (0.8)	4.2 (0.8)

B. Data from Referee Surveys:

Statistic	(1) Total sample	(2) Double- blind sample	(3) Single-blind sample
Number of referee surveys returned	1,933	1,164 (22)	769 (22)
Percentage of sample		60.2 (1.1)	39.8 (1.1)
Percentage of surveys with:			
Identifiable referee	90.0 (0.7)	89.4 (0.9)	90.9 (1.0)
Referee gender identifiable	89.3 (0.7)	88.9 (0.9)	90.0 (1.1)
Female referee	8.1 (0.7)	8.3 (0.9)	7.8 (1.0)
Referee institution identifiable	89.9 (0.7)	89.3 (0.9)	90.8 (1.0)
Percentage of surveys from:			
University ranked 1-5	16.7 (0.9)	16.7 (1.2)	16.6 (1.4)
University ranked 6-10	7.2 (0.6)	6.5 (0.8)	8.3 (1.0)
University ranked 11-20	21.6 (1.0)	21.7 (1.3)	21.5 (1.6)
University ranked 21-50	17.8 (0.9)	17.8 (1.2)	17.9 (1.5)
University ranked above 50	12.5 (0.8)	13.8 (1.1)	10.7 (1.2)
College	3.3 (0.4)	3.6 (0.6)	2.7 (0.6)
U.S. government	2.8 (0.4)	2.9 (0.5)	2.6 (0.6)
U.S. private firm/research institution	7.2 (0.6)	6.7 (0.8)	8.0 (1.0)
Foreign, academic/nonacademic	10.8 (0.7)	10.3 (0.9)	11.6 (1.2)

Note: Standard errors reported in parentheses.

percent come from graduate departments ranked 21-50, 25 percent are from universities not in the top 50, and 17 percent come from foreign nationals. The remaining 14 percent are spread across the other categories. Thus, paper submissions to the *AER* come from economists at quite a broad spectrum of institutions.

On average, it takes 22 weeks for a final publication decision to occur at the *AER*. This varies greatly between acceptances and rejections, however, with an average length of time to rejection of 18 weeks, and an average length of time to acceptance of 54 weeks.

The median paper is sent to two referees. Only a few papers (5.7 percent) are rejected with no outside review, and only a small percentage of papers are sent to more than two referees.

From reviewers of these 1,498 papers, I received 1,933 completed referee surveys. A total of 2,538 referees evaluated these papers, indicating a response rate of 76.2 percent.[19] This seems good, given that the referee survey was explicitly not part of the required evaluation and was to be filled out and returned in a separate envelope.[20]

The information from the referee surveys is summarized in the second part of Table 7.3. I can identify the referee on 90 percent of the surveys. It is clear that the characteristics of referees do not mirror the characteristics of authors. Women referee only about 8 percent of the papers, less than the 12 percent of submitted papers that have women's names on them. Almost half (45.5 percent) of all referees are at the top 20 departments, while only 28.2 percent of the papers come from these departments. These differentials do not necessarily indicate any potential bias in the refereeing process. In fact, one would expect that better-known individuals would be asked to referee more papers. However, these differences do raise the question of whether referee institution and gender influence referee decisions.

B. Comparing the Double-Blind and Single-Blind Samples: Are They Randomized?

Columns 2 and 3 in Table 7.3 present information on the comparative characteristics of papers in the double-blind and single-blind samples. (Note that, from this point, papers reviewed double-blind will be referred to as the "blind" sample, i.e., blind to the referee; papers reviewed single-blind will be referred to as the "nonblind" sample, i.e., nonblind to the referee.) Among all papers, 832 (55.5 percent) were blind, and 666 (44.5 percent) were nonblind. The reason for the different numbers in these two categories are the special submissions and comments received by the *AER*, which are necessarily nonblind. The editorial assistant logging in papers automatically assigned any paper that she felt could not be handled as a blind paper to the nonblind category. As noted above, all special submissions and comments were deleted from the data set, leaving the nonblind category with fewer observations.

A randomized experiment occurs when two groups are identical across all measures except the one being investigated. In this case, random assignment to the blind and nonblind categories should imply that the blind and nonblind samples are composed of papers from a statistically identical set of authors. The only difference should be that one group's papers were refereed blind while the other group's paper were refereed nonblind. Thus, any differences in acceptance rates or referee ratings between the two samples can be ascribed to the blind/nonblind effects and not to any other difference between the two samples.

Columns 2 and 3 of Table 7.3 indicate that these two samples are indeed identical and that the randomization was effective. The confidence intervals indicated by the standard errors on the mean characteristics overlap in both samples on virtually every characteristic.[21] Of the blind papers, 12.3 percent had at least one female author, very close to the 12.6 percent among the nonblind papers. The distribution of papers across institutions is quite similar, although the nonblind category has a few more submissions from foreign academics. The numbers of weeks to rejection are statistically identical in the two samples. The mean number of weeks to acceptance is higher in the nonblind sample, but this is primarily because of a few unduly lengthy acceptance processes, which raise the mean in this category. The numbers of assigned referees are also similar in the two samples.

While the papers assigned to the blind and nonblind sample were randomized, assuring identical samples, the selection of who returned a referee survey was not. Referee survey response may have been influenced by whether a paper was blind or nonblind. The data in part B of Table 7.3 indicate that there was a higher response rate on the referee surveys for the blind papers than for the nonblind papers.[22] The question asking referees of blind papers to identify the author clearly generated interest among these referees and may have led them to return their surveys at a higher rate.

Despite this return-rate differential, the referees returning the surveys for the blind and nonblind papers appear to be identical. Statistically, the same fraction are identifiable and are female, and they are distributed across the institutions in a similar manner in both samples. Thus, the data on referee surveys in Table 7.3 indicate that any differences in referee ratings between the blind and nonblind papers are not due to differences in the referees and can be ascribed to differences in their response to the two refereeing systems.

IV.   IS BLIND REVIEWING REALLY BLIND?

One crucial piece of information from the referee survey is whether referees can identify the authors of ostensibly blind papers. As noted above, supporters of single-blind reviewing often claim that few papers are really anonymous. Table 7.4 presents information on this issue.

Among all referee surveys received for blind papers, slightly over half (50.9 percent) claim to know the author. Ten percent of these referees are incorrect, however, so that only 45.6 percent of the authors in the blind sample are correctly identified.[23] In general, there are two accurate statements about these results. On the one hand, a substantial fraction – almost half – of the blind papers in this experiment could be identified by the referee. This indicates the extent to which no reviewing system can ever be fully anonymous. On the other hand, more than half the papers in the blind sample were completely anonymous. A substantial fraction of submitted papers are not readily identified by reviewers in the field.

I will refer to referees of blind papers who cannot correctly identify the author as "truly blind" and to those who can as "pseudo-blind." These referee-survey results can be mapped back into the sample of papers for which referee surveys were returned. Table 7.4 indicates that for 46.9

Table 7.4 Referee Ability to Identify Authors in Blind Sample

A. *Among All Referee Surveys Received on Blind Papers* (N = 1,164)		
Percentage of referees claiming to know author:	50.9	(1.5)
Percentage who correctly identify author:	45.6	(1.5)
B. *Among All Blind Papers with Returned Referee Surveys* (N = 736)		
Percentage truly blind (none of referees can identify author):	46.9	(1.8)
Percentage pseudo-blind (all referees can identify author):	36.7	(1.8)
Percentage mixed blind (some referees can identify author/some cannot):	16.4	(1.4)

Note: Standard errors are reported in parentheses.

percent of the blind papers all referees were truly blind, while for 36.7 percent of these papers all referees were pseudo-blind. The remaining 16.4 percent of the blind papers had a mix of truly blind and pseudo-blind referees.

It is important to note that the methodology of a randomized experiment, investigating the effects of double- and single-blind reviewing on an identical sample of papers, can only be applied to the blind/nonblind samples, and not to the truly-blind/not-truly-blind samples. Those blind papers that are correctly identified by the referees are not a randomized sample of all blind papers, but are skewed in favor of authors who are better known or who belong to networks that distribute their working papers more widely. Thus, there is selectivity in the truly blind sample which does not exist in the randomized comparison between the overall blind and nonblind samples.

V.   A LOOK AT THE RAW DATA

The advantage of a randomized experiment is that it does not require a substantial amount of statistical analysis. Because both samples start with an identical group of papers, a simple comparison of outcomes between the blind and nonblind samples should indicate whether these two reviewing practices produce different results. Thus, Table 7.5 presents the primary data of interest in this paper: the difference in acceptance rates between the blind and nonblind samples, in total and by author's gender and institutional rank.

Table 7.5 Data on Acceptance Rates in the Total, Blind, and Nonblind Samples

Sample	(1) Number of papers	Acceptance rates			(5) Difference: Blind & non-blind
		(2) Total sample	(3) Blind sample	(4) Non-blind sample	
1) All papers	1,498	12.1	10.6	14.1	-3.5
		(0.8)	(1.1)	(1.4)	(1.8)
By gender:					
2) Female-authored papers	180	10.6	10.0	11.2	-1.2
		(2.3)	(3.0)	(3.5)	(4.6)
3) Male-authored papers	1,266	12.7	11.0	15.0	-4.0
		(0.9)	(1.2)	(1.5)	(1.9)
By institutional rank:					
4) Universities ranked 1-5	149	28.9	29.5	28.2	1.3
		(3.7)	(5.2)	(5.3)	(7.4)
5) Universities ranked 6-20	274	16.4	13.4	20.9	-7.5
		(2.2)	(2.7)	(3.9)	(4.7)
6) Universities ranked 21-50	239	12.1	10.1	15.0	-4.9
		(2.1)	(2.6)	(3.6)	(4.4)
7) Colleges/universities ranked > 50	426	6.6	6.2	7.1	-0.9
		(1.2)	(1.5)	(1.9)	(2.4)
8) U.S. nonacademic institutions	134	6.7	4.1	10.0	-5.9
		(2.2)	(2.3)	(3.9)	(4.5)
9) Foreign	276	10.1	8.2	12.0	-3.8
			(1.8)	(2.4)	(2.7) (3.6)

A. Acceptance Rates in the Blind and Nonblind Samples

Row 1 of Table 7.5 presents the percentage of accepted papers in the total, blind, and nonblind samples.[24] Blind papers have a significantly lower acceptance rate (10.6 percent vs. 14.1 percent). The confidence intervals for these two point estimates, as defined by their respective standard errors, do not overlap. A likelihood-ratio chi-square test of whether accept/reject rates are identical for the blind and nonblind samples can be rejected at a 3.5 percent level of significance. These results indicate that blind papers were accepted at a lower rate than nonblind papers over the sample period. As will be seen below, it is also true that blind papers have worse referee ratings. Given that all other aspects of these papers are identical in both samples, this indicates that these two reviewing practices do not produce identical results.

B. Acceptance Rates by Gender in the Blind and Nonblind Samples

Rows 2 and 3 of Table 7.5 present the acceptance rates separately for men and women in the overall, blind, and nonblind samples. Women's aggregate 10.6 percent acceptance rate is somewhat below men's 12.7 percent acceptance rate, but this result by itself says nothing about gender bias in the journal acceptance process, since it does not control for differences in age, experience, or institutional affiliation between men and women. This difference is also not statistically significant. The confidence intervals of the two estimates overlap, and a likelihood-ratio chi-square test cannot reject the hypothesis that the acceptance rates for males and females are identical.

Columns 3 and 4 of rows 2 and 3 show acceptance rates by gender in the blind and nonblind samples. One can compare acceptance rates between the blind and nonblind samples without other control variables because the randomization process guarantees that papers by women (and men) in each sample have identical distributions of characteristics. For women, there is no significant difference in acceptance rates between the two samples. For men, acceptance rates are significantly higher in the nonblind sample.

In comparing men's and women's acceptance rates, note that the important comparison is not whether men's acceptance rates differ from women's, but whether the ratio of male to female acceptance rates in the nonblind sample is different from that in the blind sample. In both samples, women's acceptance rates are lower than men's, but the differential in the blind sample is smaller. While women in the blind sample have an acceptance rate only 1 percentage point below that of men, their rate is 3.8 percentage points lower in the nonblind sample. The number of observations for women is small enough, however, that these differences are not statistically significant. A likelihood-ratio chi-square test of the hypothesis that the ratio of male to female acceptance rates are identical in both samples cannot be rejected.

The lack of significance for the gender differences in Table 7.5 reflects the small number of women's papers in the data set. It is true that these differences would be significant with a larger sample of papers. The lack of statistical significance, however, indicates that one cannot assume that a larger sample of papers would produce the same results.

C. Acceptance Rates by Institutional Rank in the Blind and Nonblind Samples

Rows 4-9 of Table 7.5 show acceptance rates by author's institutional rank in the overall, blind, and nonblind samples. It is clear that authors from the five highest-ranked universities have a substantially higher aggregate acceptance rate than other authors; their rate of 29 percent is well above the

12-16 percent acceptance rates at second-tier universities. Acceptance rates are 7 percent for authors from colleges and universities not ranked in the top 50 and for authors from U.S. nonacademic public or private settings. Foreigners have a slightly higher acceptance rate of 10 percent. These differences are highly significant, as the standard errors indicate.

Columns 3 and 4 present the blind and nonblind samples separately. Again, the issue is not whether there are differences in acceptance rates across institutional rank, but whether the ratio of acceptance rates between institutional ranks in the blind sample differs from the corresponding ratio in the nonblind sample.

The experimental results by institutional rank in Table 7.5 are somewhat surprising, since many would predict that authors at highly ranked schools would do worse under blind refereeing and authors at lower-ranked schools would do better. In fact, the two groups whose acceptance rates are largely identical in the blind and nonblind samples are those at top-ranked departments and those at colleges and low-ranked universities. All other groups have substantially lower acceptance rates in the blind sample than in the nonblind sample. Two groups that are particularly affected by blind reviewing are those at near-top-ranked universities, whose acceptance rate drops by more than 7 percentage points, and those at U.S. public and private research institutions, whose acceptance rate falls by 6 percentage points. In the blind sample, acceptance rates at the top-ranked schools are 2.2 times higher than the next-highest category; in the nonblind sample, this ratio is only 1.3. These differences are only mildly significant, however. The null hypothesis that the relative ratio of acceptance rates across all institutional ranks is identical in the blind and nonblind samples cannot be rejected at any conventional level of significance.

VI.   STATISTICAL/ANALYSIS ESTIMATING THE DETERMINANTS OF ACCEPTANCE/REJECTION RATES

Because of the nature of a randomized experiment, the results presented in Table 7.5, based on simple comparisons of the raw data between the blind and the nonblind samples, are the full set of experimental results. There is no need to do more complex statistical analysis, because the differences between the blind and nonblind samples are uncorrelated with any other variables in the data; both samples have an identical set of papers along all other dimensions. This section explores accept/reject decisions in a standard multivariate-regression context, which allows more concisely for the interaction of gender and institutional effects, but the basic conclusions regarding the effect of double-blind reviewing on acceptance rates by gender and institutional rank will not change.

The sample of papers in this data set has an explicit dependent variable, namely, whether the paper is accepted or rejected. One obvious way of summarizing the data is to estimate the determinants of acceptance across the entire sample, including controls for gender and institutional rank. The re-suits of the randomized experiment on blind reviewing can be estimated by interacting a dummy variable denoting inclusion in the blind sample with the other variables in the model. The coefficients on these interaction terms will measure the differential effect on acceptance rates between the blind and nonblind samples.

Table 7.6 presents the results from a linear probability model of the determinants of publication at the *AER*[25] and, in contrast to Table 7.5, conveniently allows one to control for both gender and institutional rank at the same time.[26] This will remove from the gender coefficients any effects that are due to a differential distribution of women across institutions. The first group of variables shows the experimental effects of double-blind reviewing, interacting gender and institutional rank with a dummy variable for inclusion in the blind sample. The coefficients on these variables should be robust to the inclusion of any other variables in the model, since they come from two experimental samples that are identical in all other characteristics. As expected, the results are quite similar to those in Table 7.5.

Once institutional rank is controlled for, the gender effect of being in the blind sample is virtually zero. This indicates that the (admittedly insignificant) closer relative acceptance rates between men and women in the blind sample occurred because more women are in institutional settings that are less negatively affected by blind refereeing, particularly lower-ranked universities and colleges. The institutional-rank effects of being in the blind sample are the same as those shown in Table 5, with the lower acceptance rates for authors from near-top-ranked schools and in U.S. nonacademic settings.

The variables at the bottom of Table 7.6 (the nonexperimental results) show the further effects of gender, institutional rank, and multiple authorship on the accept probability. However, it is not clear how to interpret the coefficients on these variables, because they are contaminated by excluded variables. For instance, while women in general have lower acceptance rates than men, as noted above it is not clear whether this is a gender effect or whether it is caused by the omission of other crucial variables from the model, such as age and experience in the profession. Likewise, scholars in more highly ranked departments have higher

Table 7.6--Determinants of Acceptance

Variable	Coefficient	SE
Experimental effects:		
Blind × female	0.8	5.2
Blind × university rank 1-5	1.8	5.3
Blind × university rank 6-20	-7.0	4.1
Blind × university rank 21-50	-5.3	4.3
Blind × college/university rank > 50	-0.9	3.3
Blind × U.S. nonacademic institution	-6.3	5.8
Blind × foreign	-3.6	4.2
Other variables:		
Female	-2.3	3.9
University rank 1-5	23.0	4.4
University rank 6-20	16.2	3.7
University rank 21-50	11.2	3.7
College/university rank > 50	3.2	3.0
U.S. nonacademic institution	6.7	4.6
Foreign	8.8	3.5
Multiple authorship	1.2	1.8
Controls for field of editor	yes	
Number of observations:	1,446	

Notes: The results are based on linear probability models in which the dependent variable equals 1 if the paper is not rejected. All coefficients and standard errors are multiplied by 100.

acceptance rates, but it is unclear whether this is the cause of high acceptance rates or the result.

Table 7.6 indicates how completely the raw data from a randomized experiment describe the results. The multivariate linear probability model provides another way to analyze the impact of blind refereeing on acceptance rates, but it provides little in the way of new results.

VII.   DO REFEREE RATINGS SHOW THE SAME RESULTS?

The analysis of acceptance and rejection rates is problematic, since these decisions involve co-editors as well as referees. Although the above discussion assumes that the measured effects are the result of differences in referee behavior under a blind system, they may also reflect differences in how the co-editors handled blind papers. In order to measure the effects of blind reviewing on referee behavior, one needs a measure of referee evaluations that is not contaminated by co-editor behavior. This is provided by the referee ratings of papers from the referee surveys. This referee survey data set also has another advantage: it includes information on referee gender and institution, so that the comparative responses of referees from different backgrounds to blind reviewing can also be investigated.

As Table 7.3 indicated, the referees of blind and nonblind papers have identical distributions of characteristics, as one would expect if referees were assigned without regard to whether the paper was blind or nonblind. In addition, experimental randomization guarantees that the blind and nonblind papers have identical distributions of author characteristics. This means that differences in the referee ratings of these two groups must be solely due to differences in referee responses to different reviewing procedures and will not be contaminated by other variables.

A. Overall Experimental Effects on Referee Ratings

Table 7.7 presents the raw data on mean referee ratings of the overall quality of each paper.[27] Recall that the referee survey (Appendix A) asked referees to rate papers from 1 (high) to 5 (low); therefore, higher numbers in Table 7.7 indicate more critical ratings.[28] As row 1 indicates, the mean rating for overall quality is 3.43. It is also clear in row 1 that referees are more critical of papers in the blind sample; the difference in mean ratings between the blind and nonblind samples is statistically significant, as indicated by the standard errors. This implies that the lower acceptance rates for blind papers are not due solely to co-editor behavior, but reflect more critical referee evaluations.

Rows 2 and 3 indicate the differences in referee ratings between male- and female-authored papers. Referees are more critical of blind papers for both groups. The differences in mean ratings indicate that women appear to benefit more in terms of referee ratings from nonblind reviewing, but these differences are not significant. Thus, as with acceptance rates, there is no statistically measurable difference in referee evaluations of male-and female-authored papers.[29] It is also worth noting that referee evaluations of women's papers are lower in general, as were acceptance rates among women. As noted above, this cannot be easily interpreted, however, since these aggregate gender effects are likely to be contaminated by missing variables, such as experience and tenure.

Rows 4-9 indicate the differences in referee ratings among papers written by authors from different institutional ranks. In general, referees are far less critical of papers from the top-ranked or near-top-ranked schools, as would be expected from the higher acceptance rates for papers from these schools. The differences in referee ratings between blind and nonblind papers, however, do not identically mirror the results on acceptance rates. Recall that acceptance rates for blind papers from authors at near-top-ranked schools were substantially lower than for nonblind papers, while acceptance

Table 7.7 Data on Referee Ratings in the Total, Blind, and Nonblind Samples

Sample	(1) # of papers	Referee ratings			(5) Difference: blind-nonblind
		(2) Total sample	(3) Blind sample	(4) Non-blind sample	
1) All referees	1,900	3.43	3.47	3.37	0.10
		(0.02)	(0.03)	(0.04)	(0.05)
By gender of author:					
2) Female-authored papers	158	3.61	3.68	3.51	0.17
		(0.08)	(0.11)	(0.12)	(0.16)
3) Male-authored papers	1,691	3.40	3.44	3.35	0.09
		(0.02)	(0.03)	(0.04)	(0.05)
By institutional rank of author:					
4) Universities ranked 1-5	205	2.96	2.91	3.03	-0.12
		(0.07)	(0.09)	(0.10)	(0.14)
5) Universities ranked 6-20	391	3.38	3.36	3.41	-0.05
		(0.05)	(0.06)	(0.09)	(0.11)
6) Universities ranked 21-50	327	3.39	3.46	3.27	0.19
		(0.05)	(0.07)	(0.08)	(0.11)
7) Colleges/universities ranked > 50	500	3.61	3.67	3.52	0.15
		(0.05)	(0.06)	(0.07)	(0.09)
8) U.S. nonacademic institutions	155	3.47	3.52	3.37	0.15
		(0.09)	(0.11)	(0.15)	(0.18)
9) Foreign	322	3.53	3.62	3.45	0.17
		(0.06)	(0.08)	(0.08)	(0.11)
By gender of referee:					
10) Female	136	3.54	3.42	3.72	-0.30
		(0.09)	(0.11)	(0.14)	(0.18)
11) Male	1,562	3.44	3.49	3.36	0.13
		(0.03)	(0.03)	(0.04)	(0.05)
By institutional rank of referee:					
12) Universities ranked 1-5	280	3.34	3.41	3.24	0.17
		(0.06)	(0.08)	(0.10)	(0.13)
13) Universities ranked 6-20	499	3.44	3.46	3.40	0.06
		(0.05)	(0.06)	(0.07)	(0.09)
14) Universities ranked 21-50	306	3.55	3.56	3.54	0.02
		(0.06)	(0.08)	(0.08)	(0.11)
15) Colleges/universities ranked > 50	271	3.42	3.40	3.48	-0.08
		(0.06)	(0.07)	(0.09)	(0.12)
16) U.S. nonacademic institutions	170	3.43	3.58	3.22	0.36
		(0.08)	(0.10)	(0.11)	(0.15)
17) Foreign	374	3.40	3.45	3.32	0.13
		(0.05)	(0.07)	(0.08)	(0.11)

Notes: Standard errors are reported in parentheses.

rates were nearly identical for blind and nonblind papers from top-ranked schools and low-ranked universities and colleges. In contrast, referee ratings of papers from top-ranked and near-top-ranked schools are virtually identical. Authors of blind papers from near-top-ranked schools did not receive worse referee evaluations. Their lower acceptance rates must therefore have reflected differential co-editor decisions. In addition, referee ratings of papers from low-ranked universities and colleges are significantly more critical in the blind sample, although there is no significant difference in acceptance rates. Thus, it is possible that co-editors were somewhat affected in their decisions by this experiment; in particular, they viewed blind papers by authors from near-top-ranked schools less favorably and viewed blind papers from authors at low-ranked schools more favorably than did referees. Referee ratings for authors from other institutional-rank categories largely mirror the patterns seen in accept/reject decisions.

The results for referee ratings in Table 7.7 are largely consistent with those based on acceptance rates. Referees are more critical of blind papers and show no significant difference in their treatment of male-authored and female-authored papers. Papers written by foreign authors, nonacademic U.S. authors, and authors from universities ranked 21-50 receive more critical referee ratings when their papers are blind. Authors from top-ranked universities receive identical referee ratings whether their papers are blind or nonblind. However, referees are less critical of blind papers from near-top-ranked universities and more critical of blind papers from low-ranked universities and colleges than acceptance rates would indicate.

B. Experimental Effects on Referee Ratings, by Gender and Institutional Rank of the Referee

Rows 10-17 of Table 7.7 provide new information on the effects of blind reviewing. The referee survey data make it possible to analyze the effect of referee gender and institutional rank on referee ratings of blind versus nonblind papers. In other words, rather than focusing on whether different authors receive different treatment under blind reviewing, these rows investigate whether different referees behave differently under blind reviewing.

Rows 10 and 11 investigate the effect of referee gender on referee ratings. The results are quite striking. Female referees are significantly more critical of nonblind papers, while male referees are significantly more critical of blind papers. The overall lower referee ratings for blind papers reflect the fact that male referees are more numerous than female referees. While differences in relative referee ratings between male- and female-authored papers were not significant, differences in referee ratings between male and female referees are indeed statistically significant. The ratio of female ratings to male ratings among blind papers is 0.98, while this ratio is 1.11 among nonblind papers.

Rows 12-17 investigate the effect of referee institutional rank on referee ratings of blind versus nonblind papers. There are few measurable effects. Only referees from nonacademic U.S. institutions appear to treat blind and nonblind papers significantly differently, by being more critical of the blind papers.

In general, the referee's institutional affiliation does not appear to affect substantially referee evaluations of blind versus nonblind papers. Referee gender, however, does seem to be important. Female referees rate blind papers more favorably, while male referees rate nonblind papers more favorably.

C. How Correlated are Referee Ratings on the Same Paper?

One question of interest in the referee survey data is the degree of correlation between referee ratings of the same paper. As noted above, there is evidence in the existing literature that referee responses may be highly random. I investigate this question using the set of papers for which I have exactly two referee reports returned.[30]

Correlations between the ratings given by each of the two referees are fairly low. The correlation between the theory ratings of two referees on the same paper is 0.28; it is 0.24 for empirical ratings, 0.23 for contribution to field, and 0.24 for overall paper quality. This seems to indicate a relatively low degree of referee agreement.

This result is further demonstrated in the pattern of ratings between the two referees. For only 33 percent of the papers did both referees give an identical rating on overall paper quality. Identical ratings for the other three dimensions are even less frequent. Thus, the evidence from this sample appears to indicate that there is quite a bit of randomness in the ratings any paper receives from referees.

This randomness does not imply that referee ratings contain no information or that they are not useful to the co-editors. In fact, as Table 7.7 indicates, the referee ratings show quite similar results to those derived from an analysis of accept/reject decisions. This implies that the co-editors are following the referee's advice quite closely. A linear probability model estimating the probability of a paper's acceptance as a function of its mean rating on overall quality across all returned referee surveys produces the coefficients shown in Table 7.8. In short, co-editor decisions are highly correlated with the mean rating received by papers. If it is true that there is substantial variance across referee ratings and that co-editors largely follow

Table 7.8 Referee Ratings and Corresponding Probabilities of Acceptance

Mean referee rating	Estimated probability of acceptance (SE)
1-1.5	71.4 (11.3)
1.5-2.5	50.0 (2.7)
2.5-3.5	17.1 (1.5)
3.5-4.5	3.5 (1.4)
4.5-5	1.0 (2.2)

Note: these results are based on a regression that includes observations from all papers with returned referee surveys (1,223 papers).

referee advice, then soliciting additional referees is clearly an effective strategy for improving co-editor decisions.

VIII. WHAT IS THE IMPACT OF A PAPER BEING TRULY BLIND?

The discussion so far has focused on the effects of blind reviewing, as measured by the experimental randomization of papers into blind and nonblind samples. This section leaves that question entirely and focuses on another unique piece of information in the data: whether a blind paper was truly blind to a referee. (Recall from the discussion in Section IV that a truly blind paper is a blind paper whose author could not be identified by the referee; a pseudo-blind paper is a blind paper whose author was identifiable by the referee.) This section investigates the effect of true anonymity on a paper's probability of acceptance[31] and shows how the randomized data on refereeing practices can be used to create instruments to estimate the effect of being in the nonrandom truly anonymous sample, purged of all other correlations.

The analysis above relied upon the randomization of papers into blind and nonblind samples. One could compare acceptance rates between these two samples only because randomization assured that all other characteristics of these two samples were identical. In contrast, a comparison of truly blind and pseudo-blind papers involves a nonrandom comparison. The factors that make a paper likely to be truly blind are strongly correlated with a large number of author and referee characteristics. Papers are less likely to be truly blind if they are written by more famous or more senior authors, or if their authors are at schools whose working papers are widely distributed. Thus, one would expect that truly blind papers would have lower acceptance rates even if they were not truly blind, because they are likely to be written by less experienced and less famous economists.

A. Differences Among the Truly Blind, Pseudo-Blind, and Nonblind Samples

Table 7.9 uses the referee survey data to tabulate the percentages of blind papers that are truly blind among different groups; Table 7.9 also presents acceptance rates within the truly blind, pseudo-blind, and nonblind samples.[32] About half (47 percent) of the blind papers have authors who are not identifiable to the referees. Acceptance rates among these truly blind papers are substantially lower than in the pseudo-blind or nonblind samples, but as noted above, this is due to at least two factors: these papers are refereed entirely anonymously and they are more likely to be papers by less experienced and less well-known economists. In fact, the selectivity of these papers is verified by the fact that acceptance rates among pseudo-blind papers are above those for the nonblind sample.

Rows 2 and 3 of Table 7.9 indicate that there is little difference in the distribution of truly blind papers between men and women authors. In fact, women's papers are slightly less likely to be truly blind, but the differences are not statistically significant. There are large differences among the acceptance rates in the truly blind, pseudo-blind, and nonblind samples, both for men and for women. These differences are statistically significant for men but not for women (which is not surprising, given the much smaller number of observations on women's papers). In addition, the differences in acceptance rates between men and women in the different samples are not statistically significant.

Rows 4-9 of Table 7.9 investigate these questions across institutional rank of authors. Here there is more evidence of the nonrandom selection of truly blind papers. Only 29 percent of papers by authors from the top-ranked universities are truly blind, while 57 percent from colleges and low-ranked universities are in this category. As before, in each institutional-rank category, the acceptance rates among the pseudo-blind papers are higher than those among the nonblind papers, while the truly blind papers have lower acceptance rates.

Table 7.9 verifies that there are indeed lower acceptance rates for the truly blind papers than for the pseudo-blind or nonblind papers. However, Table 7.9 also verifies the fact that there is quite a bit of selectivity in terms of which papers are truly blind, as shown by the different distribution of truly blind papers among authors from different institutional ranks and as shown by the higher acceptance rates in the pseudo-blind sample than in the nonblind sample.

Table 7.9 Share of Truly Blind Papers and Acceptance Rates in the Truly Blind, Pseudo-Blind, and Nonblind Samples

			Acceptance rates		
	(1)	(2)	(3)	(4)	(5)
	Number of papers	Percentage of blind papers that are truly blind	Truly blind sample	Pseudo-blind sample	Non-blind sample
Sample					
1) All papers	1,223	46.9	5.5	16.4	15.0
		(1.8)	(1.2)	(1.9)	(1.6)
By gender:					
2) Female	150	41.6	8.1	11.5	8.2
		(5.2)	(4.5)	(4.4)	(3.5)
3) Male	1,036	47.5	5.4	17.5	16.3
		(2.0)	(1.3)	(2.1)	(1.8)
By institutional rank:					
4) Universities ranked 1-5	129	29.2	23.8	35.3	26.3
		(5.4)	(9.3)	(6.7)	(5.2)
5) Universities ranked 6-20	239	36.2	7.3	17.5	17.2
		(3.9)	(3.5)	(3.8)	(4.0)
6) Universities ranked 21-50	203	42.3	3.8	15.5	18.7
		(4.5)	(2.7)	(4.3)	(4.4)
7) Colleges/ universities ranked > 50	334	57.4	5.8	7.9	8.8
		(3.4)	(2.1)	(2.9)	(2.5)
8) U.S. nonacademic institutions	102	54.5	0.0	10.0	8.3
		(6.1)	–	(5.5)	(4.6)
9) Foreign	216	53.5	1.6	15.1	13.7
		(4.7)	(1.6)	(4.9)	(3.4)

Notes: The data are based on all papers with returned referee surveys. Standard errors are reported in parentheses.

B. Estimating the Effects of Being in the Truly Blind Sample on Acceptance Decisions

Because of the selectivity in terms of which papers are truly blind, it is not possible simply to compare acceptance rates between truly blind and pseudo-blind papers and to conclude that this is the effect of anonymity in the refereeing process, as was possible with the randomly selected blind and nonblind samples. Even if true anonymity had no effects whatsoever, one would still expect truly blind papers to have lower acceptance rates, because they are disproportionately written by authors who, even under identical refereeing processes, would have a lower probability of acceptance.

To estimate the effects of a paper being truly anonymous, purged of the contaminating effects that result from the selectivity of the truly blind sample, one needs an instrument for the variable "truly blind" that is uncorrelated with authors' ability, experience, or fame. Normally such instruments are very difficult to find. The randomized experiment that separated the data into a blind and nonblind sample, however, provides a perfect instrument. By design, authors of papers in the blind sample are identical to authors in the nonblind sample. Thus, inclusion in the blind sample is an effective instrument for inclusion in the truly blind sample. By estimating the probability of inclusion in the truly blind sample as a function of inclusion in the blind sample, one can derive an estimate of "truly blind" that is based only on the randomized experimental data and that is independent of any nonrandomized elements. This estimate can in turn be used as a replacement for the "truly blind" variable in a second-stage equation to estimate the effect of true anonymity on acceptance rates.

This is a standard instrumental-variables procedure. To implement it, let $\mathbf{X}^{\text{TB}}$ be a vector of endogenous truly blind interaction variables that I want to purge of any effect other than that created by the anonymity of the paper in the refereeing process. ($\mathbf{X}^{\text{TB}}$ contains the variables "truly blind $\times$ female author," "truly blind $\times$ university ranked 1-5," etc.) Let $\mathbf{X}^{\text{BL}}$ be a vector of the instruments, namely, the equivalent set of interaction variables defined from the blind/nonblind sample. ($\mathbf{X}^{\text{BL}}$ contains the variables "blind $\times$ female author," "blind $\times$ university ranked 1-5," etc.) Let $\mathbf{Z}$ be all other exogenous variables in the model ("female," "university ranked 1-5," "multiple-authored," etc). In the first stage, I estimate each variable in the vector $\mathbf{X}^{\text{TB}}$ as a function of the instruments and all the other included variables in the model. If $\mathbf{X}^{\text{TB}}$ has J elements, then this is a set of J linear probability regressions, where the following equation is estimated for each endogenous variable j:

$$X_j^{\text{TB}} = \mathbf{X}^{\text{BL}}\beta + \mathbf{Z}\gamma + \varepsilon_j \qquad (7.1)$$

Using the coefficients from these equations, if one computes an estimate for each of the J endogenous variables that is orthogonal to all effects except the randomized experimental effects embedded in the instruments, one obtains

$$\hat{X}_j^{\text{TB}} = \mathbf{X}^{\text{BL}}\hat{\beta} + \mathbf{Z}\hat{\gamma} \qquad (7.2)$$

If A is the 0/1 dichotomous variable indicating acceptance, one can then estimate a second-stage linear probability model as

$$A = \hat{\mathbf{X}}^{TB}\boldsymbol{\alpha} + \mathbf{Z}\boldsymbol{\delta} + v \tag{7.3}$$

The estimated coefficients for $\boldsymbol{\alpha}$ indicate the effect of the variables in the $\mathbf{X}^{TB}$ vector on the probability of acceptance, purged of their correlations with anything except the randomized effects.[33]

Intuitively, this instrumental-variables procedure estimates the size of the truly blind effect by assuming that all the difference in acceptance rates between the blind and the nonblind sample is due to differential acceptance rates within the truly blind sample. The first-stage equation replaces a dummy variable indicating inclusion in the truly blind sample with an instrumented variable that is equal to the percentage of the blind sample that is truly blind. The result is to scale up the estimated effect of being in the blind sample (seen in the estimates from Table 7.5), producing coefficients that indicate how large the effect in the truly blind sample would have to be in order to produce the measured effect within the overall blind sample. In essence, this procedure is almost equivalent to dividing the coefficient on the blind interaction term by the share of the blind sample that is truly blind, which would be the indirect least-squares approach to this problem.

The results of estimating the effect of being in the truly blind sample on acceptance probabilities are shown in Table 7.10. Columns 1 and 2 show the estimation results when a dummy variable indicating actual inclusion in the truly blind sample is interacted with the gender and institutional-rank variables. Columns 3 and 4 show the results when the instruments are used instead, purged of all correlations with anything except true anonymity. The point estimates on most of the instrumented variables are large, but so are the standard errors.

The most striking difference between the estimates in columns 1 and 3 occurs for authors from the top-ranked schools in the truly blind sample. Simply controlling for inclusion in the truly blind sample in column 1 would lead to the conclusion that there is a small, insignificant, negative effect of being in the truly blind sample for this group. However, this is a group for which the selectivity associated with truly blind papers might be quite large. Indeed, when the instrumented (purged) variable is used instead, the effect of being in the truly blind sample among this group becomes positive and large, although poorly estimated.

Papers in the truly blind sample by authors from lower-ranked universities generally have lower acceptance rates, but the only group that is significantly affected by being truly anonymous contains papers by authors

Table 7.10 Effect of Truly Blind Refereeing on Probability of Acceptance

Variable	Using actual data on truly blind		Using IV for all variables involving the truly blind interaction	
	(1) Coef- ficient	(2) SE	(3) Coef- ficient	(4) SE
Truly blind effects:				
Truly blind × female author	8.0	6.6	10.5	12.0
Truly blind × university ranked 1-5	-6.7	7.9	21.3	27.4
Truly blind × university ranked 6-20	-11.1	5.1	-8.6	13.4
Truly blind × university ranked 21-50	-15.5	5.4	-21.8	12.1
Truly blind × college/university ranked > 50	-3.8	3.8	-4.6	5.3
Truly blind × U.S. nonacademic institution	-11.1	6.9	-7.5	9.6
Truly blind × foreign	-14.4	5.3	-11.2	8.3
Other variables:				
Female	-5.6	3.4	-6.4	3.1
University ranked 1-5	25.8	3.9	20.7	4.9
University ranked 6-20	13.2	3.2	12.2	3.2
University ranked 21-50	13.9	3.3	15.2	3.5
College/University ranked > 50	5.2	3.0	5.1	2.3
U.S. nonacademic institution	6.1	4.5	4.4	4.0
Foreign	11.2	3.5	9.8	3.2
Multiple-authored	0.2	2.0	0.1	1.8
Controls for field of co-editor	yes		yes	
Number of observations:	1,186		1,186	

Notes: The results are based on linear probability models in which the dependent variable equals 1 if the paper is not rejected. All coefficients and standard errors are multiplied by 100. The standard errors in column 4 are corrected for the instrumental-variables (IV) transformation.

from universities ranked 21-50, whose probability of acceptance falls almost 22 percentage points. This is in sharp contrast to the estimates in column 1, where the effect of true anonymity is contaminated by the selectivity associated with the truly blind sample. In column 1, papers by authors in four of the five categories of lower-ranked institutions appear to be significantly and negatively affected by being in the truly blind sample. Column 3 generally shows smaller and less significant effects for most of these categories. There is also no significance to the large positive effect on acceptance of being in the truly blind sample for papers by women.

Studying the effect of a paper's being truly blind is not easy, because the sample of truly blind papers would likely have a lower acceptance rate even if the papers were not anonymous. The randomized sample of blind/nonblind papers provides a way to look at the effect on acceptance rates of a paper's being truly blind, purged of the selectivity problems, and indicates that the effects are generally smaller and less significant than a simple comparison of acceptance rates between truly blind papers and other papers would indicate.

IX.   CONCLUSIONS

This paper has investigated the effects of single-blind versus double-blind reviewing using a unique experimental dataset from the *AER*. The primary conclusions are as follows:

1) There is a different pattern of acceptance rates under a single-blind reviewing system than under a double-blind system. The most striking effect is that acceptance rates are lower and referee reports are more critical under a double-blind system.

2) There are differences in the acceptance rates across institutional categories between single-blind and double-blind reviewing. In general, authors at the top-ranked institutions and those at colleges or low-ranked institutions are little affected. However, authors at institutions ranked 6-50 have lower acceptance rates under blind reviewing, as do foreign authors and authors from nonacademic institutions.

3) While there is some indication in these data that women do slightly better under a double-blind system, both in terms of acceptance rates and referee ratings, these effects are relatively small and statistically insignificant. Thus, this paper provides little evidence that moving to a double-blind reviewing system will substantially increase the acceptance rate for papers by female economists.

4) Referee ratings are generally highly correlated with accept decisions, indicating that co-editors follow the advice of referees fairly closely. Thus, referees are more critical of blind papers in general. The only substantial difference between referee ratings and accept decisions is that

5) Referees tend to rate both blind and nonblind papers from near-top-ranked schools virtually identically, while blind papers from these schools were accepted at a lower rate than nonblind papers.

6) Female referees tend to give lower ratings to nonblind papers than do men and tend to give higher ratings to blind papers, while male referees

show the opposite pattern. Referees from different institutional settings do not appear to respond differently to blind versus non-blind papers.

7)   While a substantial number of referees of blind papers can identify the author, a substantial number cannot. It is not true that "you can always guess who wrote the paper." Slightly under half of the ostensibly blind papers in this data set are actually not blind to the referees, but more than half are truly blind.

8)   Those papers that are truly blind are a selected group of the blind papers. The estimated point effects of complete anonymity on acceptance rates are large for some groups, but generally poorly determined. The effect of being in the truly blind sample is not as large or as significant once all effects other than true anonymity are purged from the data.

As with any experiment, there are some caveats that should be noted. First, this experiment was not kept secret within the economics profession.[34] Thus, referees who knew that such an experiment was ongoing, might have behaved somewhat differently when they reviewed and evaluated papers than they would in the absence of such an experiment.[35]

Knowledge of the nature of the experiment could lead referees and co-editors to be more concerned with the fairness of their decisions, particularly regarding women's papers and papers from authors at lesser-ranked schools. This might lead to somewhat higher acceptance rates for these papers than would occur in the absence of the experiment. Thus, the significant differences in evaluation and acceptance between the single-blind and double-blind samples in the data from a publicly acknowledged experiment might be minimum estimates of the effect in the absence of such an experiment.

There may, however, be at least one offsetting effect. This experiment was run by a journal generally known for using a review process that is single-blind. The results from the double-blind sample in this experiment may not duplicate the results that would occur if the *AER* announced that it was going to use a permanently double-blind system. Once it is known that all papers will be reviewed double-blind, authors who want to be sure that their papers are identified by the referee can do so through careful attention to citations and writing. Any author can "outsmart" a double-blind system by throwing in numerous references clearly labeled as his or her own previous work. While it is more difficult for an author to assure anonymity, careful writing can make it more likely. If a substantial amount of this type of "gaming" starts to occur on the part of authors when a double-blind system is permanently utilized, then the results of this experiment would overstate the differences between single- and double-blind reviewing.[36]

Finally, while a major finding of this paper is that acceptance rates are lower under double-blind reviewing, this result is almost surely not generalizable to a situation in which a journal is fully double-blind. Editors have to accept a certain number of papers in order to meet their publication schedules. Because of the unique nature of this experiment, co-editors at the *AER* could respond to more critical referee ratings in the double-blind sample by accepting fewer of these papers while this experiment was running. This would not be possible if the journal were fully double-blind. The generalizable conclusion is not that acceptance rates would fall if the *AER* implemented double-blind reviewing, but that a double-blind system would lead to more critical referee reports and a different mix of accepted papers across institutions.

APPENDIX A

Referee Survey

Dear Referee,

We ask you to fill out this page at the same time that you send back your referee's report. This is part of a special *AER* research project. This page will not be seen by the editors or the authors. Confidentiality will be strictly protected. Please return this page in the attached pre-stamped envelope. Use the envelope only for the questionnaire.

1. File number (from front page of paper)
2. Paper title
3. Please evaluate the quality of this paper by circling the appropriate number:

	First rate				Seriously deficient	Does not apply
Theoretical exposition	1	2	3	4	5	0
Empirical analysis	1	2	3	4	5	0
Contribution to the field	1	2	3	4	5	0
Overall quality of paper	1	2	3	4	5	0

4. Please answer this last question only if the author(s) name(s)and affiliation were deleted from the paper:

Do you believe you can identify the author(s)?
    Yes
    No

If yes, who do you believe the author(s) to be?

Thank you for providing this information.

APPENDIX B

Rankings of Economics Departments

Top Five:
  MIT
  Harvard
  University of Chicago
  Princeton
  Stanford
6-20:
  Yale
  University of Minnesota
  University of Pennsylvania
  Columbia
  UCLA
  UC-Berkeley
  University of Wisconsin
  Northwestern
  University of Michigan
  Rochester
  New York University
  Brown
  University of Maryland
  Cornell
  UC-San Diego
21-50:
  Carnegie Mellon
  Johns Hopkins
  CalTech
  Duke

21-50 (cont.)
  University of Virginia
  University of Washington
  Michigan State
  Virginia Polytechnic Institute
  University of Illinois
  University of North Carolina
  University of Southern California
  Washington University
  Texas A&M
  Purdue
  Vanderbilt
  UC-Davis
  Iowa State
  Boston University
  University of Massachusetts
  Ohio State
  SUNY-Stony Brook
  UC-Santa Barbara
  University of Florida
  University of Texas
  University of Iowa
  University of Pittsburgh
  Claremont Graduate School
  Penn State
  Indiana University
  North Carolina State

Source: Jones et al. (1982 pp. 54-63 [column 08]).

NOTES

1. See Table 7.2. "Single-blind" refers to the fact that the author does not know who the referee is; "double-blind" means that the referee is also not informed about the author. A few journals (not in economics) use an entirely "nonblind" system, wherein the referee signs the report sent back to the author.
2. An eloquent argument favoring single-blind reviewing, which is difficult to summarize, is contained in Angus Deaton et al. (1987).
3. The data in Table 7.1 come from Miller and Punsalan's (1988) guidebook on publication practices in economics. A survey conducted in the winter of 1989 of 50 top economics journals, asking about their use of single-blind or double-blind reviewing, produced almost identical results (see Blank, 1989).
4. For earlier tabulations of refereeing practices in economics, see Linda N. Edwards and Marianne A. Ferber (1986), Ferber and Michelle Teiman (1980), and Robert K. Coe and Irwin Weinstock (1967).
5. Questionnaries were sent to 50 journals, selected as the top journals in these nine fields by a senior reference librarian at Princeton University. Forty-seven questionnaires were returned; nine journals reported making little or no use of outside referees. The remaining 38 responses are tabulated in Table 7.2.
6. In response to an open question about why a particular referee system was utilized, the responses match those often given in economics. The single-blind journal respondents indicated that the identity of the authors can often be guessed, that double-blind reviewing causes administrative inconvenience, or that the tradition of the field was long-established. The double-blind journal respondents mentioned issues of fairness.
7. The most striking problems are the small number of observations in each discipline and the potentially nonrandom selection of journals.
8. The attempt was to signal a low-status institution, so Harvard, for instance, was changed to The Tri-Valley Center for Human Development.
9. In 1973, a new editor initiated a nine-month experiment with double-blind reviewing. He became convinced that a double-blind procedure was perceived as fairer and that it did not have any serious costs associated with it (George Borts, 1974), and he implemented double-blind reviewing for the remainder of his term as editor. The editor appointed in 1979 returned the journal to a single-blind system.
10. The original research design proposed that papers sent to more than one referee should alternate between double-blind and single-blind. If the *AER* had a centralized staff dealing with all papers from beginning to end, such a research design might have been feasible, but these papers were handled out of four different offices around the country. Effective monitoring and training of the changing secretarial staff in all of these offices over the two-year period, to insure adequate implementation of this research design, would have been almost impossible.
11. A peer-reviewing system typically requires that the editor know the author of submitted papers, simply to avoid sending a paper to its own author or to the author's departmental colleagues for review.
12. In reality, papers that are not rejected long after their initial submission date are highly likely to be accepted; typically they are simply involved in a lengthy

"revise and resubmit" delay. In a few cases, a file may remain open because an author has sent (or even published) the paper elsewhere without informing the *AER* staff.

13. Referees did not sign the surveys. When only one referee was used, the identity was obvious. For papers with multiple referees, I identified referees by matching the date on which a survey was received in the *AER* office with the dates when referee reports on that paper were received by the co-editors (part of a paper's official record card). In most cases, surveys and referee reports could be clearly matched by date. In some cases with multiple referees, however, I was not able to identify which referee sent in which survey and thus could not identify referee gender or institutional ranking (unless they were similar for all referees on the paper).

14. The primary reason to believe that co-editors might have been more sensitive to the question of bias against women than to the question of bias against lesser ranked institutions is that there are few papers submitted by women but many papers submitted by individuals in lower-ranked departments. It is thus easier to "notice" the women's papers when they appear.

15. First, economics colleagues at Princeton were shown the list and asked to identify anyone they knew. Second, foreign students were asked to look at the unfamiliar foreign names and see whether they could determine gender. Third, if the author listed an affiliation with an institution in the United States or Canada, this institution was called and queried about the gender of that person. Fourth, for those listing only initials, the directory of the American Economic Association was used to see whether full names were available.

16. Much of the analysis has been duplicated using the two alternative definitions. The results are generally similar, with higher standard errors.

17. This document measures departments along 18 dimensions. For this study, I used the rankings associated with measure 8, the most broadly cited quality measure, which is the mean rating of the scholarly quality of program faculty.

18. Tests of similarity across these groupings indicate that little information is lost by this grouping. Note that all authors from a given institution are coded with the same institutional rank, even though these rankings refer only to economics departments. For example, economists from Harvard Business School are ranked in the top five, although that ranking is based solely on the quality of the Harvard Department of Economics.

19. Actually, the response rate is better than this. In one editor's office, surveys were mailed only to referees of double-blind papers for several months before the mistake was corrected, so not all referees received surveys.

20. Given the length of time that papers sit on some referee's desks and the confusion that reigns in some referee's offices, this may be a surprisingly high referee response rate.

21. The estimated characteristic, plus and minus its standard error, provides a one-standard-deviation confidence interval, indicating that 68 percent of the data falls within this range. If a 90 or 95 percent confidence interval were calculated, the range would be even larger.

22. The return rate for referee surveys in the blind sample is 82.5 percent, while it is 67.5 percent in the nonblind sample. As noted in footnote 19, this is partly due to a problem in the office of one of the co-editors, but even among the

other co-editors, the response rate was higher in the blind sample. The result is that 60.2 percent of the referee-survey data comes from blind papers, although only 55.5 percent of the papers were blind.

23. Multiple-author papers are considered to be correctly identified if any of the author's names are known.

24. Acceptance rates throughout the rest of this analysis are defined as the percentages of papers that are not rejected, including both fully accepted papers and papers for which decisions are not yet final. As noted in footnote 12, most papers involved in long decision delays are ultimately accepted. Duplicating the analysis using only finally accepted papers in the "accept" category makes no difference to the results.

25. The accept/reject decision is a dichotomous variable and technically should be modeled with either a probit or logit specification. Either of these estimating techniques provides results that are indistinguishable from the linear probability model shown here, which treats the dichotomous variable as a continuous variable.

26. Neither a constant nor an aggregate control for being in the blind sample is included in Table 7.6, since the sum of the university-rank variables is collinear with the constant, and the sum of the interactions between the blind sample and the university-rank variables is collinear with the blind dummy variable.

27. A more complex statistical alternative to looking at differences in mean ratings between the blind and nonblind samples would be to estimate ordered probit models, using the five-point referee rating scale as the dependent variable. Experimental effects could be measured by including variables such as gender and institutional rank, interacted with a dummy variable indicating inclusion in the blind sample. Because of the experimental nature of the data, there is little gained by this more complex econometric approach; such estimates produce results virtually identical to those discussed here. The estimated coefficients from such models are available from the author.

28. Referee ratings on theoretical exposition, empirical analysis, and contribution to the field show similar patterns to ratings for overall quality. In all cases, blind papers receive more critical (higher) ratings. I report the overall quality rating, since this seems to be the most inclusive measure. Also, 98.3 percent of the referees provided a rating for overall paper quality, while only 93.0 percent gave a theoretical-exposition rating and only 50.9 percent give an empirical-analysis rating.

29. It is interesting that the point estimates indicate that women gain more in referee ratings by moving from a blind to a nonblind reviewing system. This is the opposite of what the point estimates showed for acceptance rates, where the probability of acceptance rose more for men than for women under a nonblind system. The lack of statistical significance on these differentials, however, makes it impossible to draw inferences from these results.

30. Thirty-seven percent (555 papers) of the papers had exactly two referee surveys returned. Note that this is not a randomized sample. Papers with more referees were more likely to have more returned surveys, but papers with more referees were also more likely to have had referee disagreements, inducing the co-editor to solicit additional referee reports. Thus, because of the sample selection, these

estimates are probably an overstatement of the degree of referee disagreement across all papers.

31. Note that this question has little to do with the question of how double-blind reviewing affects publication outcomes. As shown in Table 7.4, almost half the referees are able to identify the authors of blind papers in these data; the effect of a double-blind reviewing process necessarily includes the fact that many ostensibly blind papers are only pseudo-blind.

32. The sample for Tables 7.9 and 7.10 is based on all papers for which referee surveys were received. Truly blind papers are those for which no referee could identify the author. Pseudo-blind papers are those for which at least one referee could identify the author (this includes both those papers listed as "pseudo-blind" and as "mixed" in Table 7.4).

33. The standard errors resulting from the estimation of equation (7.3) are incorrect, since they do not account for the fact that the instruments are estimated with error. The standard errors reported in column 4 of Table 7.10 are corrected for this problem.

34. Indeed, that would have been impossible, given the referee survey and the sudden appearance of double-blind papers sent to referees from the *AER*.

35. My own conversations with economists over the past several years regarding this project seem to indicate that a small number of economists at a few (primarily highly ranked) departments were fully aware of the experiment, but that most others, even those who served as referees for the *AER* over the experimental time period and filled out referee surveys, had little awareness that something unusual was occurring.

36. It is also possible that authors' decisions about where to submit their papers may be influenced by refereeing practices. Thus, a permanent double-blind system could result in a somewhat different selection of submitted articles. It seems reasonable to expect such an effect to be small.

REFERENCES

Blank, Rebecca M. (1989), "Which Journals Practice Blind Refereeing?" *Newsletter of the Committee on the Status of Women in the Economics Profession*, pp. 5-6.

Borts, George (1974), "Report of the Managing Editor," *American Economic Review* (Papers and Proceedings), **64**, 476-82.

Ceci, Stephen J., and Douglas P. Peters (1982), "Peer Review Practices of Psychological Journals: The Fate of Published Articles, Submitted Again," *Behavioral and Brain Sciences*, **5**, 187-252.

Ceci, Stephen J., and Douglas P. Peters (1984), "How Blind is Blind Review?" *American Psychologist*, **39**, 1491-4.

Coe, Robert K., and Irwin Weinstock (1967), "Editorial Policies of Major Economic Journals," *Quarterly Review of Economics and Business*, **7**, 37-43.

Coughlin, Cletus C., and Anthony O'Brien (1985), "Non-blind Refereeing as a Barrier to Entry: Is There a Dual Labor Market in the Economics Profession?" unpublished manuscript presented at the December 1985 ASSA meetings, New York.

Crane, Diane (1967), "The Gatekeepers of Science: Some Factors Affecting the Selection of Articles for Scientic Journals," *American Sociologist*, **2**, 195-201.

Deaton, Angus, Roger Guesnerie, Lars Peter Hansen, and David Kreps (1987), "*Econometrica* Operating Procedures," *Econometrica*, **55**, 204-6.

Edwards, Linda N., and Marianne A. Ferber (1986), "Journal Reviewing Practices and the Progress of Women in the Economics Profession: Is There a Relationship?" *Newsletter of the Committee on the Status of Women in the Economics Profession*, pp.1-7.

Ferber, Marianne A., and Michelle Teiman (1980), "Are Women Economists at a Disadvantage in Publishing Journal Articles?" *Eastern Economic Journal*, **63**, 89-93.

Gordon, Michael, (1979), "Peer Review in Physics," *Physics Bulletin*, **30**, 112-13.

Jones, Lyle V., Gardner Lindsey and Porter E. Coggeshall (1982), *An Assessment of Research-Doctorate Programs in the United States: Social and Behavioral Sciences, Report of the Committee on the Assessment of Quality-Related Characteristics of Research-Doctorate Programs in the United States*, Conference Board of Associated Research Councils, Washington, DC: National Academy Press.

Mahoney, Michael J. (1977), "Publication Prejudices: An Experimental Study of Confirmatory Bias in the Peer Review System," *Cognitive Therapy and Research*, **1**, 161-75.

Miller, A. Carolyn, and Victoria J. Punsalan (1988), *Refereed and Nonrefereed Economic Journals: A Guide to Publishing Opportunities*, New York: Greenwood Press.

Peters, Douglas P., and Stephen J. Ceci (1980), "A Manuscript Masquerade: How Well Does the Review Process Work?" *Sciences*, **20**, 16-19.

Zuckerman, Harriet, and Robert K. Merton (1971), "Patterns of Evaluation in Science: Institutionalisation, Structure and Functions of the Referee System," *Minerva*, **9**, 66-100.

8. Favoritism versus Search for Good Papers: Empirical Evidence Regarding the Behavior of Journal Editors*

David N. Laband and Michael J. Piette

Abstract: Journal editors who publish papers authored by colleagues and former graduate students have been charged with practicing favoritism, with the implication that the papers in question are of lower quality than those written by scholars with no ties to the editor. Using citation analysis, we find strong evidence that although journal editors occasionally publish subpar papers authored by colleagues and former graduate students, on balance their use of professional connections enables them to identify and "capture" high-impact papers for publication. This implies that a practice interpreted as "favoritism" by many scholars in fact serves to enhance efficiency in the market for scientific knowledge.

I. INTRODUCTION

Of 15 editorial practices considered in a survey of 328 marketing faculty by Sherrell, Hair, and Griffin (1989), the two deemed least ethical were (1) favoritism to friends and personal associates by an editor or reviewer and

* Reprinted with permission of the copyright holder from the *Journal of Political Economy*, Vol.102, No.1, 1994, pp. 194-203.

Salisbury State University and Economic Research Services, respectively. Helpful comments received from John P. Sophocleus, Rebecca M. Blank, John D. Jackson, Anna Maria Turner Lomperis, Melayne Morgan, seminar participants at Auburn University and George Mason University, and an anonymous reviewer and computer programming support provided by Edward T. Novak are gratefully acknowledged. We assume full responsibility for remaining errors of commission or omission.

(2) selection of reviewers that have a strong bias (pro or con the manuscript's content area or methodology) in order to ensure acceptance or rejection. Indirectly, charges of editorial favoritism have been leveled at the *Journal of Political Economy*. Gerrity and McKenzie (1978) claimed and Laband (1985) offered evidence to the effect that a large fraction of articles published in the *JPE* were authored by scholars with ties to the University of Chicago. Siegfried (1992) presents additional evidence on this score but also finds that the fraction of Chicago-affiliated authors in the *JPE* has declined over the past 40 years.

Authors have strong feelings about editorial favoritism, for two reasons. First, we suspect that most academic scholars believe that journal editors *should* serve as disinterested gatekeepers (Crane 1967) rather than self-interested deal cutters. The shared perception of scientific advancement as a steady progression, however slow, from error to truth is an illusion that is seemingly shattered by the practice of editorial favoritism. Second, editorial favoritism implies a wealth redistribution in favor of certain members of the scientific community at the expense of other members; the latter are liable to object vociferously.[1]

Basing charges of editorial favoritism on the fraction of papers published by authors with ties to an editor is problematic. The distribution of submissions may well support the observed publication outcomes, or even suggest that the editors shy away from publishing papers written by scholars with whom they share some affiliation. The issue of concern, it seems to us, is whether there are qualitative differences between the papers authored by scholars with personal ties to an editor and those authored by scholars with no ties to an editor.

There are two competing arguments about the nature of the relationship between quality of papers published in scientific journals and personal ties between the author(s) and the editor. On one hand, editors may publish substandard papers written by their personal friends or professional allies. That is to say, the publication standard applied by the editor to papers submitted by these individuals is lower than the one that must be met by individuals with no connection to the editor, and perhaps substantially lower than the standard that must be met by individuals whom the editor dislikes. We are painfully aware that we have no ready answer to the question "Why would editors do this?" except to emphasize that, to our knowledge, no widely accepted theory of editorial behavior has ever been articulated. This difficulty notwithstanding, editorial favoritism of this form implies that papers authored by individuals with personal ties to the editor will be of lower quality than those written by individuals unconnected to the editor, ceteris paribus.

In stark contrast to this view stands the argument made to us by numerous journal editors (independently) over the years: the personal feelings of authors to the contrary notwithstanding, there is a consistent shortage of truly good papers authored by scholars in economics. Journal editors compete to identify and publish the (few) papers with relatively great substantive impact. The role of the editor in this competitive process was spelled out recently in private correspondence to one of us by Harold M. Hochman, editor of the *Eastern Economic Journal*:

> It [author/editor connection] also implies lower transactions costs, in particular, lower costs of information – i.e., more output, given other input costs. *Editors compete with each other for good papers.* ... If one of my colleagues has a good paper, I'm more likely to know about it than other editors and, conversely, my colleague is more likely to be comfortable with my ability to choose competent referees.
>
> ... *All I want are good papers, whatever their source, and there are few enough of them that I don't agonize about the so-called fairness issues with which so many of our fellow economists are preoccupied.* [Emphasis added]

As part of this competitive process, editors attend professional meetings to learn about research papers in the "presubmission" stage. Many universities housing journal editorships maintain active seminar series that become de facto, and valuable, inputs in this search process. In addition, journal editors solicit information from their colleagues about good paper prospects. This information is likely to prove valuable for the simple reason that journal editors tend to be affiliated with major universities; their faculty colleagues and graduate students are liable to be among the best scholars in the profession.

The two explanations are not mutually exclusive. An editor might occasionally publish a substandard paper by a personal friend or departmental colleague while simultaneously using his or her connections to search assiduously for high-impact papers. The empirical question that we explore is whether, *on balance*, editors' use of personal connections results in publication of higher-impact papers than those published for which no author/editor connection is apparent-

II.   DATA, METHODOLOGY, AND FINDINGS

We compiled detailed information on 1,051 full articles published in 28 top economics journals in 1984.[2] We then examined the extent to which an author's personal ties to the editor of a journal influenced subsequent citations to published articles, controlling for author, article, and journal-specific characteristics that might influence citations.

We employed an ordinary least squares (OLS) regression to estimate numerous alternative specifications of the following model of the determinants of citations to an article:

$$\text{citations}_i, 1985\text{-}89 = a_0 + a_1\text{length}_i$$
$$+ a_2\text{lead articles}_i + a_3\text{gender}_i$$
$$+ a_4\text{author's mean age}_i + a_5\text{connection}_i$$
$$+ a_6\text{author's}_i\text{ stock of citations, 1979-83}$$
$$+ a_7\text{journal quality}_i + e_i \qquad (8.1).$$

Citations were obtained from the *Social Sciences Citation Index*; we excluded self-citations. Article length was standardized to *AER*-equivalent sized pages. We defined an author/editor connection to exist whenever any of the authors of an article received his or her Ph.D. from the same university that the editor, coeditor, or any associate editor of the journal that published the paper was affiliated with in 1984 or received his or her Ph.D. degree from, or if any of the authors of a paper was affiliated in 1984 with the same university that the editor, coeditor, or any associate editor was affiliated with in 1984 or received his or her Ph.D. degree from. Journal quality is a normalized measure of the relative prestige of the journals in our sample, based on citations per character space, as reported by Liebowitz and Palmer (1984).

Following Laband (1986), we expect signs on a_1, a_6, and a_7 to be positive. Conventional wisdom (and the behavior of journal editors) suggests that lead articles are published in that position precisely because the editors expect these articles to have special relevance to the readership.[3] We therefore expect lead articles to be cited more than other articles; a_2 should sign positive. We have no strong feeling a priori about the impact of author's mean age or gender on predicted citations.

Finally, we included a variable that partially reflects connections between authors and the journal editors who published their work. We concede that our connection variable does not account for the full range of methods employed by editors to identify and "capture" good articles. However, it does capture the informational network of same-school colleagues and graduate students. We rely on the data to inform us about the sign and importance of a_5.

Empirical Results

As in Leamer (1983, 1985), numerous alternative specifications of equation
(8.1) were estimated, including models with linear and squared terms of
several variables, as well as a variety of interaction terms. Since citations
arguably are distributed nonnormally (with most papers receiving few or no
subsequent citations), we logged the two citations variables as a check on
the robustness of the OLS results. As a further check on the accuracy of our
results, we estimated equation (8.1) using the ordered probit technique. We
ordered citations by quintile, since the large percentage of articles in our
sample receiving zero citations (21 percent) precluded an ordering by
deciles. Our results, reported in Table 8.1, were consistent across all our
regression and ordered probit estimations.[4]

As expected, article length, author reputation, and relative quality of
publishing journal all demonstrate positive and statistically significant
explanatory power with respect to subsequent citation of an article. Our
results indicate that journal editors correctly select high-impact papers for
publication as lead articles. We found no gender-based differences in
citations to the articles in our sample, whether defining female authorship as
at least one woman on a coauthored paper or all women on a coauthored
paper.

The estimated impact of author/editor connection (a_5) on citations is
positive and highly significant. This finding provides empirical support for
the contention that the editorial process is competitive and that editors use
their connections to actively search out high-impact papers for publication
in their journals. These findings were consistent across all our estimations.

Nearly one-quarter of the papers published in our entire sample were
characterized by at least one type of author/editor connection, in terms of
current affiliation or degree-granting institution. To investigate more fully
the efficacy of editorial search via connections for good papers, we split our
sample by connection status. Variable means and standard errors for each
sample are reported in Table 8.2. Using the regression equation reported in
Table 8.1, we then generated predicted mean residual citations for each
sample and examined the proportion of residuals in the two tails of the
distribution that were associated with editor/author connections.

Table 8.1   *OLS Regression and Ordered Probit Estimation Results: Equation (8.1)*

Variable	OLS RESULTS		ORDERED PROBIT RESULTS: Dependent Variable: Citations, 1985-89 (N = 1,051)
	Dependent Variable: Citations, 1985-89 (N = 1,051)	Dependent Variable: Log of Citations, 1985-89 (N = 790)	
Constant	.21599	.37584*	.05096
	(1.77145)	(.08334)	(.18050)
Length	.51949*	.01849*	.07617*
	(.04361)	(.00199)	(.00550)
Lead article	2.31690**	.14418*	.32740*
	(1.11090)	(.04894)	(.11660)
Log of author's stock of citations, 1979-83		.10060*	
		(.02157)	
Author's stock of citations, 1979-83	.00400*		.00025*
	(.00108)		(.00012)
Author's mean age	-.13785*	--.00910*	-.01714*
	(.04181)	(.00208)	(.00433)
Author/editor connection	4.13239*	.13062*	.35170*
	(.74062)	(.03363)	(.08240)
Gender female = 1	.45534	.03037	.08507
	(1.11170)	(.05229)	(.12140)
Journal quality	.08630*	.00441*	.01294*
	(.01281)	(.00061)	(.00146)
R^2	.2382	.2442	
F_{reg}	46.5831*	37.4171*	
Log likelihood			-1,500,812
χ^2			334.690*

Notes: * Significant at the .01 level.   ** Significant at the .05 level.

Table 8.2 Variable Means/Standard Errors by Author/Editor Connection Status for 1,051 Papers Published in 28 Economics Journals in 1984

Variable	Entire Sample (N = 1,051)	Connection (N = 250)	No Connection (N = 801)
Citations, 1985-89	7.057	12.288	5.424
	(11.173)	(16.600)	(8.177)
Length	11.721	14.130	10.969
	(7.301)	(8.954)	(6.529)
Lead article	.091	.148	.074
	(.288)	(.356)	(.261)
Author's stock of citations, 1979-83	132.382	250.104	95.639
	(302.683)	(383.391)	(262.325)
Author's mean age	38.221	38.667	38.082
	(7.737)	(8.994)	(7.302)
Review process double-blind	1.461	.456	.462
	(.499)	(.499)	(.499)
Author/editor connection	.238	1.000	.000
	(.426)		
Journal quality index	49.370	52.833	48.289
	(23.926)	(21.477)	(24.553)

Twice as many of the articles authored by individuals with our measure of connection to the editor were published as lead articles as compared with papers whose authors had no connection to the editor. Mean actual citations of articles published for which we identify an author/editor connection (12.288) were more than twice as great as citations of articles without such a connection (5.424). Some portion of this differential results from differences in author, article, and journal-specific characteristics that generate a large difference in mean predicted citations between articles with author/editor connections and those without such connections. However, with these factors accounted for, papers written by individuals with our measured connections to editors received 29 percent more citations, on average, than predicted, whereas papers written by authors without our measured connections to editors received 13.74 percent fewer citations, on average, than predicted. These results suggest quite strongly that, on balance, journal editors use their professional connections to search out good papers, rather than print substandard material written by their colleagues or buddies. This is not to deny the possibility of the latter. The evidence, however, clearly indicates that the beneficial aspect of search/screening by editors dominates any harm derived from favoritism they may exhibit.

Indeed, our results arguably understate the true impact and importance of this search process by editors. A broad range of editorial connections is not incorporated in our particular measure. For example, editors acquire information about papers by attending professional conference, seminar, and workshop presentations, as well as by word of mouth from individuals not affiliated with their university or degree-granting institution. The presumably positive residuals associated with these papers are incorporated into the set of papers that we treat as being "unconnected." This inevitably inflates the mean residual ascribed to the papers described as lacking any author/editor connection and may deflate the mean residual ascribed to the papers described as having an author/editor connection.

However, not all that glitters is gold. When one examines the connection status of papers at the tail end of the distribution of residuals, it becomes apparent that the use of connections is costly. Over two-thirds of the papers with residual citations at least one standard deviation below their predicted values were published by editors with our version of connection to the authors. Whether these type 1 error papers were published by design or through carelessness or represent an inefficiency inherent to this mechanism for extracting information about good papers is an issue beyond the scope of our present inquiry.

In regression analyses not reported herein, we identified separately the author/editor connections defined by authors who were departmental colleagues of editors and those defined by authors who were former graduate students of the department of which the editor was a member. These analyses revealed that the source of the most heavily cited papers is editors' colleagues, not former graduate students of the department.

III. FINAL COMMENTS

One implication of a model of journal editors as active competitors on the production side of the market for scientific information is that the value of a journal ranking scheme based on citations is lower than it would be if editors were completely passive brokers of submitted papers. Editorial activism in the submission stage generates noise in such rankings, because the variance around the mean quality of papers published by a specific journal is greater than it would be without editorial activism. Consider the case of editors of specialty journals using their professional contacts to identify and "capture" high-quality papers that might otherwise have been published by the good general-interest journals. This not only raises the mean citation counts of papers published by the specialty journals but also increases the variances around those means and *lowers* the mean citation counts of papers published by the general-interest journals, which probably also raises the variances around those means. The effect of such competition is to make it more difficult for scholars to allocate their scarce reading time among articles. High-impact articles may be found in any number of journals, not just the most highly cited general-interest journals.

Our findings also have implications regarding editorial favoritism, defined in our terms as publication of papers authored by an editor's "friends" that do not meet the same qualitative standard for publication required of authors having no connection to the editor. It seems possible, if not probable, that part of the implicit compensation offered to journal editors is the opportunity to publish low-quality papers, relatively speaking, written by professional friends (including himself) and allies. Indeed, to the extent that an editor can arrange quid pro quos in the form of invitations to give paid lectures, attend prestigious conferences, join esteemed societies, and the like, this prerogative may, on the margin, be one of the more powerful inducements motivating the supply of editors. If this prerogative were denied journal editors, either the quality of editors would decline or we would have to pay more for subscriptions (to fund the increase in nominal compensation required to make journal editors no worse off). Indeed, since new journals are established occasionally by individuals who seek to become editors, the supply of journals may also be adversely affected. If, on balance, the losses due to editors' occasionally publishing substandard material written by friends/allies are more than made up for by the marginal impact of this prerogative in attracting editors who are more efficient than the next-best editors available in the absence of such a prerogative, then any restrictions placed on the exercise of editorial favoritism would result in a net loss of efficiency in the market for scientific knowledge.

NOTES

1. Beyer (1978, p. 75) argues this point: 'any factors that increase the probability of particularistic decisions or increase their consequences are not likely to benefit

the majority of scientists. A relatively small proportion of such decisions spread over time may serve to give some groups and individuals substantial cumulative advantage, because publication itself is convertible into the scarce "evidence" of competence that makes future selection for further advantage then based upon competence, and therefore universalistic. Thus, a particularistic advantage can soon be transformed into a universalistic one.' See also Vandermeulen (1972).

2. These journals are *American Economic Review, American Journal of Agricultural Economics, Brookings Papers on Economic Activity, Canadian Journal of Economics, Econometrica, Economic Inquiry, Economic Journal, Economica, International Economic Review, Journal of Econometrics, Journal of Economic Literature, Journal of Finance, Journal of Financial Economics, Journal of Human Resources, Journal of International Economics, Journal of Law and Economics, Journal of Mathematical Economics, Journal of Monetary Economics, Journal of Money, Credit and Banking, Journal of Political Economy, Journal of Public Economics, National Tax Journal, Quarterly Journal of Economics, Rand Journal of Economics, Review of Economic Studies, Review of Economics and Statistics, Scandinavian Journal of Economics,* and *Southern Economic Journal.*

3. For example, the editors of *Economic Inquiry* published 'Economical Writing' as a lead article in 1985, and they continue to emphasize their commitment to the message contained therein in their style guidelines to authors. Several top journals routinely publish Nobel lectures and presidential addresses as lead articles.

4. We investigated the possibility that the impact of some or all of our control variables differs by type of review process employed, by estimating separate regressions for the single-blind and the double-blind papers. Although large differences in coefficient estimates on certain variables were apparent, the only statistically significant difference, as determined by estimating eq. (8.1) with review process interaction terms to all other explanatory variables, occurred on journal quality. The estimated impact of journal quality, on citations was approximately twice as great for articles reviewed double-blind as for those reviewed single-blind, these results are available on request.

REFERENCES

Beyer. Janice M. (1978), "Editorial Policies and Practices among Leading journals in Four Scientific Fields," *Sociological Quarterly*, **19**, 68-88.

Crane, Diana. (1967), "The Gatekeepers of Science: Some Factors Affecting the Selection of Articles for Scientific Journals," *American Sociologist*, **2**, 195-201.

Gerrity, Dennis M., and Richard B. McKenzie (1978), "The Ranking of Southern Economics Departments: New Criterion and Further Evidence," *Southern Economic Journal*, **45**, 608-14.

Laband, David N. (1985), "Publishing Favoritism: A Critique of Department Rankings Based on Quantitative Publishing Performance," *Southern Economic Journal*, **52**, 510-15.

Laband, David N. (1986), "Article Popularity", *Economic Inquiry*, **24**, 173-80.

Leamer, Edward E. (1983), "Let's Take the Con out of Econometrics," *American Economic Review*, **73**, 31-43.

Leamer, Edward E. (1985), "Sensitivity Analyses Would Help," *American Economic Review,* **75**, 308-13.

Liebowitz, Stanley J., and John P. Palmer (1984), "Assessing the Relative Impacts of Economic Journals," *Journal of Economic Literature*, **22**, 77-88.

Sherrell, Daniel L.; Joseph F. Hair, Jr., and Mitch Griffin (1989), "'Marketing Academicians' Perceptions of Ethical Research and Publishing Behavior," *Journal of Academic Marketing Science*, **17**, 315-24.

Siegfried, John J. (1992), "Trends in Institutional Affiliation of Authors Who Publish in the Three Leading General Interest Economics Journals," Manuscript. Nashville: Vanderbilt University.

Vandermeulen, Alice (1972), "Manuscripts in the Maelstrom: A Theory of the Editorial Process," *Public Choice*, **13**, 107-11.

9. Why Referees are not Paid (Enough)[*]

Maxim Engers and Joshua S. Gans

Referees for journals are often paid nothing for their work. Even those journals that do offer something for timely review (e.g., *The American Economic Review*) typically pay considerably less than referees can receive for their time spent elsewhere (such as consulting, for example). This paper provides a possible explanation of why referees are paid so little.

The first puzzle is why some referees are willing to perform their task without payment. Since the task requires costly time and effort there must be an offsetting benefit to the referees. But such benefits, while necessary, are not sufficient to explain the absence of payments. Just because some referees will work without pay does not rule out the use of payment to induce better performance.[1] The second conundrum, therefore, is why publishers do not find it worthwhile to pay referees and hence improve their performance and consequently the quality of their journals.

In this paper, we provide a motivation for referees that can resolve both puzzles. We assume that, while referees dislike the refereeing task, they are concerned about the quality of academic journals and, in particular, about their own impact upon this. This could be because of a dedication to the profession or simply because the referees themselves publish and read

[*] Reprinted with permission of the copyright holder from the *American Economic Review*, Vol.88 No.5, 1998, pp. 1341-50.

University of Virginia and University of Melbourne, respectively. We thank Simon Anderson, Vivek Chaudhri, Patrick Francois, Simon Grant, John Lott, Leon Mann, Robert Marks, Shannon Mitchell, Koji Shimomura, Scott Stern, seminar participants at the Australian National University and the Universities of Melbourne and Virginia, and two anonymous referees for helpful comments. This research was done while Engers was a visitor at the University of New South Wales. Responsibility for any errors lies with the authors.

articles in the journal. Editors face a free-rider problem in motivating referees for, given any journal quality, an individual referee would prefer not to incur the private costs of refereeing. Nonetheless, individual referees may choose to review an article when they perceive their own impact on journal quality to be sufficiently large.[2]

We focus on a referee's decision to participate in the reviewing process. The key point here is that the higher the general level of participation of referees, the greater is journal quality, as current research is published sooner and better articles are attracted by the quick reviewing process. This increase in quality, however, lowers a referee's costs of declining to review and, thus, greater payments are required to maintain the higher participation rate. Indeed, we show that, under quite general conditions, this can mean that editors and publishers optimally set referee pay to zero. Any improvements in journal quality are too costly relative to overall monetary compensation paid. Thus, using incentives to motivate referees, while resulting in an improvement in journal quality, is so costly that it makes such incentives unprofitable.

I.   A SIMPLE ILLUSTRATION

We begin by providing a simple model to illustrate how monetary payments, while capable of motivating referee performance, are not, in equilibrium, used by editors. We model the interaction between the editor-publisher of a journal (whom we refer to as the editor) and a potential referee, and focus on the referee's decision whether to agree to review a paper. In general, referees have the option to refuse to review.

Referees incur a cost, $c > 0$, if they choose to review the article. Note that this cost could, in principle, net out any benefits from deciding to referee that would be otherwise lost.[3] We suppose that this cost is known to the referee but that the editor knows only the distribution, $F(c)$, of such costs over the population of potential referees. This distribution is continuous with support, the compact interval, $[\underline{c}, \overline{c}], \underline{c} < \overline{c}$.

If a referee opts not to review the paper, delay costs are imposed on the journal. Each time the article is sent back to the editor unreviewed, the delay costs increase by a fixed amount, δ, and the editor must send the article out again. If all referees with a cost lower than $\hat{c}$ review the article, the probability of a randomly chosen referee agreeing to review the paper is $F(\hat{c})$ and there are no other costs to delay.[4] Thus, the expected total delay cost, D, when the editor[5] sends out the article satisfies the following recursive equation: $D = (1 - F(\hat{c}))(\delta + D)$ which yields,

$$D = \frac{(1 - F(\hat{c}))}{F(\hat{c})} \delta \qquad (9.1).$$

From their perspective, referees returning a paper unreviewed will expect total delay costs to be:

$$\delta + D = \delta + \frac{(1 - F(\hat{c}))}{F(\hat{c})} \delta = \frac{\delta}{F(\hat{c})} \qquad (9.2).$$

Note that as $\hat{c}$ rises, expected delay costs fall. In the model below, the cost of the threshold referee, $\hat{c}$, will be determined endogenously.

A. Case I: Identical Interests in Journal Quality

Consider the benchmark case in which the editor and referees share the same interest in journal quality. That is, referees in deciding whether to review a paper will compare their private time cost of c and expected delay imposed on the journal for a single submission, $\delta / F(c)$. Therefore, in the absence of monetary incentives, a referee with cost, c, will review the article as long as $c \leq \delta / F(\hat{c})$. Without monetary incentives, we can define 80 as the threshold level of costs with only referees with a lower cost reviewing the paper. As such, $\hat{c}_0 = \delta / F(\hat{c}_0)$. There is a unique solution $\hat{c}_0$ to this equation for all $\delta > 0$.[6]

When no monetary incentives are used, the editor's payoff is simply $-\delta(1 - F(\hat{c}_0)) / F(\hat{c}_0)$. Suppose, however, that a positive monetary transfer, w, is paid to any referee agreeing to review the article. This raises the threshold referee cost for agreement to $\hat{c}_w$, resulting in a payoff to the editor of $-\delta(1 - F(\hat{c}_w)) / F(\hat{c}_w) - w$. This threshold, $\hat{c}_w$, is the unique solution to:

$$\hat{c}_w = w + \frac{\delta}{F(\hat{c}_w)} \qquad (9.3).$$

Note that $\hat{c}_w \geq \hat{c}_0$, with a strict inequality if $\hat{c}_0 < \overline{c}$. Thus, positive pay can potentially motivate more referees to agree to review the paper, reducing the expected delay costs. However, raising the review rate, $F(\hat{c}_w)$, means that referees can expect to impose lower delay costs on the journal by not reviewing the paper. While the monetary payment raises the referees' benefits of reviewing a paper, the effect on quality lowers the costs of declining to review. To compensate for this countervailing effect, payments must rise further. This means that the pay required to elicit a greater review rate is higher than that which simply offsets the costs of the marginal referee.

When this countervailing effect is considered, the benefit an editor obtains from a higher review rate is more than offset by the costs of higher pay. The editor's payoff for any chosen $\hat{c}_w$, becomes:

$$-\left(\hat{c}_w - \frac{\delta}{F(\hat{c}_w)}\right) - \delta\left(\frac{1-F(\hat{c}_w)}{F(\hat{c}_w)}\right) = \delta - \hat{c}_w \qquad (9.4).$$

This is declining in $\hat{c}_w$ and thus the editor chooses not to let the threshold rise above $\hat{c}_0$. Hence, it is never optimal for the editor to set $w > 0$.

B. Case II: Similar Interests in Journal Quality

The countervailing pay effect occurs as long as referees have any interest in journal quality. To show this, we assume that referees put weight α on journal quality. For example, suppose that a referee who does not review an article incurs a private cost of $\alpha\delta / F(\hat{c})$, with $\alpha = 1$ corresponding to Case I above. Therefore, α can be regarded as parameterizing goal congruence. Now the threshold, $\hat{c}_w$, satisfies $w = \hat{c}_w - \alpha\delta / F(\hat{c}_w)$. Thus, the editor's costs become:

$$\hat{c}_w + (1-\alpha)\frac{\delta}{F(\hat{c}_w)} - \delta \qquad (9.5).$$

Note that, as before, $\hat{c}_0$ is the threshold value when $w = 0$, i.e., $\hat{c}_0 = \alpha\delta / F(\hat{c}_0)$.

Under certain distributional assumptions, zero payment can still be the unique equilibrium. Assume the following:

(A1) $f(c) / F(c)^2$ is decreasing on $[\underline{c}, \overline{c}]$.

This is a weaker requirement than assuming that the likelihood ratio, $f(c)/F(c)$ is nonincreasing or equivalently that $\ln F(c)$ is concave, a property that holds for many commonly specified distributions. Under (A1), there is zero pay in equilibrium if and only if:

$$1 \geq (1-\alpha)\delta \frac{f(\hat{c}_0)}{F(\hat{c}_0)^2} = (1-\alpha)\frac{\hat{c}_0 f(\hat{c}_0)}{\alpha F(\hat{c}_0)} \tag{9.6}.$$

where the last equality follows from the fact that $\delta = \hat{c}_0 F(\hat{c}_0)/\alpha$. Inequality (9.6) is more likely to be satisfied as a rises and the referees' and editor's interests in journal quality become more aligned.

C. Comparative Statics

We next examine how changes in delay costs and the nature of the cost distribution affect the possibility of a zero pay equilibrium. Consider an increase in δ. While this would seem at first glance to reduce the possibility of a zero pay equilibrium when there is not complete goal congruence (i.e., $\alpha < 1$), this also increases the threshold, $\hat{c}_0$. Without any pay, the costs of the marginal referee who agrees to review the paper rise as δ rises. Thus, the derivative of the right-hand side of (9.6) with respect to δ is:

$$\frac{1-\alpha}{\alpha}\left(\frac{f(\hat{c}_0)}{F(\hat{c}_0)} + \frac{\partial \frac{f(\hat{c}_0)}{F(\hat{c}_0)}}{\partial \hat{c}_0} \right)\frac{d\hat{c}_0}{d\delta} \tag{9.7}.$$

The sign of this derivative is independent of α. For a uniform distribution, this is negative if and only if $1 < \hat{c}_0/(\hat{c}_0 - \underline{c})$, which is always true when $\underline{c} > 0$. Therefore, the possibility of a zero pay equilibrium rises with δ. Intuitively, when delay costs are higher, a greater proportion of referees agree to review the paper without additional motivation. Thus, the returns to positive pay are lower.

Consider now a shift in the distribution of costs toward higher costs. Let θ be a parameter that shifts $F(c)$ according to First Order Stochastic Dominance, that is, $\partial F(c)/\partial \theta \leq 0$ for all c. As θ rises, this causes $\hat{c}_0$ to rise, raising expected delay costs. This, in turn, lowers the right-hand side of (9.6), increasing the range of α for which a zero pay equilibrium exists. Intuitively, this shift in the distribution reduces the possibility that any referee can rely on others with lower costs to agree to review the paper.

Thus, the effect is similar to greater goal congruence, as it raises each referee's intrinsic motivation to review the paper. Note, however, that the review rate is lower after this shift as the identity $\hat{c}_0 = \delta / F(\hat{c}_0)$ implies that $F(\hat{c}_0)$ must vary inversely with $\hat{c}_0$.

II.   ENDOGENIZING TIMELINESS

One difficulty editors face is in motivating referees to complete their review in a timely manner. Indeed, Hamermesh (1991, 1994) identifies slow refereeing as a larger contributor to review delay than difficulties in finding a referee. Our previous model implicitly held this variable as fixed. Here we amend the basic model above to suppose that referees, by expending effort, can complete their review more quickly. In this section, we show that the countervailing effect of monetary incentives, identified above, is also present when such incentives are used to motivate referees to submit reports in a timely manner. Once again these effects arise precisely because referees care about journal quality.

Suppose that to produce a report in time τ, a referee must expend e units of effort, where e is a decreasing function of τ. The private cost of effort to referees is simply e. As in Section I, referees differ in c, the fixed costs of reviewing an article.

If they agree to review a paper, the expected benefits of timeliness on journal quality is a decreasing function, $q(\tau)$. Since $e(\tau)$ is decreasing, we can write q as an increasing function of e. We assume:

(A2) $q(e)$ is twice continuously differentiable with $q'(e) > 0$ and $q''(e) < 0$ for all e, $\lim_{e \to 0} q'(e) = \infty$ and $\lim_{e \to \infty} q'(e) = 0$.

Here we retain the assumption of Section I, subsection B, Case II, that the referee places a weight of α on journal quality. Therefore, having decided to review a paper, each referee chooses:

$$e^*(\alpha) = \arg\max_{e \geq 0} \alpha q(e) - e \qquad (9.8).$$

Note that $e^*(\alpha)$ is uniquely defined and increasing in α. Thus, by agreeing to review a paper, the referee receives a benefit, in the absence, of monetary incentives, of $\alpha q(e^*(\alpha)) - e^*(\alpha) - c$.

If a referee opts not to review a paper, expected journal quality is $Q = q(e^*(\alpha)) - D - \delta$, an increasing function of e^*, where D is the expected delay cost as defined in Section I. Thus, without editorial intervention, a referee c will opt to review the paper if $\alpha q(e^*(\alpha)) - e^*(\alpha) - c \geq \alpha Q$ or $e^*(\alpha) + c \leq \alpha(D + \delta)$.

Editors can now use monetary payments to motivate timely reviews. They can do this by specifying a time by which a report must be completed in order to receive payment. Given the correspondence between timeliness and effort, this corresponds to a minimum level of effort for referees. However, it is also the case that, in this environment, an editor could simply require a minimum effort level (i.e., a maximum time limit) without any payment and commit not to use any report failing to meet this standard. Referees knowing that another referee would be sought if the report were not timely would choose not to review the paper. Note that referees with lower fixed costs of reviewing will be more likely to meet any given minimum effort.

Editors have the choice of setting a minimum effort level (e) (i.e., maximum completion time) but also an accompanying payment (w). They choose these to maximize expected journal quality less payments to referees. If $\hat{c}_e$ is the fixed cost of the threshold referee who agrees to review the paper when the minimum effort level is imposed at e, expected journal quality from the editor's perspective is $q(e) + \delta - \delta / F(\hat{c}_e)$.

By not reviewing an article, referees anticipate that other referees will optimally comply with the standard or decline to review. The participation constraint is thus,

$$\alpha q(e) - e - c + w \geq \alpha\left(q(e) - \tfrac{\delta}{F(\hat{c}_e)}\right) \qquad (9.9).$$

Now, the no-payment, no-minimum-requirement cost threshold level is $c\hat{c}_0 = \alpha\delta / F(\hat{c}_0) - e^*(\alpha)$. Let $\hat{e}$ be the editor's choice of minimum effort standard. The following proposition then follows from solving the editor's constrained maximization problem.

PROPOSITION 1: Suppose (A1) and (A2) hold. Then the unique equilibrium involves: (i) $\hat{w} = 0$ and $\hat{e} > e^*(1)$, or (ii) $\hat{w} > 0$ and $\hat{e} = e^*(1)$. A sufficient condition for (i) is that $(1-\alpha)\delta f(\hat{c}_0)/ F(\hat{c}_0)^2 < 1$.

The proof is in the Appendix. The equilibrium involves greater referee

Referees and Editors

Figure 9.1 Zero Payment, No Minimum Standard Equilibrium

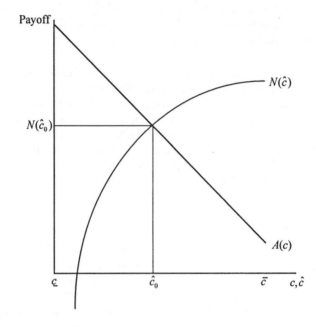

timeliness ($\hat{e}$) than would occur without editorial intervention (i.e., $\hat{e} > e^*(\alpha)$). However, this may not be accompanied by a positive payment to referees.

The intuition for this result is clearest when there is complete goal congruence between editor and referees. In this case, the result is more precise.

COROLLARY 1: Suppose that $\alpha = 1$. Then the unique equilibrium has $\hat{w} = 0$ and $\hat{e} > e^*(1)$.

A diagram is helpful in understanding this result. Suppose that $\alpha = 1$ and no payment is offered or minimum standard imposed. Then referees supply effort of $e^*(1)$. In Figure 9.1, the fixed cost is on the horizontal axis. Let $A(c)$ ($\equiv q(e^*(1)) - e^*(1) - c$)) be the payoff to a referee with cost c who agrees to review a paper. Let $N(c)$ ($(\equiv q(e^*(1)) - \delta / F(\hat{c}))$) be the payoff to a referee who does not agree to review the paper when the threshold referee has fixed cost $\hat{c}$. Thus, A is a straight line with slope -1 while N is

Figure 9.2 The Effects of a Positive Payment

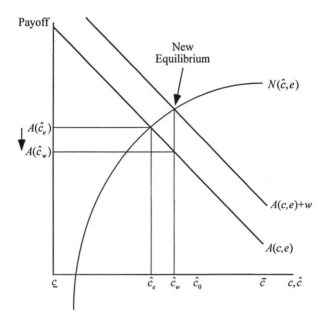

increasing and concave. Let $\hat{c}_0$ be the maximal element of the set $\{c \leq \overline{c} : A(c) \geq N(c)\}$. This will be where the two curves intersect or the endpoint, $\overline{c}$, of the distribution.

Without editorial intervention, the referees who agree to review are those whose costs satisfy $c \leq \hat{c}_0$, and the editor's payoff is $N(\hat{c}_0) + \delta$. To see whether offering a positive payment for greater referee effort is advantageous to the editor, we can compare this situation to one where the editor simply imposes that effort standard as the minimum with no wage payment. A minimum standard above $e^*(1)$ will always be imposed because raising effort slightly above this will have a zero first-order effect on $A(c)$ (that is, the derivative of $A(c)$ with respect to e is zero) since $e^*(1)$ is the optimal choice. But it has a positive first-order effect on $N(c)$, thus serving to increase the editor's payoff.

In general, $A(c)$ will shift down as the minimum standard becomes greater. Figure 9.2 depicts this minimum standard, zero payment possibility with a threshold fixed cost of $\hat{c}_e < \hat{c}_0$. From this benchmark, greater payments serve to mitigate the effects of the minimum standard on delay costs. The payment shifts the A schedule upwards by w and the threshold fixed cost to $\hat{c}_w$. But the editor's payoff becomes $N(\hat{c}_w) + \delta - w$, which can

Referees and Editors

be read off the A schedule as $A(\hat{c}_w)+\delta$, which is strictly less than $A(\hat{c}_e)+\delta$. Thus, any positive payment reduces the editor's payoff. If $\hat{c}_e = \overline{c}$, a positive payment is even less desired since it does not reduce delay costs which are already minimized.

In conclusion, if timeliness is endogenous then editors have an additional instrument other than monetary payments to improve journal quality – imposing a minimum standard. Therefore, compared with the model in Section I, editors' benefits from using monetary incentives are even less. Indeed, the sufficient condition for a zero payment equilibrium in Proposition 1 can be shown to be stronger than necessary. Hence, the range of a guaranteeing a zero payment equilibrium in the endogenous timeliness model is greater than the range in Section I, subsection B, Case II. The possibility of endogenous timeliness makes it more likely that referees will not be paid for their work.[7]

III. POLICY IMPLICATIONS

The zero pay equilibrium in each of the above cases is not Pareto optimal. Intuitively, this is because both the editor and potential referees care about journal quality but each neglects the full implications of their actions on the utility of others. Referees, when deciding whether to review the paper, consider only their own value of journal quality and not that of others. The editor, when comparing the quality benefits of a greater review rate with monetary payments, neglects the referees' concern for quality. Thus, there is a case for intervention to raise journal quality, perhaps by use of a subsidy to referee pay.

To demonstrate this we return to our simple model of Section I in which high journal quality is synonymous with low delay costs in finding a referee. We consider the expected ex ante delay costs to the editor and a representative referee in turn, bearing in mind that the payment is a simple transfer between them and, hence, has only distributional and no welfare implications. Ex ante, the editor's and expected referee costs are given by:

$$D = \left(\frac{\delta}{F(\hat{c})} - \delta \right) \text{ and } R = \frac{\alpha}{F(\hat{c})} \left(\frac{\delta}{F(\hat{c})} - \delta \right) + \frac{1}{F(\hat{c})^2} \int_{\underline{c}}^{\hat{c}} c\, dF(c) \quad (9.10).$$

where $\hat{c}$ is the threshold referee type, the referee with the highest cost who reviews the paper. Recall that in the decentralized equilibrium this threshold, $\hat{c} = \hat{c}_0$, is defined by $\hat{c}_0 = \alpha\delta / F(\hat{c}_0)$.

It is clear that raising $\hat{c}$ lowers editor costs. For referees, as $\hat{c}$ rises, expected cost changes by:

$$R'(\hat{c}) = -\frac{f(\hat{c})}{F(\hat{c})^3}\left(\alpha\delta(2 - F(\hat{c})) + 2\int_{\underline{c}}^{\hat{c}}cdF(c) - \hat{c}F(\hat{c})\right) \quad (9.11).$$

Evaluated at $\hat{c} = \hat{c}_0$, it is easy to see this derivative is negative,

$$R'(\hat{c}_0) = -\frac{f(\hat{c}_0)}{F(\hat{c}_0)^3}\left((1 - F(\hat{c}_0))\alpha\delta + 2\int_{\underline{c}}^{\hat{c}_0}cdF(c)\right) < 0 \quad (9.12).$$

So long as $\hat{c} < \overline{c}$ (or equivalently, that $\delta < \overline{c}$), raising $\hat{c}$ above the level implied by the zero wage equilibrium reduces expected referee costs.[8] Thus, costs from the perspective of both editor and referee would be reduced by raising the review rate.

What policy responses are available to deal with the inefficiency of the equilibrium outcome?[9] A direct subsidy to the pay of referees would raise $\hat{c}$. This could come from a third party such as the government or the governing body of a nonprofit academic organization, such as the American Economic Association. Such third parties will not necessarily be concerned with minimizing the amount spent to achieve a certain level of delay but also internalize the preferences of potential referees. Basically, the subsidy is a substitute for referee pay which would not otherwise emerge in equilibrium. If the third party considers a transfer to referees as having no net effect on welfare (i.e., the cost of the subsidy is exactly matched by the gain to the referees), then its problem is simply to minimize the sum of editor and referee costs. If, however, the social cost per dollar of raising the subsidy exceeds the social benefit of the transfer to the referee, the countervailing incentive effect will keep journal quality below its efficient level. This might explain why nonprofit academic organizations offer zero or very small payments to referee members: the costs in terms of reduced membership or, alternatively, higher submission fees deterring good articles might be too great.

IV.   CONCLUSION

It is often argued that academic researchers do not need financial incentives to provide peer review of articles and grants because they are motivated by a concern for their discipline. This paper presents a model in which referees are motivated by a concern for the quality of research[10] but where monetary incentives can play a role in improving this quality by eliciting speedier review or a greater review rate.[11] Moreover, under very general conditions, the model predicts the observed lack of financial rewards to refereeing. The reason is that while referees are motivated by a concern for quality, if pay can raise this quality, this reduces the need for referees to incur private costs in enhancing this quality.

Nonetheless, this paper also demonstrates that a concern for quality causes both editors and referees to fail to internalize fully the effects of their choices on others. Thus, in equilibrium, pay is zero in situations in which a positive payment would result in a socially beneficial enhancement of quality. Indeed, an appropriate subsidy to referee pay could result in social benefits.

In many ways, the primary interest of the analysis here is beyond the issue of referee pay. The issues raised in this paper seem likely to be pervasive in volunteer activities. Problems in using monetary incentives to elicit more blood donations is a case in point (see Russell D. Roberts and Michael J. Wolkoff, 1988). These considerations also arise within profit-maximizing organizations, attempting to motivate agents individually in a team environment. Suppose that agents value team output, perhaps through organizational design choice or because they derive utility from that output (as in the provision of public goods, for example). This can cause traditional free-rider problems (see Bengt Holmstrom, 1982). Thus, using individually based incentives in this environment may be costly as they may exacerbate such free-rider problems. While it may be socially efficient to use such incentives principals may choose not to do so. The extension of the considerations in this paper to more general problems represents continuing research for us.

APPENDIX:

PROOF OF PROPOSITION 1:

The following is the Lagrangian for the editor's problem:

$$q(e) + \delta - \frac{\delta}{F(\hat{c})} - w + \lambda \left(w - e - \hat{c} + \alpha \frac{\delta}{F(\hat{c})} \right)$$

Since the objective is concave, the constraint convex and the constraint qualification is satisfied, necessary and sufficient conditions for the optimum are:

(1) $q'(e) = \lambda$ (since $e > 0$ by A2).

(2) $\lambda \leq 1$ and $w \geq 0$, with complementary slackness.

(3) $\delta \dfrac{f(\hat{c})}{F(\hat{c})^2} \left(\dfrac{1}{\lambda} - \alpha \right) = 1$.

(4) $w = e + \hat{c} - \alpha \delta / F(\hat{c})$, since $\lambda > 0$, by (1).

There are two broad possibilities (i) $\lambda < 1$ and (ii) $\lambda = 1$. In (i) $\lambda < 1$ forces $w = 0$ by complementary slackness. Recall that $q'(e^*(1)) = 1$. Therefore, $\hat{e} > e^*(1)$ while (9.3) continues to hold with equality even for $\alpha = 1$.

In (ii), $\lambda = 1$, $q'(\hat{e}) = 1$. Hence, $\hat{e} = e^*(1)$. Note, however, that in this case (9.3) becomes:

$$\delta \frac{f(\hat{c})}{F(\hat{c})^2} (1 - \alpha) = 1.$$

However, this will not hold for α sufficiently close to 1. By (9.4), if $w > 0$ and then $\hat{c} > \hat{c}_0$. Hence, by (A1), the final condition of the proposition rules out an equilibrium with $\lambda = 1$.

NOTES

1. Recent literature has expressed concern regarding the quality of refereeing (see David N. Laband, 1990; Gans and George B. Shepherd, 1994; Daniel S. Hamermesh, 1994; Laband and Michael J. Piette, 1994).
2. Below we model journal quality as the performance of the referee's task in reviewing a single submission on journal quality. Therefore, one need not interpret referees as being concerned about the quality of reviewing for all papers, just the single submission they have been sent.
3. It has been suggested to us that some referees agree to review papers to curry favor with editors or to keep up with current ideas and new results. This would

be deducted from net costs, c, as a benefit to refereeing. Nonetheless, so long as there exists a subset of referees for whom these net costs are positive, the analysis here is unchanged by such additional motives.

4. While much of the editor's effort is concerned with trying to find a suitable match between the article and the referee, we abstract from this aspect of the editorial process.

5. We assume that editor and publisher incentives coincide, so that both care about journal quality and the total cost of payments of referees.

6. If the delay cost is at least as large as each referee's time cost ($\delta \geq \overline{c}$), then all referees will agree to review the paper without payment as $\hat{c}_0 \geq \overline{c}$, and zero pay is clearly optimal.

7. Similar countervailing effects on pay occur if referees differ in their marginal effort costs as well as fixed costs. This extension involves, however, considerable more complexity without the clear closed forms analyzed in this section.

8. Note that if $\alpha = 0$, this externality is not present and so any resulting equilibrium is Pareto optimal. While in this case, referees do not take into account their influence on the review rate, they do not care about it either. This is, of course, not to say that referees prefer equilibria in which they have no intrinsic interest in journal quality but this is certainly possible.

9. One policy could be to send the article to more than one referee at a time. However, referees will realize this and this will reduce each referee's incentives to agree to review the paper. This policy would be ineffective.

10. This concern for quality is distinct from altruism per se. Referees care about the quality of journals but do not internalize the costs of others (as in Julio J. Rotemberg, 1994).

11. Similar problems with the use of monetary incentives occur when editors try to motivate thorough refereeing in addition to timeliness. Of course, it is more difficult to imagine observable minimal standards in that case.

REFERENCES

Gans, Joshua S., and George B. Shepherd (1994), "How Are the Mighty Fallen: Rejected Classic Articles by Leading Economists," *Journal of Economic Perspectives*, **8**, 165-79; Chapter 4 of this volume.

Hamermesh, Daniel S. (1991), "The Appointment-Book Problem and Commitment, with Applications to Refereeing and Medicine," National Bureau of Economic Research (Cambridge, MA) *Working Paper* No. 3928.

Hamermesh, Daniel S. (1994), "Facts and Myths about Refereeing," *Journal of Economic Perspectives*, **8**, 153-63; Chapter 5 of this volume.

Holmstrom, Bengt (1982), "Moral Hazard in Teams," *Bell Journal of Economics*, **13**, 324-40.

Laband, David N. (1990), "Is There Value-Added from the Review Process in Economics? Preliminary Evidence from Authors," *Quarterly Journal of Economics*, **105**, 341-52; Chapter 6 of this volume.

Laband, David N., and Michael J. Piette (1994), "Favoritism versus Search for Good Papers: Empirical Evidence Regarding the Behavior of Journal Editors," *Journal of Political Economy*, **102**, 194-203; Chapter 8 of this volume.

Roberts, Russell D., and Michael J. Wolkoff (1988), "Improving the Quality and Quantity of Whole Blood Supply: Limits to Voluntary Arrangements," *Journal of Health Politics, Policy, and Law*, **13**, 167-78.

Rotemberg, Julio J. (1994), "Human Relations in the Workplace," *Journal of Political Economy*, **102**, 684-717.

PART THREE

To Co-Author or not to Co-Author

10. Estimates of the Returns to Quality and Coauthorship in Economic Academia[*]

Raymond D. Sauer

Abstract: Salaries of academic economists are studied to determine if individuals receive differential returns to publishing articles of varying quality and to coauthored versus single-authored articles. Estimates based on detailed data and a flexible nonlinear least-squares procedure indicate that substantial returns to quality exist and that an individual's return from a coauthored paper with n authors is approximately $1/n$ times that of a single-authored paper.

> It is enough to check the growth of science that efforts and labors in this field go unrewarded. [Francis Bacon; quoted in Merton (1973, p. 297)]

I. INTRODUCTION

The reward structure in academia has been a subject of keen interest to economists, sociologists, and historians of science. Two topics in this inquiry are of particular interest to economists: (1) the existence of incentives capable of promoting the growth of knowledge, in which economists have tended to specialize; and (2) the consequences of

[*] Reprinted with permission of the copyright holder from the *Journal of Political Economy*, Vol.96, No.4, 1988, pp. 855-66.

Clemson University. I would especially like to thank Daniel Hamermesh, Charles Nelson, Andy Rutten, and Frank Wolak for their comments and advice. In addition the comments of Orley Ashenfelter, Bob Halvorsen, Mason Gerety, Tim Sass, and an anonymous referee helped to improve this paper.

competition among scientists within the structure of rewards (see esp. Merton 1973). The chief concern of this study is a more careful documentation of the incentives academicians face.

This paper presents an empirical analysis of the earnings function for academic economists that is designed to address two questions. First and more important, what are the returns to quality in academic research? Second, what are the relative returns to single authorship versus coauthorship of published research? These questions have been neglected in previous investigations.

Earnings functions similar to the one used in this paper have been estimated in several studies for various academic disciplines. The most extensive of these is a study by Tuckman (1976, chap. 5), which examined rewards across disciplines for over 50,000 faculty at 301 institutions. Tuckman measured systematic and significant returns to publishing for 17 of 18 nonprofessional disciplines, including economics.[1] The exception, anthropology, was also the only field to lack a measurable return to administrative service. Finally, 16 of the 18 fields, including economics, failed to deliver significant salary increments for good teaching. This consistency of rewards across disciplines gives us confidence that the results of this study will not be peculiar to economics but will shed light on the incentives that exist elsewhere in academia.

Other studies with smaller samples and more narrow foci have confirmed and expanded on Tuckman's findings.[2] Yet virtually all have imposed stringent assumptions on the data that make it impossible for them to address the concerns of this paper. The nature of these assumptions and the manner in which they are relaxed in this paper are discussed in Section II. Section III outlines the estimation procedure used to calculate the returns to differences in research quality and the relative return to coauthorship. Section IV contains some concluding remarks.

II.   THE MEASUREMENT OF RESEARCH OUTPUT

A. Measurement Issues

Previous studies of academic salaries typically estimate a linear equation in which academic salary is regressed on articles published, "experience," and other productivity variables. This study proceeds in a similar fashion, with one important difference. In the past, researchers have assumed that a "publication is a publication," be it in *Economica* or *Econometrica*, be it a note or a full-length paper, be it written by one author or two. These restrictions are relaxed in this paper by utilizing more detailed data. Issues relating to each of these factors are discussed below.

Liebowitz and Palmer (1983) report results of a survey of department chairmen that indicate that chairmen ordinarily "assign a weight" to coauthored papers that exceeds $1/n$ (with n being the number of authors), presumably to encourage collaborative research. But since economists are mobile, it is ultimately the market that would determine the relative value of coauthored papers, and it is not at all obvious what the market-determined value would be.

In a market in which collaboration entailed no extra costs, one would expect to read very few single-authored papers if monetary rewards were as described above. On the other hand, if researchers were less productive at coauthored research than single-authored research, a reward scheme encouraging the former entails a considerable cost in terms of forgone research output. Clearly then, the "equilibrium" weight for coauthored work is a function of production (and "taste") parameters that are difficult to observe. Fortunately, one can estimate the sample weight for coauthored research by recording data on coauthored and single-authored productivity indicators separately, which is the approach taken in this paper.[3]

In addition, the following analysis recognizes the difference between notes and full-length articles. While few would object to the assertion that the former are less valuable than the latter, drawing a line to separate one from the other would be inappropriate. Yet if one assumes that journal editors allocate space as value maximizers, it naturally follows that articles of greater length are more valuable than those of lesser length (on average). This is addressed in the data by defining an individual's publication measure for each journal as the sum of pages published therein. Since page sizes vary between journals, pages in each journal are adjusted to pages of *American Economic Review* equivalent size (AEQ pages).

Finally, unlike the poetic rose, all 10-AEQ-page articles are not the same. Studies using citations in economics (Liebowitz and Palmer, 1984) and the natural sciences (Garfield, 1972) indicate that articles published in a small core of journals account for the majority of references in the literature.[4] Liebowitz and Palmer (1984) constructed several rankings of economics journals based on citation frequencies. The ranking that "probably comes closest to an ideal measure of the impact on the economics profession of manuscripts published in various journals" (p.83) shows a sharp decline in the impact-adjusted citation frequency as one moves down the list.[5] For example, articles in the tenth-ranked journal received 36.45 percent of the impact adjusted citations per character of the top journal; this figure is 28.06 percent for the twentieth- and 7.15 percent for the fortieth-ranked journal.

A possible method of adjusting for differences in journal quality would be to weight an article by the impact-adjusted citation frequency of the journal in which it is published. Although this adjustment may be too severe, it does raise the question of just how steep the quality gradient may be. This question is examined in detail in Section III.

B. The Data Set

The data set used in this study consists of 140 academic economists who are members of the associate or full professor rank at seven "top 40" departments. These departments are those that responded fully to a request for salary information and vitae of senior faculty that was sent to the top 40 departments listed in Graves, Marchand, and Thompson (1982). The average rank of the departments in the sample is 24.

The data were tabulated in light of the issues discussed above. Measures of research productivity were based on information provided on the vitae and in the *Social Science Citations Index*, with coauthored work recorded separately.[6] The data on each individual consist of the following variables (see the Data Appendix for details): SALARY: 9-month salary for the 1982-83 academic year; PROD: a single-author productivity vector consisting of PAGES: AEQ pages in each of the top 100 journals ranked in Liebowitz and Palmer (1984), OPAPERS: other papers listed on the vitae, BOOKS: number of books written, and CITES: citations received to published work, 1976-82; COPROD: the coauthored counterpart to PROD; EXPER: years since receipt of the Ph.D.; YRAD: years of administrative service; and DUMMY: a department-specific 0-1 dummy variable.

Means and standard deviations for these variables (using the sum of PAGES for each individual) are listed in Table 10.1. Also listed are means for the number of single- and coauthored articles (in ranked journals), which are 6.7 and 4.3, respectively.[7] But how does this sample compare with the universe of publishing economists? One available yardstick is citation frequency. Liebowitz and Palmer (1983) compiled a frequency distribution of citations for over 3,000 academic economists from more than 100 departments. Table 10.2 lists the number of economists from this sample within each percentile. It seems that the sample distribution encompasses a broad range of the profession. If anything, the top 20 percent of Liebowitz and Palmer's tabulation is over-represented here, as one might expect since the sample is restricted to the top 40 departments.

Table 10.1 Means and Standard Deviations of 1982 9-Month Salary and Personal Indicators for 140 Economists at Seven Universities

Variable	Mean	Standard Deviation
SALARY	42,935	10,797
PAGES ($\alpha = 0$)	67.2	73.8
COPAGES	48.2	56.0
CITES	95.4	184.9
COCITES	39.0	68.9
OPAPER	17.2	17.2
CO-OPAPERS	5.2	6.8
BOOKS	1.0	2.2
COBOOKS	.4	.7
EXPER	17.7	8.9
YRAD	1.1	3.5
QPAGES ($\alpha = \alpha^{*}$)	47.5	60.0
COQPAGES	29.4	38.2
ARTICLES	6.7	7.1
COARTICLES	4.3	4.9

Note: QPAGES is the sum of single-authored AEQ pages in each journal weighted by $(w_j)^{\alpha^{*}}$ where w_j is the impact-adjusted citation frequency for journal j, and α^{*} is the optimal exponent obtained in Section III.

Table 10.2 Average Citations per Year for the Sample Relative to the Profession

Number of Citations	Percentile for Profession	Sample Frequency	Sample Percentage
≥ 167	99	1	.7
$61 \leq x < 167$	95	5	3.6
$30 \leq x < 61$	90	17	12.1
$12 \leq x < 30$	80	27	19.3
$6 \leq x < 12$	70	21	15.0
$4 \leq x < 6$	60	13	9.3
$2 \leq x < 4$	50	22	15.7
$1 \leq x < 2$	40	21	15.0
0	< 40	13	9.3

Note: Coauthored citations are weighted at $1/n$.

Before we go any further, it is useful to consider the possible effects of the sample selection process on the results. Perhaps the biggest concern is self-selection among the respondents. For the most part, departments in this sample keep vitae on file. Thus the chief criterion for inclusion in this study is the low cost of detailed information on faculty members.[8] Offers of information on self-selected faculty were turned down from two departments. However, one department voluntarily sent such information, which was retained. In this case, a reasonable conjecture is that nonresponse is concentrated among the less productive. This is unfortunate if nonresponse entails a reduction in pages published in lower-ranked journals since it would make estimates of differential returns to quality less precise.

III.   ESTIMATION OF THE RETURNS TO QUALITY AND COAUTHORSHIP

A. Specification of the Model

The two primary questions of interest are the relative return to quality and the relative return to coauthorship of published research. These questions are addressed using an iterative nonlinear least squares procedure to find the optimal adjustment of AEQ pages for differences in quality.[9] Quality-adjusted AEQ pages for each individual is given by

$$\text{QPAGES} = \sum_{j=1}^{100} p_j \cdot w_j^{\alpha}, \quad 0 \le \alpha \le 1,$$

where p_j is pages and w_j is the impact-adjusted citation frequency for journal j. The transformation w_j, for $0 \le \alpha \le 1$, is useful since it encompasses a wide range of alternatives. Using $\alpha = 0$ results in no distinction between journals. For $\alpha = 1$, the quality weights are simply the impact-adjusted citation frequencies, which would force an AEQ page in the fortieth journal to equal 7.15 percent of an AEQ page in the top journal. Intermediate values of α yield more modest declines as one moves down the journal rankings. The calculated QPAGES replaces PAGES in PROD and COPROD.

The following equation was estimated using values of $\alpha = (0.00, 0.05, 0.10, 0.15, ..., 1.00)$ in sequence:

$$\text{LOG(SALARY)} = \text{INTERCEPT} + \beta_1 \cdot \text{PROD} + \beta_2 \cdot \text{PROD}^2$$
$$+ \Gamma \cdot \beta_1 \cdot \text{COPROD} + \Gamma \cdot \beta_2 \cdot \text{COPROD}^2$$
$$+ \beta_3 \cdot \text{EXPER} + \beta_4 \cdot \text{EXPER}^2 + \beta_5 \cdot \text{YRAD}$$
$$+ \beta_6 \cdot \text{YRAD}^2 + \beta_7 \cdot \text{DUMMY} + \varepsilon$$

where β_1 is the estimated coefficient vector for single-authored research indicators (β_2 for the squared variables), and Γ the estimated weight for coauthored research. The value of α that minimized the sum of squared residuals was taken to be the optimum. The resulting estimates are listed in the first column of Table 10.3.

These estimates all have the expected signs and are reasonably precise. However, regression diagnostics (see Belsley, Kuh, and Welsch, 1980) identify five observations with excessive influence on the coefficient and variance estimates. Three of these are heavily cited "superstars," whose effects are to dramatically reduce the coefficient estimate for CITES.[10] In the light of this evidence, it was determined to calculate the returns to quality using estimations from both the full sample of 140 and a restricted sample that excludes these observations.

The specification search outlined above was repeated with the restricted sample. The coefficient estimates for the regression equation employing the optimal value $\alpha^* = 0.30$ are listed in column 2 of Table 10.3. Note that for either sample a test of the hypothesis that $\alpha = 0$ against $\alpha = \alpha^*$ is rejected at the .01 level.

It is clear from these estimates that citations and journal articles are the most important of the productivity indicators in determining salary. The coefficient estimates for BOOKS and OPAPERS are both low and imprecise. This result is in accord with earlier studies and may reflect the relatively poor measurement of these research indicators. The returns to administrative service are sizable, although they decline very fast. Given the opportunity costs involved, it may pay to be the chairperson, but not for very long.

The estimated Γ is 0.56 with a standard error of 0.18. Such a point estimate cannot tell us whether coauthors each receive returns more than $1/n$ times that of a single author ($1/n = 0.50$ here), yet it does indicate that some form of discounting takes place. In particular, the maintained hypothesis that $\Gamma = 1$ that has commonly been used can be rejected at the .05 level.[11]

Table 10.3 Coefficient Estimates of the Monetary Returns to Publication

Variable	Full Sample (1)	Restricted Sample (2)
Page weight (α^*)	.15	.30
Intercept	10.06	10.08
	(150.9)	(131.4)
Γ	.614	.560
	(3.2)	(3.2)
QPAGES	.0030	.0033
	(4.6)	(3.2)
QPAGES^2	-7.2E-06	- 1.4E-05
	(2.8)	(2.0)
CITES	.0005	.0021
	(2.2)	(3.9)
CITES^2	- 1.6E-07	- 4.6E-06
	(.7)	(3.3)
BOOKS	.0014	.0122
	(.1)	(.5)
BOOKS^2	.0005	-.0047
	(.6)	(.8)
OPAPERS	.0012	.0011
	(.6)	(.5)
OPAPERS^2	- 1.6E-05	- 1.5E-05
	(.6)	(.6)
EXPER	.0178	.0129
	(3.3)	(1.9)
EXPER^2	- 2.SE-04	1.3E-04
	(2.1)	(.7)
YRAD	.0565	.0560
YRAD^2	(4.9)	(4.9)
	-.0024	-.0024
	(3.8)	(3.8)
Standard error	.0212	.0198
R^2	.696	.656

Note: Numbers in parentheses are t-statistics. Γ is the estimated weight for coauthored research relative to single-authored research. Department-specific 0-1 dummy variables (DUMMY) range from -.074 to .209 for the col.2 equation are jointly significant at the .01 level. Pages in each journal are weighted by $(w_j)^{\alpha^*}$, where w_j is the impact-adjusted citation frequency for journal j and α^* is the optimal weight.

Following Leamer (1983), a battery of regressions were run to examine the sensitivity of the regression estimates to alternative specifications. The range of the Γ estimates was 0.429-0.689 with a mean of 0.555. We thus know that the Table 10.3 estimate of Γ is not an outlier and can have some confidence in asserting that the weight for coauthored work is not much different from $1/n$.[12]

B. Calculation of the Quality Gradient

Publication of an article appears to have a measurable impact on salary independent of citations.[13] The estimates in column 2 indicate that the incremental return from an AEQ page in the top-ranked journal (1.6 pages in the *J.P.E.*) is 0.17 percent of salary at the sample mean ($72.27 in 1982 dollars). The gradient is such that an article of equivalent size in the tenth-ranked journal returns (0.3645)-30 or 73.9 percent of an article in the top journal. Subsequent benchmarks are 45.3 percent for the fortieth- and 21.0 percent for the eightieth- ranked journals.

The full return from publication includes the additional effects from being cited. Articles published in the top journal during the 1975-79 period received 0.2522 citations per AEQ page in 1980 (Liebowitz and Palmer, 1984). With a constant citation rate over the 7 year "citation period" in this study, the average 10-AEQ-page article in the top journal would yield an increment of 17.65 citations, which are estimated to yield 0.12 percent each, for a 2.09 percent increase in salary. For other journals, citations are less frequent. The estimated returns from citations as a percentage of the top journal range from 51.5 percent for the tenth-ranked journal to 17.2 percent for the eightieth-ranked journal.[14]

The full return to a 10-AEQ-page article in the top journal is thus estimated to be a 3.80 percent increase in salary ($1,602 in 1982 dollars), which seems a sizable sum. For other journals, the return as a percentage of the top journal declines to 18.9 percent at the eightieth rank. This quality gradient is presented in greater detail in the first row of Table 10.4. A gradient using the full-sample results is also presented in this table. Both estimates for the full return in the top journal are large, and the gradients are steep. Once one moves below the twentieth- or fortieth-ranked journal, returns drop to roughly one-half the return from the top journal. These figures clearly indicate that there are significant monetary returns to high-quality research in the economics profession.

Table 10.4 Estimates of the Quality Gradient

Average Full Return to 10 AEQ Pages in the Top Journal	Returns for Other Journals as a Percentage of the Top Journal			
	No. 10	No. 20	No. 40	No. 80
Restricted Sample				
.0380	61.6	53.1	34.1	18.9
Full Sample				
.0286	74.3	68.5	53.0	36.2

Note: The full-turn includes the calculated return for QPAGES and expected CITES. Each row is on the corresponding coefficient estimates in Table 10.3, the quality weights w_j^{α}, and the expected citations for each journal.

IV.   CONCLUDING REMARKS

The estimates given in this paper are obtained from a sample of academic economists from seven of the top 40 departments in the United States. While estimates of the coefficients of interest are both reasonably precise and insensitive to alternative specifications, the calculated monetary values will not be representative of particular departments, much less other disciplines. However, the broad commonalities in academic reward structures discussed above imply that qualitative inferences for other fields can be made from this study. Hence, one may infer that monetary returns to research quality in academia are measurably large and provide nonnegligible incentives to produce high-quality research. How effective these incentives are at influencing the behavior of scientists is a question that awaits further investigation.

DATA APPENDIX

This Appendix provides a more detailed description of the data collection and definition procedures. First, note that all coauthored work was recorded separately from single-authored work. Coauthored work with $n > 2$ authors was weighted at $2/n$ times work with two authors. Hence, for an article with three authors, each would receive 2/3 of what authors contribution to a two-author paper would receive. This means that if the coauthorship weight in the sample does not differ substantially from $1/n$ ($\Gamma = 0.50$), the three coauthors would receive a monetary return of 1/3 of that of a single author.

Journal pages for articles listed on the vitae were recorded for each individual. Only articles published in the 108 journals listed in Liebowitz and Palmer (1984) were recorded under this variable. More often than not, recording pages entailed looking up in the journal in which the article was published since page numbers were infrequently listed on the vitae. Comments and replies were not counted. Articles in annual conference proceedings (including the *A.E.R. Papers and Proceedings*) were included in the OPAPERS category.

All citations for the period 1976-82 other than self-citations and citations to textbooks were counted. Note that since the *Social Science Citations Index* attributes citations only to the first listed author, making an accurate count of citations to coauthored work often required searching for particular citations listed under a coauthor's name. The 1976-82 period was used for two reasons. First, it is unclear whether a stock of lifetime citations or the flow of very recent citations is the appropriate variable to use. Selecting a 7-year period since the *Social Science Citations Index* has a 5-year cumulative volume for 1976-80, which substantially reduces the cost of looking up citations for several years. The years 1981 and 1982 were included since current citations are likely to measure current influence.

Any working paper or publication not listed in Liebowitz and Palmer (1984) was classified in OPAPERS. Similarly, any published book other than a textbook was counted in BOOKS. The varying qualities of the members of these variables may be partly responsible for the lack of precision in their estimated coefficients. Adopting a more rigorous classification scheme for these research indicators may yield more informative estimates but is beyond the scope of the current paper.

The ranking used in the paper is based on impact-adjusted citation frequencies. To calculate monetary returns from expected citations, estimates of (unadjusted) citation frequencies were used rather than actual measures. This was done to avoid problems stemming from the nonmonotonic relationship between two actual measures. However, the differences between quality gradients based on the estimated and actual citation frequencies are very minor. Note also that Oromaner (1981, p. 89) and others have found that the frequency of citations to an article is "quite stable during the first (post-publication) decade." Hence, the simple method used to estimate the increment of citations due to publication of an article (cites per page times pages times years) has empirical justification.

NOTES

1. Tuckman reported that the median number of articles published was in the 5-10 category for 11 of the 18 fields. The figure was lower for music and higher for psychology and all the natural sciences. Further, in the natural sciences and psychology, a greater number of articles were required to obtain significant salary differentials than in other fields. Tuckman speculated that these differences were due to differential costs in producing an 'article' (note that he did not distinguish coauthored articles). Merton (1973, pp. 470-74, 547) found that in the natural sciences, articles are shorter, more likely to be coauthored, and less likely to be rejected, which is consistent with Tuckman's conjecture.

2. These include Siegfried and White (1973), Tuckman and Leahey (1975), Tuckman and Hagemann (1976), Hansen, Weisbrod, and Strauss (1978), Hamermesh, Johnson, and Weisbrod (1982), and Diamond (1986).

3. Coauthored work with $n > 2$ authors was weighted at $2/n$ times work with two authors. This was necessary because of the small number of papers written by three or four individuals. The Data Appendix discusses the implications of this weighting scheme.

4. Citations have also been used to construct loose rankings of scientists. Quandt (1976, p. 741) stated that citation counts permit 'tentative predictions as to who future Nobel prizewinners will be.' Time has supported this conclusion. Quandt's list of the 26 most cited economists in 1970 contains seven subsequent prizewinners (among them the 1987 laureate) along with three who had been honored before the article was published. Similar figures for the natural sciences are reported in Garfield (1978) for both Nobel prizes and other highly regarded honors.

5. This ranking is their Table 10.2, col. 2, ranking. The impact adjustment refers to an iterative weighting scheme that gives greater weight to citations received from higher ranked journals.

6. The period for which citations were collected was 1976-82, which is something of a compromise between conflicting notions about the proper period for this analysis (see the Data Appendix for further discussion). Making an accurate count of the number of citations and coauthored citations, given the multiple listings of most authors, required an undue amount of patience and attention to detail. The great care taken by M.C. Matheson in collecting the data is much appreciated.

7. The journals most frequently published in by this sample are *American Economic Review, Journal of Political Economy, Review of Economics and Statistics, Econometrica*, and *Quarterly Journal of Economics*, accounting for 37 percent of all articles.

8. Not all the schools in this sample are public. Chairs of some public departments gave as a reason for nonresponse the cost of gathering together the information; others were unwilling to report salary figures.

9. Quality adjustment is made only on journal pages and not on citations. Where citations occur is probably significant (and expensive to record), although

frequency and quality are likely to be more CIOSCIY related here than with journal pages.

10. The minimum effect of adding only one of these three observations to the remainder of the sample is to reduce the coefficient estimate for CITES by .001 (about 1/2 the value when the remainder of the sample is used).

11. With a χ^2 test based on the likelihood function, a 95 percent confidence interval for gamma was calculated as the range (0.29, 0.93).

12. The alternative specifications used were all possible subsets obtained by (a) deleting all variables other than QPAGES, CITES, and DUMMY and (b) repeating the procedure above using (unlogged) salary as the dependent variable. Note that fairly narrow ranges for the incremental returns from QPAGES and CITES in *a* were obtained; these were 0.0012-0.0017 and 0.0012-0.0019, respectively, at the sample means.

13. One would naturally expect QPAGES and CITES to be highly correlated, which is indeed the case. However, an analysis of the variance decompositions suggested by Belsley et al. (1980) revealed that the coefficient estimates for QPAGES and CITES are not degraded by collinearity problems. However, there is a 'moderate' linear dependency between the intercept, EXPER, and EXPER2, which may help explain the imprecise estimates of the latter coefficients.

14. See the Data Appendix for details on the construction of these estimates.

REFERENCES

Belsley, David A., Edwin Kuh, and Roy E. Weisch (1980), *Regression Diagnostics: Identifying Influential Data and Sources of Collinearity*, New York: Wiley.

Diamond, Arthur M., Jr. (1986), "What is a Citation Worth?" *Journal of Human Resources*, **21**, 200-215.

Garfield, Eugene (1972), "Citation Analysis as a Tool in Journal Evaluation," *Science*, **178**, 471-9.

Garfield, Eugene (1978), "The 300 Most-Cited Authors, 1961-1976," *Current Comments*, **39**, 1-26.

Graves, Philip E., James R. Marchand, and Randall Thompson (1982), "Economics Departmental Rankings: Research Incentives, Constraints, and Efficiency," *American Economic Review*, **72**, 1131-41.

Hamermesh, Daniel S., George E. Johnson, and Burton A. Weisbrod (1982), "Scholarship, Citations and Salaries: Economic Rewards in Economics," *Southern Economic Journal*, **49**, 472-81.

Hansen, W. Lee, Burton A. Weisbrod, and Robert P. Strauss (1978), "Modeling the Earnings and Research Productivity of Academic Economists," *Journal of Political Economy*, **86**, 729-41.

Leamer, Edward E. (1983), "Let's Take the Con out of Econometrics," *American Economic Review*, **73**, 31-43.

Liebowitz, Stanley J., and John P. Palmer (1983), "Assessing Assessments of the Quality of Economics Departments," Manuscript. Rochester, N.Y.: Univ. Rochester.

Liebowitz, Stanley J., and John P. Palmer (1984), "Assessing the Relative Impacts of Economics Journals," *Journal of Economic Literature*, **22**, 77-88.

Merton, Robert K. (1973), *The Sociology of Science: Theoretical and Empirical Investigations*, Chicago: University of Chicago Press.

Oromaner, Mark (1981), "Articles in Core Economics Journals: A Citation Analysis," *Knowledge*, **3**, 83-96.

Quandt, Richard E. (1976), "Some Quantitative Aspects of the Economics Journal Literature," *Journal of Political Economy,* **84**, 741-55.

Siegfried, John J., and Kenneth J. White (1973), "Financial Rewards to Research and Teaching: A Case Study of Academic Economists," *A.E.R. Papers and Proc.,* **63**, 309-15.

Tuckman, Howard P. (1976), *Publication, Teaching, and the Academic Reward Structure*, Lexington, Mass.: Heath.

Tuckman, Howard P., and Robert P. Hagemann (1976), "An Analysis of the Reward Structure in Two Disciplines," *Journal of Higher Education*, **47**, 447-64.

Tuckman, Howard P., and Jack Leahey (1975), "What is an Article Worth?" *Journal of Political Economy*, **83**, 951-67.

11. Trends in Multi-Authored Papers in Economics[*]

John Hudson

Several decades ago, the overwhelming majority of papers appearing in leading journals of economics had a single author. In 1950, for example, only 6 percent of the papers published in the *Journal of Political Economy*, and just 8 percent of the papers published in the *American Economic Review*, were written by more than one author. These figures have changed dramatically. By 1993, the proportion of multi-authored papers in these two journals had risen to 39.6 percent and 54.9 percent, respectively. These figures are illustrative of a general trend, as this paper will show by examining the publishing trends in eight leading journals. The paper will then consider some possible reasons for this trend and its possible consequences.

THE TREND OF MULTI-AUTHORSHIP OVER TIME

To illustrate the trend in multi-authorship, I will focus on eight leading journals: *American Economic Review, Economic Journal, Econometrica, Review of Economics and Statistics, Review of Economic Studies, Journal of Political Economy, Quarterly Journal of Economics* and *Economica*. These eight journals were all well established in 1950 and remain important or "core journals" today (Laband and Piette, 1994; Diamond, 1989). They represent a mix of generalist and more quantitative journals as well as American and British journals.[1] The data are annual and cover the period 1950-1993.

[*] Reprinted with permission of the copyright holder from the *Journal of Economic Perspectives*, Vol.10, No.3, Summer 1996, pp. 153-9.

University of Bath. I am grateful to Timothy Taylor, Alan Auerbach and Alan Krueger for helpful comments and encouragement.

Figure 11.1 Multi-Authorship in Eight Leading Journals

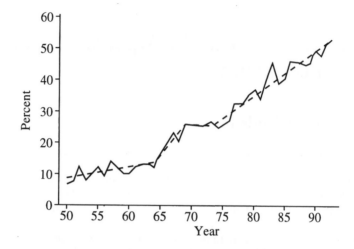

The jagged line in Figure 11.1 shows the proportion of multi-authored papers in all eight journals. It confirms that there has been a steady and substantial increase in multiple authorship since 1950. This is found in all eight of the journals. In the period 1950-1965, the highest proportion of multi-authored articles for any of the eight journals was 15.6 percent (in *Econometrica*). In the period 1974-1993, the lowest proportion for any journal was 35.5 percent (*Economica*). Apparently, the economist of the early postwar years was typically a solitary worker, while the economists of today are much more inclined to hunt in packs of at least two.

To determine whether this increase has been steady or more spasmodic, we estimate a trend line broken into four segments. This is known as a "linear splice" technique; essentially, it involves a search procedure for whether or where the slope of the data line changes significantly. In this case, the search for the first join point ranged over the period 1955-1982; the second from 1959-1986; and the third from 1963-1990. This procedure found that the slope of the data changed significantly (at the 1 percent level) in 1965, 1970 and 1974.[2] The results are shown in Figure 11.1 as the smoother line with four segments. The empirical work indicates no significant trend in the data until 1965; a significant positive upward trend from 1965 until 1970; virtually no upward trend from 1970-1974; and then again a significant upward trend between 1974 and the end of the data series in 1993. This pattern, with some slight variation in dates, is repeated in all eight journals. The increase in multi-authorship over time has been spasmodic rather than continuous, with the most rapid rise occurring in the period 1965-1970 and a further substantial and prolonged rise in the period since 1974.

POTENTIAL REASONS FOR THE RISING TREND IN MULTI-AUTHORSHIP

The potential for useful collaboration has probably been increasing since the early 1950s for at least three reasons: the growth in the subject areas covered by economics; the increasingly technical nature of the discipline, on both the theoretical and the quantitative sides; and the growth in the size of the profession from which suitable collaborators can be found. Thus, even as it has become more difficult for one individual to cover the whole of the subject, a greater range of collaborators are available. A typical "core journal" paper in economics at the present time tends to display at least two of the following three characteristics: a good and/or novel idea; high-powered theoretical/mathematical analysis; or high-powered empirical/econometric analysis. Many papers satisfy all three of these criteria. An increased emphasis on analysis, whether theoretical or empirical, has come about partly because of advances in economic knowledge and partly because developments in computer hardware and software make projects feasible for a small group of researchers that would not have been feasible 30 years ago.

Evidence for this view comes from Table 11.1, which offers some more detailed information about multi-authored papers at the eight journals considered here. The first row of Table 11.1 offers overall figures for multi-authored papers. The second row shows that multi-authorship is more prevalent in the more quantitative journals, by which I mean the *Review of Economics and Statistics* and *Econometrica*, particularly the former. Until 1970, these two journals were ranked first and second in terms of the proportion of multi-authored papers. This has also been the case since 1974, although *Econometrica* has moved back to the pack, while the *Review of Economics and Statistics* retains easily the highest proportion of multi-authored papers.

The probable increase in the likelihood of finding suitable collaborators has occurred because of the growth in the size of the profession (Lovell, 1973). Departments of economics are bigger than they used to be, and there are more of them. Technological developments such as direct dialing, the floppy disk, word processing packages, fax and e-mail have increased the ease of collaborating with colleagues in other departments and other countries. It appears reasonable to suppose that the more individuals an

Table 11.1 Proportion of Multi-Authored Papers

Journal	1950-1993	1950-1965	1966-1970	1970-1974	1974-1993
All Eight Economics Journals	26.4%	10.9%	22.8%	25.1%	40.0%
Quantitative Journals	30.8%	13.8%	30.8%	33.2%	44.2%
British Journals	24.5%	9.4%	20.2%	23.0%	37.6%
American Generalist Journals	25.5%	10.4%	20.0%	21.7%	39.5%
Economic History Review	7.8%	4.0%	5.4%	6.2%	11.7%

economist has to choose from as potential collaborators, the greater is the probability of finding someone with whom to strike up an effective working relationship, although at the same time this may have also made the screening process more complex.

Because the number of economists in the United States is greater than in the United Kingdom and individual departments are bigger, one would expect that U.S. journals would exhibit a greater tendency to multi-authored papers, although it should be noted that there has been an increasing trend over the years for British journals to publish American-authored papers. Limited evidence for this can be found in the third row of Table 11.1, which shows multiple-authorship slightly lower in the three British-based journals (*Economica, Economic Journal* and the *Review of Economic Studies*) than in the American generalist journals, particularly since 1974, although prior to that date the picture is more mixed.

Much of this discussion has emphasized the importance of technological factors in explaining the growth of multiple authorship. Evidence for this conclusion lies not just with greater incidence of multiple authorship in quantitative journals, but with the uneven nature of the increase in multi-authored papers. The two critical periods – the mid-1960s and the period since the mid-1970s – approximately coincide with two major technical developments. The early 1960s saw the mainframe computer become established as an important tool for quantitative economic research with TSP, the first major econometrics software package, becoming available in 1967. The mid-1970s and later saw the introduction of the personal computer, with 1977 marking the launch of both the Apple II and the Commodore Pet, and 1981, the IBM PC. Since then, developments have centered around the speed and memory size of personal computers, together with an enormous growth of sophisticated software and a communications revolution.

Further support for the technical explanation for the growth of multiple authorship is given by the much more modest rise in multi-authorship in the *Economic History Review*, as can be seen from the final row of Table 11.1. Economic history is clearly less quantitative and technical than economics as a whole. The onset of the mainframe in the 1960s made little impact on the study of economic history, as initially did the introduction of the personal computer. Since then, it is possible that the impact of new technology in improving the ease with which people can work together is to some extent the explanation for the slight increase in multiple authorship we have witnessed in this area.

The link with increasingly sophisticated econometric techniques has also been made by Figlio (1994) in explaining the growth of empirical papers, particularly in "top journals." This growth is itself likely to be linked with the proliferation of multi-authored papers. However, it would be a mistake to lean too heavily on technological developments to explain all of the changing patterns in multi-authorship that we have found. In particular, the 1974 join point seems too early to be accounted for by the advent of the personal computer. One alternative explanation is that the chaotic nature of economic events in the 1970s helped break down former walls of specialization between colleagues and encouraged a burst of collaborative work, with new personal computer technologies continuing this trend into the 1980s and beyond. It is also conceivable that the possible tendency of some grant-giving agencies to favor collaborative research may also have been a significant factor in explaining the growth of multi-authored papers.

DISCUSSION

From the view of the profession as a whole, is the growth of multi-authored papers a good thing? The answer will in part depend upon the motivation for the collaboration.

The major gain possible from collaborative work is that it allows for an efficient division of labor. For example, an economist working for a government statistical agency might combine with a mathematical economist and a labor economist in academia to write a quantitative paper on job search that none could have written on their own. The gains from collaborative work might result either from harnessing skill complementarities or from a sort of synergy where multiple contributors develop ideas that none would have developed on his or her own. Synergy differs from skill complementarity, in the sense that it can exist between individuals with very similar skill sets. When collaborative work draws upon such complementarities and synergies, it is most likely to represent a gain in knowledge to the economics' profession.

However, there must also be disadvantages to collaboration – otherwise all economics papers would be collaborative, and the number of collaborators would be very large. These disadvantages would appear to be threefold.

First, collaborative work involves compromise. An individual author working with a group will have to agree to a certain approach, certain text, even certain conclusions that that person might not enunciate in the same way if working alone. Because multiple authorship inevitably involves compromise, my own intuition is that it tends to reduce risk taking in academic papers. The result may be more technically proficient papers than in the past, but at the cost of the imaginative leap forward that starts economics in a new direction or gives fresh impetus to an old subject area. At an extreme, a multi-authored paper may be somewhat more likely to end up as a patchwork of text lacking a direction or theme. This may not be too much of a problem with just two authors, but if the number of authors grows to the totals often seen in medical journals, one might expect to see a growth in impenetrable prose and confused arguments.

Second, multi-authored papers impose costs of organization and communication that may lead to diseconomies of scale. These are probably greater if all the collaborators are equally involved with all parts of the research and all parts of the paper. Developments in technology in recent years may have reduced the threshold at which these problems occur, but at some level they surely continue to exist.

Finally, any net advantage of collaboration may disappear altogether if some individuals combine even though the sum of what each could achieve working alone exceeds their combined efforts. This may occur if an economist can achieve a greater gain in academic reputation from multi-authored rather than single-authored papers. This would be true, for example, if the reputation gain from two coauthored papers exceeded the gain from one single-authored paper (holding quality of journal of publication and other things equal). In this situation, there would clearly be a professional incentive for individuals to combine, despite the possibility that their combined publications may have less value than the sum of what each would produce on their own. If professional rewards tend to favor a lengthy curriculum vitae – and it is arguable that this has increasingly been the case in recent years in both the United States and the United Kingdom – then collaborative work may be undertaken under pressure for quantity rather than quality. The actual discount rate that the profession applies to a multi-authored paper as opposed to a single-authored paper is a subjective notion, and one that is difficult to quantify other than by asking what economists feel about certain papers and individuals. But it is my impression that at least for work done with only one or two coauthors, an equivalent number of multi-author papers do count for more than one single-authored paper.

Given the development of the subject of economics and the new technological possibilities, a certain increase in the number of multi-authored papers in the field of economics was probably inevitable. But it is reasonable to question whether this trend has gone too far, and whether it is continuing for reasons that are socially productive for the economics profession.

NOTES

1. There are no non-British but European journals in the list. as there were no such journals in 1950 that remain "core journals," as defined by Diamond (1989), today.
2. If readers want further details on how these join points were calculated, or on any other aspect of the data and calculations described in this paper, I would be happy to provide it. For a general description of linear spline methods, the interested reader might begin with Johnston (1984, pp. 392-6).

REFERENCES

Diamond, Arthur M. (1989), "The Core Journals of Economics," *Current Contents*, **1**, 4-11.

Figlio, David (1994), "Trends in the Publication of Empirical Economics," *Journal of Economic Perspectives*, **8**, 179-87.

Johnston, J. (1984), *Econometric Methods*. 3rd ed., New York: McGraw-Hill.

Laband, David N., and Michael J. Piette (1994), "The Relative Impacts of Economics Journals: 1970-1990," *Journal of Economic Literature*, **32**, 640-66; Chapter 15 of this volume.

Lovell, Michael C. (1973), "The Production of Economic Literature: An Interpretation," *Journal of Economic Literature*, **11**, 27-55.

12. First-Author Conditions[*]

Maxim Engers, Joshua S. Gans, Simon Grant and Stephen P. King

Abstract: This paper provides a theoretical explanation for the persistent use of alphabetical name orderings on academic papers in economics. In a context in which market participants are interested in evaluating the relative individual contribution of authors, it is an equilibrium for papers to use alphabetical ordering. Moreover, it is never an equilibrium for authors always to be listed in order of relative contribution. In fact, we show via an example that the alphabetical name ordering norm may be the unique equilibrium, although multiple equilibria are also possible. Finally, we characterize the welfare properties of the noncooperative equilibrium and show it to produce research of lower quality than is optimal and than would be achieved if coauthors were forced to use name ordering to signal relative contribution.

I. INTRODUCTION

In coauthored work, the assignment of priority on published material can be a delicate matter. When the actual contribution of each author is not

[*] Reprinted with permission of the copyright holder from the *Journal of Political Economy*, Vol.107, No.4, 1999, pp. 859-83.

University of Virginia, University of Melbourne, Australian National University and University of Melbourne, respectively. We wish to thank Jurgen Eichberger, Rohan Pitchford, John Quiggin, and an anonymous referee for helpful comments. We would also like to thank Ray Over for references to the empirical literature on name ordering and Ross Milbourne for suggesting the title of this paper. All errors and omissions remain our responsibility.

Table 12.1 Ordering Patterns in Economics Journals, 1978-97: Percentage of Papers with Names Listed in Alphabetical Order by Number of Coauthors

Journal	Multi-authored (%)	Two	Three	Four+	All
Journal of Political Economy	39.8	89.6	73.2	61.5	86.5
American Economic Review	43.7	90.1	63.1	57.7	86.3
Econometrica	42.2	88.0	85.6	100	87.6
Quarterly Journal of Economics	47.3	89.8	80.4	61.5	87.2
Review of Economic Studies	41.4	92.0	90.7	85.7	91.7

readily observable to outside interests (such as academic employers), priority may send an ordinal signal as to which author contributed more to the research. Moreover, authors themselves will be interested in sending such signals, if it is in their favor to do so.

A cursory glance at any economics journal, however, reveals a puzzle: authorship on the overwhelming majority of coauthored papers is ordered *lexicographically*, on the basis of the alphabetical ordering of authors' names. This pattern is illustrated in Table 12.1 for five major journals over the last two decades. Of coauthored papers in the sample, more than 85 percent had names listed alphabetically. In the absence of any clear correlation between name order and research productivity, it appears that coauthors are jointly deciding not to use priority as a signal of contribution either directly or indirectly, say on the basis of an ordering of seniority.[1]

When one looks at other disciplines for this phenomenon, it appears that the further afield from economics, the less prevalent the use of a lexicographical ordering. In Table 12.2 we present ordering patterns in six other academic journals. While those closest to economics exhibit the same alphabetical convention, the *American Journal of Sociology* and others in the physical sciences exhibit orderings potentially unrelated to the spelling of the authors' names. This suggests that the attribution norms in economics may differ from those of other disciplines.

The comparative differences, while interesting, are not the main focus of this paper. We focus our attention on how a convention of lexicographic ordering may be self-sustaining. To this end, we construct a model that

Table 12.2 Ordering Patterns in Other Academic Journals, 1978-97: Percentage of Papers with Names Listed in Alphabetical Order by Number of Coauthors

Journal	Multi-authored (%)	Two	Three	Four+	All
Journal of Finance	59.2	85.4	82.0	85.7	84.6
Journal of Economic History	23.3	83.8	62.5		81.7
Yale Law Journal	13.1	83.6	100		83.9
American Journal of Sociology	45.1	49.4	29.7	8.3	43.5
American Psychologist	40.8	53.3	18.7	13.3	39.3
Angewandte Chemie	38.9	64.3	41.4	13.1	52.6
New England Journal of Medicine	96.4	48.0	16.5	1.1	5.9

resolves the tension between the apparent convention of lexicographic ordering and the interests of parties in sending and receiving a more informative signal. In doing so, we demonstrate that lexicographic ordering is an equilibrium outcome of a game that involves bargaining among the coauthors under full information about their relative contributions and the rational interpretation of signals by employers. Our result is not based on altruistic or cooperative explanations for the lexicographic ordering.[2] It occurs despite the fact that individual coauthors and (potential) employers care exclusively about the individual productivity of a researcher. Moreover, we show that the very existence of the possibility of a lexicographic ordering rules out the existence of an equilibrium in which name ordering signals relative contribution, even though such an ordering may in principle be agreed on by coauthors. Indeed, with some additional, quite intuitive restrictions, we can demonstrate that the lexicographic ordering equilibrium is unique. Finally, we compare different signaling outcomes and demonstrate that the total quality of research would increase if coauthors were compelled to use priority as a signal of relative contribution.

The intuition for our basic existence result is as follows. The key to understanding it lies in the nature of bargaining. Coauthors in economics can rarely bind themselves to a specific ordering rule ex ante. While coauthors may agree on an ordering rule before commencing research, once relative contributions are known, coauthors can renegotiate this rule. Therefore, we model bargaining as taking place after the coauthors have information regarding the relative contributions to the paper. In such bargaining, the lexicographic and relative contribution orderings have two important characteristics: (i) when the lexicographic order is violated, it is obvious to all; and (ii) this recognizability is asymmetric. Using a different ordering will be observable only if that order does not match the lexicographic one. Orders themselves have an ordinal (!) quality making them highly imperfect indicators of research input.

This second characteristic means that bargaining is an issue only when the author whose name is lower in the lexicographic ordering has actually contributed more to the article. In these circumstances, authors will bargain realizing that outsiders will draw an inference of contribution from the name order. If this "market inference" is inconsistent with the bargained shares – in particular, if outsiders place too low a value on the contribution of authors who are not first under relative contribution ordering – then the only way to manipulate these perceptions is to use a lexicographic ordering. The authors agree to place more weight than outsiders expect on the lexicographic ordering as a means of compensating the author whose surname is first in the alphabet.

Clearly, in equilibrium, the market inference about relative contributions must match both the actual contributions and the shares negotiated by the authors when the lexicographic and relative contribution orderings do not happen to coincide. But why does this process push players away from a relative contribution rule and toward a lexicographic ordering? Two additional factors lead to our strong results. First, we rely on the Nash cooperative bargaining solution for our results. This means that bargaining is not too biased toward the author who is first under a relative performance rule. As such bargaining leads to a more equitable share of the surplus than would be inferred by the market, the relative performance rule cannot be an equilibrium. Second, the market's inference, when it observes different alphabetical orderings, is asymmetric. A nonalphabetical name order sends a clear signal to the market that the author who is listed first has actually contributed more and should receive a greater proportion of the credit. On the other hand, conforming to the lexicographic ordering sends a mixed signal to the market that places some weight on the possibility that the first author in that instance might actually have contributed more. As a result, reversals harm authors whose name is earlier in the alphabet more than these authors would benefit from the lexicographic ordering. Therefore, authors whose name is early in the alphabet can be compensated only by the relatively weak inference associated with lexicographic ordering. To achieve any agreed sharing of the surplus from the published article, the authors must place a relatively greater weight on the lexicographic ordering than on orderings that send a clearer signal. Of course, in response to this increased use of lexicographic rather than relative contribution ordering, outsiders will reduce their inference about the relative contribution of the first author when the lexicographic ordering is observed. The more authors rely on lexicographic ordering to compensate an author whose name is early in the alphabet, the less the market infers from this ordering. In the extreme, the combination of ex post bargaining and asymmetric inference from ordering rules may result in a lexicographic ordering norm.

While we know of no previous research on name ordering in economics, it has received some attention in the broader scientific literature. That literature confirms our evidence that alphabetical ordering is more common in economics than in other disciplines. Zuckerman (1968) examined the difficulties in inferring relative contributions from name ordering. Indeed, she found that Nobel laureates were less likely to be listed first on scientific papers, often being listed last. Nonetheless, in chemistry, physics, and biological sciences, alphabetical orderings occur more frequently than chance alone would dictate. Spiegel and Keith-Spiegel (1970) looked at name ordering among psychologists and surveyed the attitudes of members of that profession. They found that attitudes were consistent with those stated in the *Ethical Standards of Psychologists* of the American Psychological Association (1970): "Credit is assigned to those who have contributed to a publication, in proportion to their contribution, and only to these. ... The experimenter or author who has made the major contribution to a publication is identified as the first listed" (quoted by Over and Smallman, 1973, p.161).

Indeed, when asked what should occur when contributions among collaborators were deemed to be equal, only 33 percent of respondents argued that an alphabetical ordering was appropriate, with 60 percent opting for a coin toss. Over and Smallman (1970) note that alphabetical name ordering is mandatory practice at some journals. Looking at one such journal, the *Journal of Physiology*, they found less collaborative publication by scientists in the lower (P-Z) part of the alphabet than in other journals in the field. Finally, Over and Smallman (1973), in an examination of practices among psychologists, demonstrated that alphabetical name orderings were more prevalent when more than two coauthors were involved. These studies argue that the use of alphabetical name orderings is related to the lack of desire of collaborators to send a signal regarding relative contribution. In contrast, we argue that even when this motive is present, there are strong market-based forces driving the prevalence of alphabetical name orderings, especially when no other information is available.

The paper is outlined as follows. In Section II, we construct the model, which involves three stages: a research effort stage, followed by a complete information bargaining game between two coauthors over name ordering, and finally the market's updating of its beliefs. Section III characterizes the equilibrium of the full game, and Section IV compares this with the first-best outcome. Section V presents conclusions and offers thoughts regarding future research.

II.   THE SETUP

We model the game between two coauthors, Abigail and Ben, labeled A and B, respectively. These researchers put effort into the production of a paper. The cost-of-effort function is the same for both authors and is given by $c(e_i)$, $c(0) = 0$, $c',c'' > 0$, $i = A$, B. Paper quality is random, with its distribution a function of the two effort choices. We assume that the relative contribution of author A to the paper's quality can be described by the random variable S_A. The total quality of the paper is given by the random variable V. Moreover, we assume that quality can be realized only through collaborative work: there is no method by which individual authors can appropriate parts of that value on their own. For any pair of effort choices $(\bar{e}_A, \bar{e}_B)$ in $\mathbb{R}_+ \times \mathbb{R}_+$ of authors A and B, we further assume that (1) S_A is distributed with density on [0, 1] with

$$\Pr[S_A > \tfrac{1}{2}] = q(\bar{e}_A, \bar{e}_B)$$
$$E[S_A \mid S_A > \tfrac{1}{2}] = h(\bar{e}_A, \bar{e}_B)$$
$$E[S_A \mid S_A > \tfrac{1}{2}] = 1 - h(\bar{e}_A, \bar{e}_B)$$

where $q(\bar{e}_A, \bar{e}_B) + q(\bar{e}_B, \bar{e}_A) = 1$, $q_1 > 0$, $h_1 > 0$, and $q_2 < 0$, $h_2 < 0$; (2) V is distributed with density on $\mathbb{R}_+$ and mean $\bar{V}(e_A, e_B)$, where $\bar{V}$ is a concave symmetric function with positive partial first derivatives; and (3) V and S_A are independent.

The presence of uncertainty is important in generating a market signaling problem. The independence of V and S_A means that the market's (equilibrium) belief about S_A is not affected by the value of V that is observed by the market. This greatly simplifies the updating procedure of the market that we model below without any significant loss in generality.

We model the collaborative process of producing a jointly authored paper as a game in three stages. The first stage of this process entails the actual effort expended by the two authors to produce the joint paper. Although some degree of (mutual) monitoring may be possible by authors, we view the amount of effort committed by each author as essentially private knowledge for that author, or at the very least extremely difficult to verify to an outside observer. Hence we model this stage by the simultaneous choice of effort levels e_A and e_B by A and B, respectively.

The second stage loosely corresponds to the journal "publication pipeline" process. The transformation of the efforts expended by the two authors in the first stage into "value added" for the joint research project is by its very nature an activity whose actual outcome is uncertain at the time the activity is undertaken. So although the paper has already been written at this stage, we assume that the actual effort choices of the two coauthors cannot be determined by an inspection of the paper. It does not seem unreasonable to suppose, however, even if they are still uncertain about what the actual value their paper will command once published in the "marketplace of ideas," that the two authors can identify their relative contributions to this joint paper. So at the beginning of this stage we assume that the two authors observe the realization of S_A, which signals the relative contribution of author A to the project.

Knowing their respective contributions, although uncertain about what the total quality of the project will be, the two authors bargain over the attribution rule for the paper in this submission stage. Although nothing in our framework precludes the possibility that authors will decide on the attribution rule in the first stage, before they have committed to their respective efforts for this joint project, nothing prevents them from renegotiating the attribution rule once they have learned the size of their relative contributions. As we have not explicitly modeled a commitment device for the first stage, we believe that it is appropriate to consider the decision about attribution rules as being decided in the later stages.[3]

Formally, the attribution rule is a mapping from relative contributions into the order space, that is, $\beta:[0,1] \rightarrow \{(A, B), (B, A)\}$. To make things simple, suppose that coauthors bargain over only two "pure" attribution rules: (1) the lexicographic ordering, with $\beta(s) = (A, B)$ for all s in $[0, 1]$, arid (2) relative contribution ordering, with $\beta(s) = (B, A)$ if s in $[0, \frac{1}{2}]$ and $\beta(s) = (A, B)$ if s in $[\frac{1}{2}, 1]$.[4] We allow for the "outcome" of the bargaining procedure to be a probability mixture of these two attribution rules, where p in $[0,1]$ denotes the probability that lexicographic ordering is chosen. Without explicitly modeling the bargaining protocol, we shall assume that the outcome corresponds to Nash's (1950) well-known cooperative solution for bargaining problems.[5] After the resolution of the probability mixing (if any) for the bargaining outcome, the order of the authors for the paper is determined by the chosen attribution rule.

In the final stage, the value (or, equivalently, quality) of the project V is revealed to the market along with the order of authors. The market (say, consisting of potential or current employers) assigns weights α and $1-\alpha$ so that the payoffs to A and B are $\pi_A = \alpha V - c(e_A)$ and $\pi_B = (1-\alpha)V - c(e_B)$, respectively. The weights represent the market's beliefs regarding the relative productivity of each coauthor, conditional on the market's observation of the ordering on the paper and prior beliefs regarding the ordering rule being used by the coauthors and their effort choices.

In summary, (1) coauthors A and B simultaneously choose effort levels. (2) The value of S_A is revealed to authors, who then "bargain" over the attribution rule. If the lexicographic ordering is chosen or $S_A \geq \frac{1}{2}$, then the order of coauthors is (A, B); otherwise the order of coauthors is (B, A). (3) The value of V and the order of authors are revealed to the market. The market attributes α of V to A (and the remainder to B), where α is the market's "best" guess of A's relative contribution given the publicly available information and the market's equilibrium beliefs about the other variables.

To economize on notation, we denote the alphabetical ordering (A, B) by (+) and the reverse alphabetical ordering (B, A) by (–).

A. Stage 3: The Market's Weight Assignment Problem

As we shall see in the next subsection, the two coauthors are indifferent as to which attribution rule is used if both attribution rules lead to the same ordering. This occurs in the event $S_A \geq \frac{1}{2}$, in which case the ordering of coauthors is (+). In the complementary event (i.e., when $S_A < \frac{1}{2}$), the ordering depends on the outcome of the bargaining. The order can be either (+) if lexicographic ordering is agreed on or (–) if relative contribution ordering is used. Hence from the market's perspective, for a given set of its beliefs about the effort choices of the coauthors (e_A^M, e_B^M), the ordering (+) is less informative about A's relatively greater contribution to the quality of the paper than the ordering (–) about B's. If we let p^M denote the market's prior belief that lexicographic ordering is chosen in the event that A's contribution is actually less than B's (i.e., in the event $S_A < \frac{1}{2}$) and $q^M = q(e_A^M, e_B^M)$, the state space can usefully be divided into four mutually exclusive and exhaustive events (Table 12.3). Thus the market's posterior belief that A's relative contribution is less than B's despite an observation of the ordering (+) is given by

$$\Pr[S_A < \tfrac{1}{2} | (+)] = \frac{(1-q^M)p^M}{q^M + (1-q^M)p^M}$$

To Co-Author or Not to Co-Author

Table 12.3

Event	Probability
$S_A < \frac{1}{2}$ and (+)	$(1 - q^M)p^M$
$S_A \geq \frac{1}{2}$ and (+)	q^M
$S_A < \frac{1}{2}$ and (−)	$(1 - q^M)(1 - p^M)$
$S_A \geq \frac{1}{2}$ and (−)	0

Hence, the weight placed on coauthor A given the observation of (+) is:

$$
\begin{aligned}
\alpha[(+)] &= \Pr[S_A < \tfrac{1}{2}|(+)]E[S_A|S_A < \tfrac{1}{2}] \\
&\quad + \Pr[S_A > \tfrac{1}{2}|(+)]E[S_A|S_A < \tfrac{1}{2}] \\
&= \frac{(1-q^M)p^M}{q^M + (1-q^M)p^M}[1 - h(e_B^M, e_A^M)] \\
&\quad + \frac{q^M}{q^M + (1-q^M)p^M} h(e_B^M, e_A^M).
\end{aligned}
\tag{12.1}
$$

In contrast, from the observation of the ordering (−), the market knows with certainty that the relative contribution ordering rule was used, and hence the weight placed on coauthor A is

$$
\begin{aligned}
\alpha[(-)] &= E[S_A|S_A < \tfrac{1}{2}] \\
&= 1 - h(e_B^M, e_A^M).
\end{aligned}
\tag{12.2}
$$

The asymmetric nature of market beliefs indicates the importance of the lexicographic assumption as opposed to an ordering that sent no signal per se. That is, when A contributes relatively more than B, the market cannot distinguish which ordering was actually used. Thus, as long as the market places some probability on the event that the relative contribution ordering is used, the name ordering of A before B sends a partial signal, with some weight placed on the event that in fact $S_A > \frac{1}{2}$. We discuss the implications of the existence of a perfectly uninformative signaling device in Section III below.

B. Stage 2: Bargaining over the Attribution Risk

Given the realization of S_A, the coauthors' effort choices $(\bar{e}_A, \bar{e}_B)$, the market's beliefs about the coauthors' effort choices (e_A^M, e_B^M), and the market's ex ante belief that the coauthors will choose the lexicographic ordering rule when $S_A < \frac{1}{2}$ (p^M), the (gross of effort costs) expected payoffs are (a) with the lexicographic ordering rule,

$$R_A^+ = \alpha[(+)]\bar{V}(\bar{e}_A,\bar{e}_B)$$
$$\equiv \left\{ \frac{(1-q^M)p^M[1-h(e_B^M,e_A^M)]}{q^M+(1-q^M)p^M} + \frac{q^M h(e_A^M,e_B^M)}{q^M+(1-q^M)p^M} \right\} \bar{V}(\bar{e}_A,\bar{e}_B),$$
$$R_B^+ = \{1-\alpha[(+)]\}\bar{V}(\bar{e}_A,\bar{e}_B)$$
$$\equiv \left\{ \frac{(1-q^M)p^M[1-h(e_B^M,e_A^M)]}{q^M+(1-q^M)p^M} + \frac{q^M[1-h(e_A^M,e_B^M)]}{q^M+(1-q^M)p^M} \right\} \bar{V}(\bar{e}_A,\bar{e}_B);$$

(b) with the relative contribution ordering rule and $S_A > \frac{1}{2}$, payoffs are the same as in point a; and (c) with the relative contribution ordering rule and $S_A < \frac{1}{2}$,

$$R_A^- = \alpha[(-)]\bar{V}(\bar{e}_A,\bar{e}_B)$$
$$\equiv [1-h(e_B^M,e_A^M)]\bar{V}(\bar{e}_A,\bar{e}_B),$$
$$R_B^- = \{1-\alpha[(-)]\}\bar{V}(\bar{e}_A,\bar{e}_B)$$
$$\equiv h(e_B^M,e_A^M)\bar{V}(\bar{e}_A,\bar{e}_B).$$

Obviously when $S_A > \frac{1}{2}$, the two attribution rules are in agreement about the order and there is nothing to bargain over. However, when $S_A < \frac{1}{2}$, $(R_A^+ - R_A^-)(R_B^+ - R_B^-) < 0$; that is, there is a conflict between each player's most preferred rule. We consider the well-known Nash bargaining "solution" to the bargaining problem. This solution is given by the probability that the lexicographic ordering rule is used that solves the following program:

$$\max_{p\in[0,1]}[pR_A^+ +(1-p)R_A^-][pR_B^+ +(1-p)R_B^-].$$

The first-order condition for an interior maximum is

$$(R_A^+ - R_A^-)[p^* R_B^+ + (1-p^*)R_B^-] = (R_B^- - R_B^+)[p^* R_A^+ + (1-p^*)R_A^-].$$

Now since

$$(R_A^+ - R_A^-) = (R_B^- - R_B^+)\frac{q^M}{q^M + (1-q^M)p^M}[h(e_B^M, e_A^M) + h(e_A^M, e_B^M) - 1]\overline{V}(\overline{e}_A, \overline{e}_B),$$

it follows that

$$p^* R_A^+ + (1-p^*)R_A^- = p^* R_B^+ + (1-p^*)R_B^- = \tfrac{1}{2}\overline{V}(\overline{e}_A, \overline{e}_B). \qquad (12.3)$$

That is,

$$p^*\alpha[(+)] + (1-p^*)\alpha[(-)] = \tfrac{1}{2}.$$

Hence,

$$
\begin{aligned}
p^* &= \min\left\{1, \frac{\tfrac{1}{2}-\alpha[(-)]}{\alpha[(+)] - \alpha[(-)]}\right\} \\
&= \min\left\{1, \frac{[h(e_B^M, e_A^M) - \tfrac{1}{2}][q^M + (1-q^M)p^M]}{[h(e_A^M, e_B^M) + h(e_B^M, e_A^M) - 1]q^M}\right\},
\end{aligned}
\qquad (12.4)
$$

where $p^* > 0$ because $\alpha[(-)] = \tfrac{1}{2}$.

The equality of the postbargaining gross payoffs follows from the fact that the Pareto frontier is linear with slope -1 and intersects the 45-degree line (see Figure 12.1 below). As $R_A^- < \overline{V}/2 \le R_B^+$, it follows from the geometry of the Nash bargaining solution that $p^* > 0$, and indeed this is confirmed by the expression for p^* above. Thus, even if the market placed no weight on the probability that the lexicographic ordering rule is used, that is, $p^M = 0$, the researchers themselves would agree to that ordering some of the time when there was an actual name ordering conflict, that is, when the two ordering rules yielded different name orders. The reason for this is that the ordering (–) causes a much larger loss for A than the gain for B. To compensate A for this, some weight must be placed on the use of the lexicographic ordering rule. We demonstrate below that this property implies that there is no equilibrium in the full game that involves $p^* = 0$.

C. Stage 1: Coauthors' Effort Choices

Given A's belief $\bar{e}_B$, about B's effort choice and her beliefs about the market's expectations, her choice of effort problem can be expressed as

$$\max_{e_A} \pi_A(e_A, \bar{e}_B, e_A^M, e_B^M, p^M),$$

where

$$\pi_A(\cdot) = \{q(e_A, \bar{e}_B) + [1 - q(e_A, \bar{e}_B)]p^*\}R_A^+ + [1 - q(e_A, \bar{e}_B)](1 - p^*)R_A^- - c(e_A)$$

and p^* is given by the expression (12.4). Similarly, given B's belief $\bar{e}_A$, about A's effort choice, his choice of effort problem is

$$\max_{e_B} \pi_B(e_B, \bar{e}_A, e_A^M, e_B^M, p^M),$$

where

$$\pi_B(\cdot) = \{q(\bar{e}_A, e_B) + [1 - q(\bar{e}_A, e_B)]p^*\}R_B^+ + [1 - q(\bar{e}_A, e_B)](1 - p^*)R_B^- - c(e_B)$$

and p^* is given by the expression (12.4).

III.   EQUILIBRIUM OF THE FULL GAME

An equilibrium for the full game requires that, given the market's expectations about the use of the lexicographic ordering rule and the market's expectation about the effort choices of the coauthors, each coauthor finds it optimal to choose the effort choice that the market and her coauthor expects. Furthermore, the market's expectation about the probability that the authors will use the lexicographic ordering rule in the "bargaining over the attribution rule" stage equals the probability that results from their bargaining. The following definition states this formally.

DEFINITION 1. $(e_A^*, e_B^*, e_A^M, e_B^M, p^M, p^*)$ is an equilibrium of the full game if (a) $e_A^M = e_A^* \in \arg\max_{e_A} \pi_A(e_A^*, e_B^*, e_A^M, e_B^M, p^M, p^*)$; (b) $e_B^M = e_B^* \in \arg\max_{e_B} \pi_B(e_B^*, e_A^*, e_A^M, e_B^M, p^M, p^*)$; (c) $p^M = p^*$, where p^* is given by the expression (12.4).

Our central result is that a market expectation that only the lexicographic ordering rule will be employed in conjunction with exclusive use of the lexicographic ordering rule as a result of the coauthors' bargaining can be sustained in an equilibrium of the full game.

PROPOSITION 1. $p^* = 1$ (the lexicographic ordering norm) may be sustained in an equilibrium of the full game in which the authors engage in (Nash) bargaining over the ordering of authors. Moreover, in this equilibrium, both authors make the same effort choice e^{LO} characterized by

$$\frac{\overline{V}_1(e^{LO}, e^{LO})}{2} = c'(e^{LO}).$$

Proof. Suppose that the market believes that only lexicographic ordering will be used, that is, $p^M = 1$, and that both coauthors will choose the same effort choice e^{LO}. If the lexicographic ordering rule is actually used by the coauthors in stage 2, then in stage 3, *whatever* the surplus that is actually created, the outcome is the symmetric outcome in which both coauthors receive half of the realized total surplus since

$$\alpha[(+)] = \frac{\frac{1}{2} \times 1}{\frac{1}{2} + \frac{1}{2} \times 1}[1 - h(e^{LO}, e^{LO})] + \frac{\frac{1}{2} \times 1}{\frac{1}{2} + \frac{1}{2} \times 1}[h(e^{LO}, e^{LO})] = \frac{1}{2}$$

If the relative contribution ordering rule is used, however, then in the event $S_A < \frac{1}{2}$, the share going to A, $\alpha[(-)] = 1 - h(e, e)$, is less than one-half. Hence this simply means transferring utility from A to B. Given the symmetric nature of the Nash bargaining solution, this entails that lexicographic ordering is chosen with probability one. That is, $p^* = 1 (= p^M)$ is the outcome of the bargaining in stage 2.

Finally, given the expectation as to what will happen in stages 2 and 3, in stage 1, A's maximization problem collapses to

Figure 12.1 Nash Bargaining Over the Attribution Rule

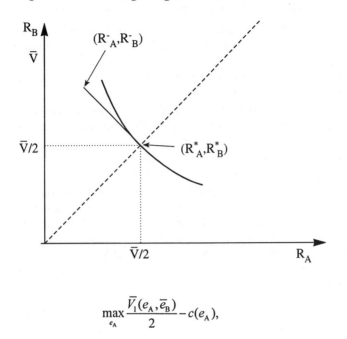

$$\max_{e_A} \frac{\overline{V}_1(e_A, \overline{e}_B)}{2} - c(e_A),$$

where $\overline{e}_B$ is A's expectation of the level of effort that B will choose. An analogous expression represents B's stage 1 maximization problem, and it is immediate that the symmetric solution entails an effort choice of e^{LO} by both coauthors. Q.E.D.

This result demonstrates that the use of the lexicographic ordering rule to send no signal about relative contribution is a noncooperative equilibrium of the full game. Figure 12.1 provides a graphical illustration of the result. Recall that with $\alpha[(+)] = \frac{1}{2}$, $R_A^+ = R_B^+ = \overline{V}/2$; hence the point (R_A^+, R_B^+) lies on the 45 degree line. Recall also that $R_A^+ - R_A^- = R_B^- - R_B^+$; hence the point (R_A^-, R_B^-) lies to the northwest of (R_A^+, R_B^+), and the line connecting them has slope -1. If this line is extended in both directions to intersect with both axes, it is obvious from the geometry that the point on that extended line for which the product of payoffs is maximized is the point (R_A^+, R_B^+). That would be the Nash solution if all points along the extended line were available, and by Nash's assumption of independence of irrelevant alternatives, it remains the solution if only convex combinations of (R_A^+, R_B^+) and (R_A^-, R_B^-) are feasible. Therefore, the convex combination (or "probability mixture") that places weight $p^* = 1$ on the point (R_A^+, R_B^+) yields the Nash outcome for the bargaining over attribution rule stage.[6]

It is very difficult either to characterize other equilibria or to show that the lexicographic ordering norm equilibrium is unique, given the general structure of the game. In particular, notice that the strategic interactions between A and B in their effort choice subgame are possibly quite complex and can potentially exhibit strategic complementarity, substitutability, neither, and multiple interior equilibria. What can be readily shown, however, is that a pure relative contribution ordering rule equilibrium does not exist.

PROPOSITION 2. There do not exist market beliefs that can sustain $p^* = 0$ as an equilibrium outcome of the full game.

Proof. In the previous section, we demonstrated that even if $p^M = 0$, $p^* > 0$. That is, in negotiations, the parties agree to some positive probability that the lexicographic ordering rule is used. Rational market expectations require that market beliefs regarding usage of the lexicographic ordering rule equal actual usage in equilibrium. Therefore, market beliefs concerning the exclusive use of the relative contribution ordering rule are unsustainable. Q.E.D.

A. Uniqueness

Uniqueness of the lexicographic ordering norm can be shown to hold if we refine the model further by making some simplifying functional form assumptions. In particular, let us remove all direct strategic interactions between the two coauthors in their effort choice subgame and leave only those determined by market interactions. Given an effort choice $\bar{e}_i$ by individual i ($i = $ A, B), suppose that i's contribution to the total quality of the paper is given by the random variable V_i, which has a gamma distribution with parameters $\bar{e}_i$ and 1.[7] Suppose further that V_A and V_B are independently distributed. Finally, assume that $c(e) = e^2/2$. These assumptions are consistent with, but stronger than, our earlier conditions for V and S_A. Under these additional restrictions we can show the following proposition.

PROPOSITION 3. $p^* = 1$ (the lexicographic ordering norm) is the unique equilibrium of the modified full game. Moreover, both authors make the same effort choice $e^{LO} = \frac{1}{2}$.

Proof. Under the assumption of a gamma distribution for V_i and the independence of V_A and V_B, it is easy to see that $V = V_A + V_B$, is also distributed gamma with parameters $\bar{e}_A + \bar{e}_B$ and 1 (and so, in particular,

$\overline{V}(e_A, e_B) = \overline{e}_A + \overline{e}_B$ and $S_A = V_A/(V_A + V_B)$ is distributed beta with parameters $\overline{e}_A$ and $\overline{e}_B$ (and so, in particular, $q(\overline{e}_A, \overline{e}_B) = \overline{e}_A/[\overline{e}_A + \overline{e}_B]$).[8] Moreover, V and S_A are independent, consistent with our earlier assumptions. We show existence first and then turn to uniqueness.

Observe that the first-order conditions for the respective coauthors' stage 1 maximization problems may be expressed as

$$\left(\frac{e_B}{e_A + e_B} + \frac{e_A}{e_A + e_B}\right)\{\alpha[(+)] - \tfrac{1}{2} + \tfrac{1}{2} = e_A \Rightarrow e_A = \alpha[(+)],$$

$$\left(\frac{e_B}{e_A + e_B} + \frac{e_A}{e_A + e_B}\right)\{\alpha[(+)] - \tfrac{1}{2} + \tfrac{1}{2} = e_B \Rightarrow e_B = \tfrac{1}{2}.$$

Imposing $p^M = p^*$, substituting $e_B = \tfrac{1}{2}$, and rearranging (12.4), we obtain

$$p^*(e_A) = \frac{[2h(\tfrac{1}{2}, e_A) - 1]q^*(e_A)}{[2h(\tfrac{1}{2}, e_A) - 1]q^*(e_A) + h(e_A, \tfrac{1}{2}) - h(\tfrac{1}{2}, e_A)}, \tag{12.5}$$

where $q^*(e_A) \equiv q(e_A, \tfrac{1}{2})$. Substituting $\alpha[(+)] = e_A$ and solving (12.1) for p^*, we also obtain

$$p^*(e_A) = \frac{q^*(e_A)[h(\tfrac{1}{2}, e_A) - e_A]}{[1 - q^*(e_A)][h(\tfrac{1}{2}, e_A) - e_A - 1]}, \tag{12.6}$$

It is straightforward to see that the right-hand sides of (12.5) and (12.6) both equal one for $e_A = \tfrac{1}{2}$. This proves existence.

A sufficient condition for uniqueness would be to rule out situations in which $p^* < p^M$. When (12.4) is rearranged, this is true if $(1 - q^M)/q^M < E[S_A | S_A > \tfrac{1}{2}]$, which is never true for $q^M < 2/3$. This condition is always satisfied as

$$q^M = \frac{e_B}{e_A + e_B} = \frac{\alpha[(+)]}{\alpha[(+)] + \tfrac{1}{2}} \le 2/3,$$

where the last inequality follows from the fact that $\alpha[(+)] \le 1$. Q.E.D.

B. Multiple Equilibria

In general, an equilibrium in which only the lexicographic ordering norm is employed need riot be the unique equilibrium of the full game. As we add strategic interactions between A and B beyond those that are generated by market relationships, it is possible that there also exist equilibria in which both the relative contribution and lexicographic ordering norms are employed. Those equilibria result in the rise of the alphabetical name ordering more likely than not, but *not* with certainty. This is consistent with observations of occasional violations of the alphabetic name ordering convention in economics journals. What is interesting, however, is that a comparison of the first-order conditions characterizing the optimum effort choices for the respective coauthors, stage 1 programs in cases in which p^* = p^M < 1 implies that $e_A^* \geq e_B^*$. Therefore, in such an equilibrium in which there is a nonzero probability that the relative contribution ordering norm may be employed, observations of an alphabetical name ordering are consistent with market beliefs ascribing a greater relative contribution from the author with a name earlier in the alphabet.

These points may be illustrated by means of the following example. To simplify the calculation and characterization of an equilibrium of the full game, suppose that each coauthor's effort choice is limited to one of three possible levels: L(ow), M(edium), or H(igh). The (common) cost-of-effort function, $c(e)$, is shown in Figure 12.2. Figure 12.3 presents the expected total value of the project, for any pair of effort levels by the two coauthors.

Figure 12.2

e	L	M	H
$c(e)$	16	78	152

Figure 12.3 $\overline{V}(e_A, e_B)$

		e_B		
		L	M	H
e_A	L	256	384	512
	M	384	512	640
	H	512	640	768

Figure 12.4

$q(e_i,e_j)$

		e_j		
		L	M	H
	L	1/2	3/8	1/4
e_i	M	5/8	1/2	3/8
	H	3/4	5/8	1/2

$h(e_i,e_j)$

		e_j		
		L	M	H
	L	23/32	45/64	11/16
e_i	M	47/64	23/32	45/64
	H	3/4	47/64	23/32

Notice that although effort choice is discrete, the relationship between an increase in effort by an author and the associated increase in that author's cost and the increase in the expected value of the project is similar to the functional specification used in the previous subsection. In particular, we see that the increment to the expected value of the project for a single increment in the effort level of one author (with the other author's effort level held constant) is always 128, but the increase in effort cost is greater going from M to H than it is going from L to M.

To complete the description of the situation, we require for any feasible pair of effort levels by the two coauthors the probability that coauthor A's contribution will be greater than B's (i.e., $\Pr[S_A > \frac{1}{2}]$) and the expected contribution of A, given that her contribution is greater than B's (i.e., $E[S_A | S_A > \frac{1}{2}]$). These quantities can be derived from the tabulations of the values of the functions $q(e_i,e_j)$ and $h(e_i,e_j)$ presented in Figure 12.4.

Recall that, given that A exerts effort level e_A and B exerts effort level e_B, $\Pr[S_A > \frac{1}{2}] = q(e_A, e_B)$, $E[S_A | S_A > \frac{1}{2}] = h(e_A, e_B)$ and $E[S_A | S_A < \frac{1}{2}] = 1 - h(e_A, e_B)$.

In addition to the lexicographic ordering norm (symmetric) equilibrium, which we know exists from proposition 1, there is also an equilibrium in which, for bargaining situations in which coauthor B's contribution to the total value of the project is greater than A's, the market expects it is equally likely that the coauthors will rise the relative contribution or lexicographic ordering norms.

PROPOSITION 4. Both (1) $(e_A^*, e_B^*, e_A^M, e_B^M, p^M, p^*) = $ (M, M, M, M, 1, 1) and (2) $(e_A^*, e_B^*, e_A^M, e_B^M, p^M, p^*) = $ (H, L, H, L, ½, ½) are equilibria of the full game.

Proof. Part 1: From the proof of proposition 1 we have $p^* = 1 \ (= p^M)$ as required, and $\alpha[(+)] = \frac{1}{2}$. So A's expected payoff following her effort choice for this putative equilibrium collapses to $[\bar{V}(M,M)/2] - c(M) = 178$. If she deviates and plays L, her expected payoff is

$[\overline{V}(M,M)/2] - c(L) = 176$. And if she deviates and plays H, her expected payoff is $[\overline{V}(M,M)/2] - c(H) = 168$. Since B's payoffs from deviating are the same as those just calculated for A, it follows that neither has an incentive to deviate from the strategy specified in the putative equilibrium. Q.E.D.

Part 2: For the putative equilibrium profile (H, L, H, L, ½, ½), we have $\Pr[S_A > ½] = ¾$, $E[S_A \mid S_A > ½] = ¾$, and $E[S_A \mid S_A > ½] = 5/16$. Hence $\alpha[(+)] = 11/16$ and $\alpha[(-)] = 5/16$ follow from (12.1) and (12.2), respectively. Substituting this into (4), we have $p^* = (½-5/16)/(11/16-5/16) = ½ = p^M$ as is required for the consistency between the market's expectation of the use of the lexicographic ordering norm and its actual use by the two coauthors. In this putative equilibrium, A's (expected) payoff is

$$(\Pr[(+)]\alpha[(+)] + \{1 - \Pr[(+)]\}\alpha[(-)])\overline{V}(H,L) - c(H)$$
$$= \left(\frac{7}{8} \times \frac{11}{16} + \frac{1}{8} \times \frac{5}{16}\right) 512 - 152 = 176$$

Deviating and playing L yields an expected payoff of only

$$\left(\frac{3}{4} \times \frac{11}{16} + \frac{1}{4} \times \frac{5}{16}\right) 256 - 16 = 136$$

And if she deviates and plays M, her expected payoff falls to

$$\left(\frac{13}{16} \times \frac{11}{16} + \frac{3}{16} \times \frac{5}{16}\right) 384 - 78 = 159$$

Coauthor B's expected payoff in this putative equilibrium is

$$\left(\frac{7}{8} \times \frac{5}{16} + \frac{1}{8} \times \frac{11}{16}\right) 516 - 16 = 168$$

If be instead plays M, his expected payoff falls to

$$\left(\frac{13}{16} \times \frac{5}{16} + \frac{3}{16} \times \frac{11}{16}\right) 640 - 78 = 167$$

And, finally, if be plays H instead, his expected payoff is reduced to

$$\left(\frac{3}{4}\times\frac{5}{16}+\frac{1}{4}\times\frac{11}{16}\right)768-152=160$$

Thus we have established that neither A nor B has an incentive to deviate from the strategy specified in the putative equilibrium. Q.E.D.

This example demonstrates that the symmetry of the bargaining outcome does not, of itself, rule out an equilibrium in which the relative contribution ordering rule is used, at least some of the time.

IV. WELFARE IMPLICATIONS

The purpose of this section is to examine the welfare properties of the lexicographic ordering norm characterized in the previous sections. So as to simplify exposition we shall continue to maintain our functional form assumptions introduced in Section III. However, our qualitative results carry over to the more general case.

We conduct our welfare analysis in two ways. First, we demonstrate that overall research quality in the lexicographic ordering norm is lower than the first-best. Second, we demonstrate that imposing restrictions on the use of the lexicographic ordering (although it is an issue how this could be enforced) would result in an improvement in research quality.

A. Joint Maximization – the "First-Best"

The first-best involves choosing research efforts to maximize total research quality less effort costs without regard to distributional issues:

$$\max_{e_A,e_B} \overline{V}_1(e_A,e_B)-c(e_A)-c(e_B).$$

This has a unique symmetric solution $\overline{e}_A = \overline{e}_B = e^{FB}$, characterized by

$$\overline{V}_1(e^{FB},e^{FB})-c'(e^{FB}).$$

Under our functional form assumptions, joint surplus maximization effort choices are $e_A^{FB} = e_B^{FB} = 1$. Therefore, the first-best research quality exceeds that of the lexicographic ordering norm. The reason for this is that individual effort has a positive spillover on the other author's payoff through the improvement in research quality. This spillover is not taken into account when there is a large market weight on the lexicographic ordering norm possibility. Hence, there is underprovision of effort akin to any model of privately provided public goods.

B. Committing to a Relative Contribution Ordering Nom

Suppose that it were possible to prohibit the use of the lexicographic ordering rule. This would mean that the relative contribution ordering rule was used with certainty and, hence, that $p^* = p^M = 0$. Under this restriction, the coauthors' stage 1 effort choice problems can be expressed as

$$\max_{e_A}\{1 - h(e_B^M, e_A^M) + [h(e_A^M, e_B^M) + h(e_B^M, e_A^M) - 1]q(e_A, \bar{e}_B)\}\bar{V}(e_A, \bar{e}_B) - c(e_A),$$

$$\max_{e_A}\{1 - h(e_B^M, e_A^M) + [h(e_A^M, e_B^M) + h(e_B^M, e_A^M) - 1]q(e_A, \bar{e}_B)\}\bar{V}(e_A, \bar{e}_B) - c(e_B)$$

The first-order equilibrium conditions are

$$\{1 - h(\bar{e}_B, \bar{e}_A) + [h(\bar{e}_A, \bar{e}_B) + h(\bar{e}_B, \bar{e}_A) - 1]q(\bar{e}_A, \bar{e}_B)\}\bar{V}_1(\bar{e}_A, \bar{e}_B)$$
$$+ [h(\bar{e}_A, \bar{e}_B) + h(\bar{e}_B, \bar{e}_A) - 1]q_1(\bar{e}_A, \bar{e}_B)\bar{V}(\bar{e}_A, \bar{e}_B) = c'(\bar{e}_A)$$
$$\{h(\bar{e}_B, \bar{e}_A) - [h(\bar{e}_A, \bar{e}_B) + h(\bar{e}_B, \bar{e}_A) - 1]q(\bar{e}_A, \bar{e}_B)\}\bar{V}_2(\bar{e}_A, \bar{e}_B)$$
$$- [h(\bar{e}_A, \bar{e}_B) + h(\bar{e}_B, \bar{e}_A) - 1]q_2(\bar{e}_A, \bar{e}_B)\bar{V}(\bar{e}_A, \bar{e}_B) = c'(\bar{e}_B)$$

Which also have a unique solution $\bar{e}_A = \bar{e}_B = e^{CO}$, characterized by

$$\frac{\bar{V}_1(e^{CO}, e^{CO})}{2} + q_1(e^{CO}, e^{CO})[2h(e^{CO}, e^{CO}) - 1]\bar{V}(e^{CO}, e^{CO}) = c'(e^{CO}).$$

Under our functional form assumptions, the equilibrium effort choices for the relative contribution ordering norm case that would arise are also symmetric: $e_A^{CO} = e_B^{CO} = e^{CO}$, with

$$e^{\text{co}} = h(e^{\text{co}}, e^{\text{co}}),$$

where

$$h(e,e) = \frac{\int_{\frac{1}{2}}^{1} s^e (1-s)^{e-1} ds}{\int_{\frac{1}{2}}^{1} s^{e-1}(1-s)^{e-1} ds}$$

Hence, $e^{CO} \approx 0.775$.

Observe that this involves an improvement in research quality over the level achieved when the lexicographic ordering norm is permitted. The reason for this is that, while the public-good aspect of each author's effort choices still militates against high effort, there is a racing aspect as well. Because a relative contribution ordering rule will be used with certainty, if one author reduces his or her effort by a small amount, this causes an even greater reduction in payoff. This creates an additional incentive to exert effort. Hence, effort levels are higher when authors can commit to the relative contribution ordering rule.

C. Efficiency of Non-Lexicographic Ordering Norm Equilibria

At first blush the previous analysis suggests that any equilibrium that involves some use of the relative contribution ordering rule might improve efficiency. However, looking to our example in Section IIIB, we can easily see that this is not the case.

In that example, notice that ex ante expected surplus is maximized when both exert high effort. That is,

$$\bar{V}(\text{H,H}) - 2c(\text{H}) = 464,$$
$$\bar{V}(\text{H,M}) - c(\text{H}) - c(\text{M}) = 410,$$
$$\bar{V}(\text{M,M}) - 2c(\text{M}) = 356,$$
$$\bar{V}(\text{H,L}) - c(\text{H}) - c(\text{L}) = 344,$$

The symmetric equilibrium outcome resulting from employing the lexicographic ordering norm is clearly inefficient. But in this particular example, it is more efficient than the asymmetric equilibrium outcome (with effort choices of H and L), which generates a project with the same expected value but at greater cost of effort.

D. A No-Signaling Option

Part of the difficulty with the lexicographic ordering rule is its asymmetric nature. Its possibility makes it difficult for A to send the market a clear signal if she has contributed more to the article. Note, however, that the authors would not agree to use the relative contribution ordering rule even when the alternative is simply to send no signal. For instance, a no-signaling option could involve a distinctive color. While bargaining would then be relevant for any realization of S_A, its ex post nature requires a solution that splits the joint surplus. The no-signaling option would allow the market to set $\alpha = \frac{1}{2}$ and could always implement an equal division of the surplus. Hence, it would be favored by the coauthors in ex post bargaining with probability one. The result would be an equilibrium that mimicked the lexicographic ordering norm.

In reality, such a no-signaling device is difficult to imagine. Our methods of citation analysis are necessarily alphabetically based, and it has been shown that this can lead to a reduction in attribution to second authors and beyond. They get lost in the et al. (Merton 1973).

V.   CONCLUSIONS AND FUTURE DIRECTIONS

The model presented in this paper represents a first step toward analyzing collaborative interactions in scientific work. It demonstrates that, under certain conditions, an alphabetical name ordering will exist as a norm in a noncooperative game with self-interested agents. In so doing, it indicates the directions that might be pursued to explain the more interesting empirical anomaly of differing patterns across disciplines. An understanding of this would be helpful in understanding both the sociology of science (Merton, 1973) and the economics of production in teams. Our earlier tabulations indicate the wealth of empirical research that could be pursued on this topic: from the relationship between attribution and team size to the existence of alternative signals of relative contribution apart from name ordering.

To this end, on a theoretical level, our model potentially can be enriched in several ways. First, the present model has the outside options of both coauthors as zero. This lies at the heart of the strong equity drive in bargaining. While this assumption might accurately characterize collaborative efforts in economics, it is less likely to hold in other disciplines. For instance, in experimental research, priority is often assigned to the laboratory head. That individual can politically appropriate most of the value of a project if others were to leave. To see how this might alter our model, suppose that one author can appropriate the entire value without the other. Suppose that such power resides with A (she can receive the entire value without B). Then the order will be alphabetical (regardless of market beliefs). On the other hand, if B can appropriate all value on his own, then the ordering will be reversed.[9] Thus, if one author, and only one author, can appropriate the entire value, the order itself is uninformative about anything except who had the strong outside option.

It would be interesting to explore situations in which outside options summed to less than the total value and situations in which the relative value of outside options was correlated with relative contribution. It is likely that the types of equilibria possible will be enriched and have to be refined by use of reasonable restrictions on market beliefs in order to derive empirically relevant results. Nonetheless, it is probable that such considerations will reduce the intensity of forces driving a pure lexicographic ordering norm and lead to a situation in which the choice between the lexicographic and relative contribution ordering norms is randomized in equilibrium. This is more consistent with observed evidence and would be necessary in order to analyze cross-disciplinary effects.

A second path modeling could take is suggested by tables 12.1 and 12.2: the greater the number of collaborators, the less likely it is that a lexicographic ordering rule will be chosen. Of course, the causation might run in the opposite direction (as suggested by Over and Smallman, 1970); that is, when market beliefs place a high probability on the use of the lexicographic ordering rule, the incentives for additional researchers to become part of the projects may be diminished. Therefore, by considering a model with an endogenous number of authors, we can consider whether team size has an effect on name ordering. Moreover, one could probably come to a better understanding about how signaling possibilities affect incentives to engage in collaborative projects.

Finally, our model does not have any observable heterogeneity among authors. If other properties such as seniority, eminence, or task-related specialization could be observed by the market, then other possible inferences could be drawn from name ordering. The apparent lack of use of an alphabetical ordering in sociology and the physical sciences should not necessarily indicate a superior efficiency in collaborative ventures. It may be that some other no-signaling norm prevails.

In a broader sense, this paper suggests that team and individual signaling problems can have an important influence on effort incentives. The implications of this for contract theory and the economics of organization remain an open area for future research.

NOTES

1. The prevalence of multi-authored papers has been on the rise in the postwar era. See Hudson (1996) for an illuminating documentation of this trend.
2. One explanation for the use of the lexicographic order arises when coauthors have an ongoing collaborative relationship with multiple outputs that involve varying relative contributions. Our model is based on a single collaborative output and is therefore independent of such explanations.
3. In Section III, we show that there exists an equilibrium of our game in which only alphabetical name orderings are used. Notice that this is observationally equivalent to a regime in which authors precommit to the use of alphabetical name orderings in stage 1. The significance of our result is that such an outcome can be sustained in a noncooperative framework, eschewing the need for an extraneous commitment device.
4. We have chosen this specification for simplicity only. As explained below, it is the symmetry of the bargaining solution when orderings do not coincide that plays an important role in our analysis. We could easily have chosen bargaining rules that mapped any realization of S_A into a probability that one ordering rule is used.
5. Our results would be unaffected if the Kalai-Smorodinsky (1975) or egalitarian bargaining solution concepts were employed instead.
6. Note that this equilibrium is "stable" in the following sense: for market beliefs, p^M, close to one, p^* exceeds p^M. Hence, the equilibrium correspondence that $p^* = p^M$ cuts the 45-degree line from above at $p^* = 1$. This can be seen by differentiating (12.4) with respect to p^M, holding effort choices and other beliefs constant (as one can do because of the continuity and convexity assumptions). It can be easily demonstrated that this partial derivative is (strictly) less than one.
7. The probability density function for V_i is then

$$f(v) = \frac{1}{\Gamma(\overline{e_i})} v^{\overline{e_i}-1} \exp(-v), \quad 0 < v < \infty$$

8. That is, the probability density function for S_A is

$$f(v) = \frac{\Gamma(\overline{e_A}, \overline{e_B})}{\Gamma(\overline{e_A})\Gamma(\overline{e_B})} s^{\overline{e_A}-1}(1-s)^{\overline{e_B}-1}, \quad 0 < s < 1$$

9. In this case there is the equivalent of an ex ante commitment device: B can simply seize the research if not placed first.

REFERENCES

Hudson, John (1996), "Trends in Multi-authored Papers in Economics," *Journal of Economic Perspectives*, **10**, 153-8; Chapter 10 of this volume.

Kalai, Ehud, and Meir Smorodinsky (1975), "Other Solutions to Nash's Bargaining Problem," *Econometrica*, **43**, 513-18.

Merton, Robert K. (1973), *The Sociology of Science: Theoretical and Empirical Investigations*, Chicago: University of Chicago Press.

Nash, John F. (1950), "The Bargaining Problem," *Econometrica*, **18**, 155-62.

Over, Ray, and Susan Smallman (1970), "Citation Idiosyncracies," *Nature*, **228**, 1357.

Over, Ray, and Susan Smallman (1973) "Maintenance of Individual Visibility in Publication of Collaborative Research by Psychologists," *American Psychologist*, **28**, 161-6.

Spiegel, Don, and Patricia Keith-Spiegel (1970), "Assignment of Publication Credits: Ethics and Practices of Psychologists," *American Psychologist*, **25**, 738-47.

Zuckerman, Harriet A. (1968), "Patterns of Name Ordering among Authors of Scientific Papers: A Study of Social Symbolism and Its Ambiguity," *American Journal of Sociology*, **74**, 276-91.

PART FOUR

The Influence of Economics Journals

13. The Journals of Economics*

George J. Stigler, Stephen M. Stigler, and Claire Friedland

Abstract: We examine the principal journals of economics, with particular attention to the communication between journals, as reflected by the network of interjournal citations during 1987-90, and the changes over the past century in the characteristics of the authors and the techniques they have used. The numerical results, and those of the statistical modeling of these results, reinforce the importance of economic theory as an exporter of intellectual influence to applied economics. The study includes an examination of the degree of specialization among different subfields of economics. A statistical model is presented for measuring the flow of intellectual influence (as measured by citations) in terms of simple univariate scores.

The full life of English-language economics journals covers almost precisely the past 100 years. Three of the still premier journals were founded at the beginning of this period: *Quarterly Journal of Economics* (1886), *Economic Journal* (1891), and *Journal of Political Economy* (1892). Today they are joined by several hundred younger journals.

Economics journals had an earlier beginning in continental Europe; for example, several German journals date from the 1860s and one *(Zeltschrift*

---

* Reprinted with permission of the copyright holder from the *Journal of Political Economy*, Vol.103, No.2, 1995, pp. 331-59.

University of Chicago. George J. Stigler, with the assistance of Claire Friedland, prepared Secs. I-V for a conference on the Role of Journals in Scholarly Communication that was held at the University of Chicago in April 1992. George J. Stigler died December 1, 1991, and Sec. VI describing the statistical model was added subsequently by Stephen M. Stigler. Sherwin Rosen has provided helpful suggestions, and Patricia Hume and Maggie Newman have expertly handled the manuscript. Financial Support was provided to Friedland by grants from the Lynde and Harry Bradley Foundation and the Amoco Foundation to the George J. Stigler Center for the study of the Economy and the State at the University of Chicago.

für die Gesamte Staatswissenschaft) from 1844. We exclude foreign-language journals from this study for a good reason and a questionable one. The good reason is that economics is predominantly an English-language science. The most numerous citations in leading European journals refer to English publications (see Stigler and Friedland 1979, p. 19), and several such journals (e.g., *Swedish Journal of Economics* and the [German] *Journal of Institutional and Theoretical Economics*) are now published in English. The questionable reason is that a reading knowledge of foreign languages is now uncommon in the English-speaking world: such knowledge was usually feeble even when required for the doctoral degree, and that requirement has since been replaced by mathematics.

The birth of the English-language journals slightly lags the development of economics as an academic calling. In the 1890s, there were perhaps a half dozen professorships of economics in Britain and probably no more than two or three dozen in the United States. Indeed, although specialization as a full-time economist was becoming common, historians and political scientists could still write on economic subjects with impunity.

Correspondingly, a good deal of professional writing of economists appeared in nonspecialist journals. In the period 1892-1901, of 377 articles published in America by 78 prominent economists including John Bates Clark, Eugen von Böhm-Bawerk, Frank Taussig, and Irving Fisher, almost 40 percent appeared in three nonspecialist journals: *Political Science Quarterly*, *Yale Review*, and the *Annals of the American Academy*.[1]

I.   THE POPULATION OF ECONOMISTS AND JOURNALS

In the mid-1890s, the recently established American Economic Association (AEA) had approximately 570 members, a number including many nonacademicians and a few foreigners and no doubt excluding many college teachers (some alienated by its early socialist tendency; see Coats (1960)).

Of the astonishingly large estimate of 220,000 employed economists with at least a bachelor's degree reported for 1988 by the National Science Foundation (1990, pp.7-9), 140,000 are employed in industry and must include a good share of the nation's MBAs. In that year, 41,800 economists were employed in education and 29,100 in various governments. Of the 18,000 economists with doctorates, 66 percent were employed in education, 15.8 percent in business, and 10.5 percent in government.

The American population of academic economists plus comparably trained business and government economists must now be on the order of

50,000-60,000. If we add in the other English-speaking nations, that number is probably increased again by half. The number of such economists has probably increased over 75-fold in the last 100 years. The profession is still predominantly academic, but government and business economists are now an important distinguishable group.

The facts that economists now have widely varied interests and technical competences and that almost every adult is interested in economic phenomena combine to make the definition of an economics journal difficult. The difficulty is illustrated by the varying practices of the AEA's many-volumed *Index of Economic Articles*. Volume 1 (1886-1924) included 11 English and five foreign-language journals, reporting, however, only English-language articles. Forty-six such foreign-language journals are included in the 1986 volume. The venerable *London Economist* has never been included in the *Index*, but the *Harvard Business Review* was included from 1922 until sometime in the 1970s. Two of the hundreds of law school reviews (Yale and Michigan) are included, and a partial selection of management science and operations research journals is included. The growth of covered journals in the *Index* from 16 in volume 1 to 312 in volume 29 reflects the complaisance of its editors as well as the growth of economics journals.

We define the body of journals devoted to the professional writing of economists as the journals economists write in and read. This involves an element of circularity because the choice of economists is itself arbitrary. (There is good precedent: Jacob Viner's famous definition of economics as "that which economists do" – and others don't?) The determination of the "core" journals of a field can be based on citation analysis, and we shall carry out such an analysis in Section III. Eugene *Garfield's Social Sciences Citation Index* (Garfield, 1987, 1988) summary volumes of journal cross-citations are available only for recent decades, however.

II.   SPECIALIZATION

The proliferation of journals in a field creates a problem of congestion. Congestion is usually a condition of demand: too many people wish to drive on a road or patronize an event. The congestion of journals is relatively mild on the demand side: a queue may arise to use the library copy. On the supply side, however, congestion is serious: How many can one examine of the two to four dozen journals that carry papers one sometimes wishes to read? Of course there are bibliographic services such as the listing of economic articles in the *Journal of Economic Literature*, but the very length of these listings is another form of congestion. (The recent introduction of an electronic database equivalent of the *Journal of Economic Literature*, EconLit, which is kept current quarterly, will greatly relieve this congestion.) The main defense of the scholar must be to rely on the specialization of some journals to his or her interests.

A famous theorem owed to Adam Smith says that specialization increases as a market grows in size. A small town will have a physician who is in general practice and one auto mechanic; a metropolis will have dozens of different medical specialists and auto repair facilities specialized by automobile brand. A small college or university will have its faculty each teaching a considerable variety of subjects; a major university will have scholars of sometimes astonishing specialization.

The specialization of journals will follow that of the scholars or professional practitioners, but the journals will seldom be tidy in their specialization. Economic theory is the authoritative central core of economics, and even the many applied economists who will not employ the advanced techniques are expected to maintain some familiarity with what is evolving in economic theory. The AEA publishes two journals (the *Journal of Economic Literature* and the *Journal of Economic Perspectives*) whose function is to give economists a survey or sample of work going on outside of their specialty (the largest specialty is no doubt doing no research of any sort).

As a consequence of the dominant status of economic theory, the major journals all emphasize this subject as their central agenda and thereby reinforce their status. The emphasis on economic theory does not exclude an interest in unconventional developments, so the *Journal of Political Economy* (with which I am most familiar) published (1) in 1948 an article on the use of experiment as a tool in economic research by Edward Chamberlin and later (1962) a more ambitious work by Vernon L. Smith on this subject; (2) in 1957 an essay by Anthony Downs that launched the application of economic theory in studies of political systems; (3) in 1968 an essay by Gary Becker on the economic theory of crime and punishment; (4) in 1973 an essay by Becker on the economic theory of marriage; and (5) in 1973 an essay by Fischer Black and Myron Scholes on option pricing, which had an immense influence on the finance literature. Conversely, none of the major journals is able to fill its pages only with articles that have primary or substantial theoretical content, although a few come fairly close. And conversely again, major theoretical contributions appear occasionally in journals outside the central core of the discipline.

III. NETWORKS OF CITATIONS

The *Social Sciences Citation Index* provides, for each year beginning with 1977, the number of times each journal cites each other possible journal (but suppresses the identities when fewer than a given number of citations, usually six, are involved).[2] The domain of the citations is approximately 1,500 journals, of which over 200 are identified as economic; the remainder include all other social science and law journals.

In Table 13.1 we present cross-citations among nine select economics journals in 1987, 1988, 1989, and 1990 combined.[3] The table orders these journals by total citations (including self-citations) within the universe of these nine journals. Other general journals that we included in the citation count are *Economica* (248 citations by the nine leading journals), *Economic Inquiry* (130 citations), and *Southern Economic Journal* (64 citations). Self-citations of journals do not have the taint of vanity associated with self-citations by individuals, but high rates of journal self-citation suggest that a journal is somewhat removed from the writings of other journals. Table 13.2 gives the breakdown of Table 13.1 totals by citing (row) journal.

One measure of the hierarchy of journals is the ratio of the number of times journal A is cited by journal B relative to the citations of journal B by journal A (see Table 13.3). Thus the *AER* was cited by the *Economic Journal* 440 times and in turn cited the *Economic Journal* 108 times. So 440/108 = 4.07 is the ratio, for this pair of journals, of citations sent to the *AER* to those sent to the *Economic Journal*. High ratios indicate that the journal in the column head of Table 13.3 is more a consumer than a producer of work in relation to the row journal, and a low ratio indicates that the column journal is a net exporter of citations. Clearly *Econometrica* and the *JPE* are the leading exporters.

These sender-receiver ratios are influenced by the varying number of citations in the articles published by each journal. That variation does not call for correction, however, if we believe that the numbers of citations in a journal's articles are related to the size and influence of the journal. In any event, the number of citations sent to the nine core journals does not vary greatly, as shown in Table 13.4 (see Stigler, 1994, p. 102).

The importance of general economic theory in all of economics is manifest in the citation patterns of journals with a strong empirical orientation. The citations to the leading journal in agricultural economics, three journals in labor economics, and a natural resources journal are tabulated in Table 13.5. The applied economics journals are seldom cited in the general journals, but the general journals are much cited by the applied journals.

Table 13.1 Citations Received from Nine Core Journals, 1987-90

Cited Core journal	Citations Received from Nine Core journals	Percentage Self-Citations
Econometrica (*Ecmca*)	4,036	22.2
American Economic Review (*AER*)	3,316	32.9
Journal of Political Economy (*JPE*)	3,037	21.3
Journal of Economic Theory (*JET*)	1,789	42.1
Review of Economic Studies (*REStud*)	1,620	18.0
Quarterly Journal of Economics (*QJE*)	1,281	17.2
Journal of Monetary Economics (*JME*)*	1,082	42.11
Review of Economics and Statistics (*REStat*)	935	61.4
Economic Journal (*EJ*)	770	47.9

Note: * Excludes citations to the *Carnegie-Rochester Conference Series*.

Source: Garfield (1987, 1988) and correspondence with Alfred Welljams-Dorof of the Institute for Scientific Information (ISI).

The three labor journals in Table 13.5 illustrate by their cross-citations the fact that almost every journal's market is somewhat removed from that of other journals in the same field. The specialization may occur in area, approach, or even editorial preference. This is essentially a universal trait: even in what appear to be journals with a common area of research, there is a preponderance of journal self-citation. The one exception to this rule that I have observed occurs in the field of finance, which for three decades has been experiencing great fundamental advances with extremely rich empirical applications. The cross-citations for three leading financial journals are presented in Table 13.6.

The economic history journals are another network, but their articles are not much noticed by the leading general journals (see Table 13.7).[4]

IV. THE AUTHORS AND THE CONTENTS

We noted that a substantial fraction – about a third – of economists with doctorates are not in academia. It is interesting to inquire about their participation in the general journals we have been studying and also discover the particular fields they cultivate.

The answer to our first question is given in Table 13.8: the general

Table 13.2 Number of Citations for Nine Core Journals, 1987-90

CITING JOURNAL	CITED JOURNAL								
	AER	EJ	Ecmca	JET	JME	JPE	QJE	REStat	REStud
American Economic Review	1,090	108	423	123	185	652	275	120	209
Economic Journal	440	369	458	103	101	375	160	55	208
Econometrica	157	44	894	269	43	170	92	35	229
Journal of Economic Theory	1233	22	669	754	7	126	100	5	252
Journal of Monetary Economics	276	17	272	107	455	362	87	27	65
Journal of Political Economy	373	61	321	108	113	646	155	75	155
Quarterly Journal of Economics	301	43	204	98	57	230	220	32	114
Review of Economics and Statistics	416	66	416	25	95	310	98	574	97
Review of Economic Studies	140	40	379	189	26	166	94	12	291
Total	3,316	770	4,036	1,789	1,082	3,037	1,281	935	1,620

Source: See Table 13.1

Table 13.3 Ratios of Citations Sent to Journal A by Journal B to Citations Received by B from A

CITING JOURNAL	JOURNAL B								
	AER	EJ	Ecmca	JET	JME	JPE	QJE	REStat	REStud
American Economic Review	1.00	4.07	.37	.90	1.49	.57	1.09	3.47	.67
Economic Journal	.25	1.00	.10	.21	.17	.16	.27	1.20	.19
Econometrica	2.69	10.41	1.00	2.49	6.33	1.89	2.22	11.89	1.66
Journal of Economic Theory	1.11	4.68	.40	1.00	15.29	.86	.98	5.00	.75
Journal of Monetary Economics	.67	5.94	.16	.07	1.00	.31	.66	3.52	.40
Journal of Political Economy	1.75	6.15	.53	1.17	3.20	1.00	1.48	4.13	1.07
Quarterly Journal of Economics	.91	3.72	.45	1.02	1.53	.67	1.00	3.06	.82
Review of Economics and Statistics	.29	.83	.08	.20	.28	.24	.33	1.00	.12
Review of Economic Studies	1.49	5.20	.60	1.33	2.50	.93	1.21	8.08	1.00
Total	.96	2.95	.48	1.15	1.54	.66	1.01	2.24	.83

Source: See Table 13.1

Table 13.4 Citations Sent to Nine Core Journals and to All SSCI Journals,
1987-90

Sending Core Journal	To Nine Core Journals	To All SSCI Journals
American Economic Review	3,198	9,836
Economic Journal	2,269	7,797
Econometrica	1,933	5,356
Journal of Economic Theory	2,058	4,658
Journal of Monetary Economics	1,668	4,010
Journal of Political Economy	2,007	5,984
Quarterly Journal of Economics	1,299	3,391
Review of Economics and Statistics	2,097	6,662
Review of Economic Studies	1,337	2,991

Source: See Table 13.1.

journals continue to be nearly monopolized by the academicians. Only in World War II did the share of academic authors fall below nine-tenths in the five journals we analyze, and that episode simply reflects the large movement of economists into government during that war.

The dominance of these five journals by academic contributors (and their academic editors) ensures that they devote much attention to economic theory. During this century, moreover, economic theory itself has been continuously more abstract and mathematical. It is not easy to characterize precisely the level of technique employed in an article: it may employ advanced techniques only at one point and hence be virtually fully comprehensible to a reader untrained in mathematics. Even when an article's text is wholly verbal, on the other hand, it will usually employ regression techniques or much more advanced econometrics. When we characterize articles by their most advanced techniques, therefore, the assignments are somewhat subjective. No faults of classification, however, could conceal the enormous movement toward mathematics in recent decades (see Table 13.9).

Table 13.5 Ratios of Citations Sent to Journal A by Journal B to Citations Received by B from A

	CITED JOURNAL					
	Land and Resources		Labor			
CITING JOURNAL	American Journal of Agricultural Economics	Land Economics	Industrial and Labour Relations Review	Journal of Human Resources	Journal of Labour Economics	Econometrica, AER, JPE
Land and resources:						
American Journal of Agricultural Economics	1,472	77	*	*	*	798
Land Economics	111	264	*	*	*	239
Labor:						
Industrial and Labor Relations Review	*	*	393	74	52	284
Journal of Human Resources	*	*	42	192	33	415
Journal of Labor Economics	*	*	120	49	108	591
General:						
Econometrica, AER, JPE	21	4	48	78	111	

Note: * No values appeared for these journals in any of the four years that were above the ISI presentation threshold. Thus they were cited a minimum of zero and a maximum of five times in each year.

Source: See Table 13.1

Table 13.6 Number of Citations for Three Leading Financial Journals, 1987-90

	CITED JOURNAL			
CITING JOURNAL	*Journal of Financial Economics*	*Journal of Finance*	*Journal of Financial and Quantitative Analysis*	*Econometrica, AER, JPE*
Journal of Financial Economics	884	317	38	247
Journal of Finance	1,281	1,289	223	822
Journal of Financial and Quantitative Analysis	492	532	201	286
Econometrica, AER, JPE	180	192	14	

Source: See Table 13.1

Table 13.7 Number of Citations for Two Leading History Journals, 1987-90

	CITED JOURNAL		
CITING JOURNAL	*Economic History Review*	*Journal of Economic History*	*Econometrica, AER, JPE*
Economic History Review	374	99	44
Journal of Economic History	107	315	164
Econometrica, AER, JPE	5	45	

Source: See Table 13.1

Table 13.8 Affiliations of Authors in Five Economics Journals

YEARS	PERCENTAGE OF TOTAL ARTICLES			TOTAL NUMBER OF ARTICLES
	Academic	Government	Other*	
1892-93	81.8	7.6	10.6	66
1902-03	74.0	5.2	20.8	77
1912-13	71.9	9.4	18.7	171
1922-23	91.4	4.6	4.0	198
1932-33	95.5	2.7	1.8	240
1942-43	79.5	16.9	3.6	279
1952-53	89.0	7.8	3.2	301
1962-63	93.4	4.3	2.3	394
1972-73[†]	88.1	3.7	8.2	503
1989-90	89.7	7.4	2.9	541

Notes: The journals are *QJE* since 1892, *JPE* since 1892, *AER* since 1912, *REStat* since 1922, and *Ecmca* since 1932.

* "Other" includes business, research institutions, other, and not available. In recent periods they are available in detail: For 1972-73, business is 2.0 percent, research institutions, 2-3 percent. and other and riot available, 3.9 percent; for 1989-90, these figures are, respectively, 0.7 percent, 1.9 percent, and 0.3 percent.

[†] *REStat* omitted affiliation of authors in 1972-73, and it as estimated from the AEA directories; hence the large percentage of "other and not available" in the note above.

Table 13.9 Highest Level of Technique in Articles in Five Economics Journals: Percentage of Total Articles

Years	Primarily Verbal Techniques	Geometry	Algebra and/or Econometrics	Calculus or More Advanced Techniques
1892-93	95	3	2	...
1902-03	92	1	6	...
1912-13	98	1	1	
1922-23	95	1	2	2
1932-33	80	1	8	10
1942-43	65	8	6	2.1
1952-53	56	6	7	3.1
1962-63	33	8	13	46
1989-90	5.3		38.8	55.9

Note: See note to Table 13.8.

Table 13.10   Highest Level of Technique in Individual Journals, 1989-90:
Percentage of Total Articles

Journal	Primarily Verbal Techniques	Algebra and/or Econometrics	Calculus or More Advanced Techniques
Economics journals:			
American Economic Review	10.3	37.4	52.3
Econometrica	1.0	2.0	96.9
Journal of Political Economy	8.7	26.1	65.2
Quarterly Journal of Economics	5.6	50.0	44.4
Review of Economics and Statistics	.8	76.3	22.9
Other fields:			
American Political Science Review	32.0	56.0	12.0
American Sociological Review	28.7	69.7	1.6

Differences among Journals – and Fields

Today economics journals make heavy use of both econometric methods – usually with attendant algebra – and mathematical analysis beginning with calculus and linear algebra and often reaching much higher levels (see Tables 13.9 and 13.10). (We classify articles by the *highest* mathematical technique; thus most of the econometric articles in *Econometrica* are reported in the last column of Table 13.10.) A journal such as *Econometrica* is simply closed to the nonmathematician, and when we take into account its low empirical content, it is indeed surprising that its articles are so extensively cited.

The Influence of Economics Journals

Table 13.11 Articles with Empirical Content, 1989-90

Journal	Percentage of Articles with Empirical Content
Economics journals:	
American Economic Review	37.4
Econometrica	17.4
Journal of Political Economy	52.2
Quarterly Journal of Economics	45.8
Review of Economics and Statistics	96.6
Other fields:	
American Political Science Review	57.3
American Sociological Review	81.2

Empirical Content

The empirical content of an article can be determined only after a most rigorous analysis. It is easy to see whether the article contains tables or data or statistical analyses of data or more informal evidence such as historical applications.[5] In fact, this is the criterion by which we have classified the empirical content of the journals analyzed in Table 13.11.[6] That criterion, however, is unsatisfactory: it treats as nonempirical a paper whose central achievement is the derivation of a set of implications with respect to real economic phenomena.

One wishes that one could state that many theoretical articles do indeed carry their analyses to the very threshold of empirical testing, but that is certainly not the impression that has been left on me after nearly 20 years of editing one of the journals of Table 13.11. Indeed, famous books such as those by Edward Chamberlin (*Theory of Monopolistic Competition*) and John R. Hicks (*Value and Capital*) have escaped serious empirical application. It is a perfectly feasible division of labor for theorists to present implications that empirical workers will utilize; this is exactly what has happened in the field of human capital theory, for example. But usually the theorist is not much interested in empirical applications and does not present his theories in a fashion calculated to facilitate such applications.

V.   EDITORS AND COMPETITION

There is considerable discussion of the possible role of editors in steering disciplines, pushing or suppressing various lines of research. it is certainly true that the tastes of an editor can influence the contents of his Journal. Davis Dewey, editor of the *AER* from 1911 to 1940, made that journal unreceptive to the growing technical rigor and formalization of economics, but the effect was a good deal stronger on the *AER* than on the profession. In effect Dewey subsidized the rise of *Econometrica*. Similarly Keynes's long reign at the *Economic Journal* probably discouraged its publication of econometric work, of which he was a skeptic, again a subsidy to *Econometrica*, and his policies also helped the *Review of Economic Studies*.

These episodes illustrate two important characteristics of journal publication. The first is the existence of competition: no journal in economics has a monopoly of the audience for articles of any general interest. The monopolies, rather quasi monopolies, have occurred in narrowly specialized lines of work: institutional economics in its latter days, Austrian economics even today. The second characteristic is the relative freedom of entry into journal publication, amply illustrated by the 300-odd journals at the present time. Entries such as the *Review of Radical Political Economy* (more than 20 years old) and *Games and Economic Behavior* (new) reveal the market's ready response to relatively few readers.

VI.   A STATISTICAL MODEL FOR CROSS-CITATIONS

The network of citations among economics journals is the product of a complex combination of factors, ranging from scientific influence and social contact to an element of pure chance in the timing of publication of accepted papers. Despite this complexity, some surprisingly revealing insights can be obtained by fitting simple statistical models to the citation data. Table 13.2 above presents four years' data on cross-citations among nine core economics journals. That table by itself is difficult to interpret, in seeming confirmation of the statement "A heavy bank of figures is grievously wearisome to the eye, and the popular mind is as incapable of drawing any useful lessons from it as of extracting sunbeams from cucumbers" (Farquhar and Farquhar, 1891, p.55). Table 13.3 represents a simplification in which at least some semblance of patterns of practice regarding imports and exports of references can be discerned. Further simplification is available through statistical modeling.

The Export Scores Model

A citation is the acknowledgment of a transfer of information. We shall refer to the source journal as sending a *reference* and the consumer of the reference as acknowledging its receipt by means of a citation. The journal that publishes the original article *exports* a reference and the receiving journal *imports* it. The citation experience of a journal will be described by its *export score*, a measure of its propensity to export references to the other journals included in the study. This propensity, which reflects the intellectual influence of the source journal on the recipient, is measured relative to another journal chosen arbitrarily as the *baseline journal*. The scores are susceptible to simple interpretations in terms of betting odds: the difference of the export scores of two journals A and B is the log odds that a citation involving A and B has B citing A as a source for a reference rather than vice versa; the export score of a single journal A is the log odds that a citation involving A and the baseline journal has the baseline journal citing A as the source for a reference rather than vice versa. The larger the export score, the greater the tendency of the journal to export references, the more attractive the journal is to citations, and hence the more influential it is, at least with regard to the collection of journals under study (Stigler, 1994).

The choice of the baseline journal is unimportant, and it may be selected, as a matter of convenience, as the journal with the largest circulation or the journal of the central professional society. The differences among the export scores *are* important. The estimation of these scores and their differences may be thought of as a form of averaging of the logarithms of the ratios of Table 13.3, carried out in the context of an established model for the analysis of categorical data of this type, one sometimes called by the unfortunately opaque name of "the model of quasi symmetry" (e.g., Agresti 1990, pp. 354-5, 382). The use of this model in effect replaces the entire Table 13.3 by a list of nine journal-specific estimated export scores, scores that both linearly order the relative flows of references among these journals and describe the relative magnitudes of these flows. The model ignores the journals' propensity for self-citation and thus succinctly summarizes the information in the $9 \times 9 - 9 = 72$ nondiagonal cells of Table 13.2 in terms of eight parameters (only eight since the choice of baseline journal is arbitrary, and thus only eight differences are needed to specify the nine scores). The model does not describe the entire set of data of Table 13.2 well, but the reasons for this are readily identifiable, and this lack of fit is itself revealing. When the model is applied to a smaller, more homogeneous subset of these journals, the agreement tends to be excellent.

Table 13.12 Export Scores for Nine Core Economics Journals

Journal	1987	1988	1989	1990	1987-90
Econometrica	1.17	.69	1.22	1.18	1.04
Journal of Political Economy	.31	.43	.52	.63	.47
Review of Economic Studies	17	.54	.46	.60	.45
Journal of Economic Theory	.13	.07	.31	.36	.21
Quarterly Journal of Economics	-.19	.17	.09	.14	.05
American Economic Review	.00	.00	.00	.00	.00
Journal of Monetary Economics	-.79	-.79	-.63	.01	-.54
Review of Economics and Statistics	- 1.38	- 1.35	- 1.33	- 1.12	- 1.30
Economic Journal	- 1.20	- 1.62	- 1.33	- 1.28	- 1.37

Note: An export score for a journal is the log odds that a counted citation involving that journal and the baseline journal (the *AER* in this study) has that journal being cited by an article in the baseline journal. The export score of the baseline journal is always 0.00.

The interpretation of the export scores model can perhaps be best explained by presenting the results of fitting it to Table 13.2. Table 13.12 gives the estimated export scores for the analysis of Table 13.2 (in the last column) and for each of the four years' data separately.

These scores can be interpreted as follows. First, the baseline journal (giving a zero point to the scale) has been arbitrarily taken to be the *AER*, the flagship journal of the major North American economic society. The scores themselves may then be directly interpreted as logarithms of betting odds: If one is told only that a citation involves *Econometrica* and the *AER*, then under the model the log odds that it is a citation from *AER* to a source in *Econometrica* (rather than the other way around) would be estimated as 1.04. This corresponds to odds of exp(1.04) = 2.83:1 (or nearly 3:1) that it is a citation from *AER* to a source in *Econometrica* rather than vice versa. Thus as regards bilateral trade in references between these two journals, the export score of 1.04 for *Econometrica* expresses a measure of the balance of trade in favor of *Econometrica* vis-à-vis the *AER*. This score (1.04) can be compared to the logarithm of the corresponding ratio in Table 13.3, namely the ratio of the number of references sent from *Econometrica* to the *AER*, divided by the number of references from the *AER* to *Econometrica*, ln(423/157) = ln(2.69) = 0.99. The statistical analysis presented here uses information involving all the transactions by the journals in the table to produce maximum likelihood estimates of the export scores.

Table 13.13 Results of Fitting the Export Scores Model to the Data of Table 13.2

CITING JOURNAL	JOURNAL B								
	AER	EJ	Ecmca	JET	JME	JPE	QJE	REStat	REStud
American Economic Review									
Observed count	1,090.0	108.0	423.0	136.0	185.0	652.0	275.0	120.0	209.0
Fitted Value		110.9	429.5	143.0	169.6	631.9	295.1	115.2	212.7
Standardized residual		-.280	-.314	-.589	1.182	.801	-1.171	.450	-.257
Economic Journal									
Observed count	440.0	360.0	458.0	103.0	101.0	375.0	160.0	55.0	208.0
Fitted Value	437.1		461.0	103.7	82.2	376.5	163.5	62.8	213.3
Standardized residual	.141		-.139	-.066	2.078	-.079	-.274	-.981	-.364
Econometrica									
Observed count	157.0	44.0	894.0	269.0	43.0	170.0	92.0	35.0	229.0
Fitted Value	150.5	41.0		283.0	53.4	176.9	79.7	39.5	215.0
Standardized residual	.530	.468		-.838	-1.419	-.519	1.383	-.711	.954
Journal of Economic Theory									
Observed count	123.0	22.0	669.0	754.0	7.0	126.0	100.0	5.0	252.0
Fitted Value	116.0	21.3	654.9		36.5	132.4	91.1	5.4	246.4
Standardized residual	.654	.145	.551		-4.887	-.555	.936	-.191	.359

Journal of Monetary Economics

Observed count	276.0	**17.0**	272.0	**107.0**	455.0	362.0	87.0	27.0	65.0
Fitted Value	291.4	**35.8**	261.6	**77.5**		348.7	92.7	39.0	66.3
Standardized residual	-.902	**-3.146**	.641	**3.357**		.712	-.589	-1.924	-.158

Journal of Political Economy

Observed count	373.0	61.0	321.0	108.0	113.0	646.0	155.0	75.0	155.0
Fitted Value	393.1	59.5	314.1	101.6	126.3		152.2	56.2	158.2
Standardized residual	-1.016	.198	.389	.634	-1.182		.228	2.536	-.253

Quarterly Journal of Economics

Observed count	301.0	43.0	204.0	98.0	57.0	230.0	220.0	32.0	114.0
Fitted Value	280.9	39.5	216.3	106.9	51.3	232.8		26.9	124.3
Standardized residual	1.200	.557	-.839	-.863	.791	-.184		.991	-.927

Review of Economics and Statistics

Observed count	416.0	66.0	416.0	25.0	95.0	310.0	98.0	574.0	97.0
Fitted Value	420.8	58.2	411.5	24.6	83.0	329.0	103.1		92.7
Standardized residual	-.236	1.019	.220	.090	1.319	-1.047	-.506		.442

Review of Economic Studies

Observed count	140.0	40.0	379.0	189.0	26.0	166.0	94.0	12.0	291.0
Fitted Value	136.3	34.7	393.0	194.6	24.7	162.8	83.7	16.3	
Standardized residual	.321	.903	-.705	-.404	.260	.249	1.130	-1.055	

Note: The standardized (Pearson) residual equals $(O-E)/\sqrt{E}$. The diagonal entries are ignored in fitting the model. For this fit, $G^2 = 106.1$ and $\chi^2 = 93.3$, both with 28 degrees of freedom; the contribution to the χ^2 statistic from the three highlighted cells alone is 45.1.

The scores describe more than just the set of bilateral trades between the core journals and the *AER*; through their differences they describe the entire network of all bilateral trade in references. For example, if we wish to inquire about the bilateral trade between the *Journal of Economic Theory* and the *Economic Journal*, we need only compute the difference of estimated scores $0.21 - (-1.37) = 1.58$; this estimates the log odds that a citation involving these two journals comes from the journal with the lower score to a source in the higher. (As we mentioned earlier, we may think of the scores as representing the relative attractiveness of the journals to citations and hence relative influence.) Thus in the given example, the odds are estimated to be about $\exp(1.58) = 4.85:1$ (nearly 5:1) that the citation goes from the *Economic Journal* to the source *Journal of Economic Theory* rather than vice versa. Log odds of 0.0 would correspond to odds of 1:1, a precise balance of trade.

There is virtue in the simplicity of a model that permits us to describe all $\binom{9}{2} = 36$ bilateral arrangements in terms of but eight scores in an additive fashion. The model has been used in population studies to describe migratory patterns in terms of a one-dimensional scale of geographical attractiveness. The problem with the simplicity of the model is that we have no right to expect that such a complex situation can be adequately described in such simple terms (see, e.g., Eagly, 1975; Quandt, 1976; Garfield, 1979; Leijonhufvud, 1991). Indeed the model does exhibit lack of fit. The log likelihood ratio statistic for this fit is $G^2 = 106.1$ and $\chi^2 = 93.3$, either of which should be compared to a χ^2 distribution with 28 degrees of freedom (for 28 degrees of freedom, the 1 percent point of the χ^2 distribution is 48.3). Still, this is not all that bad with such a large sample size, and it suggests looking to see whether the lack of fit can be traced to a few significant interactions. This does indeed seem to be the case. Table 13.13 gives the fitted values for this model and the standardized (Pearson) residuals.

This residual analysis reveals that the preponderance of lack of fit involves the *Journal of Monetary Economics*, and by far the most significant interaction involves the cross-citations between the *Journal of Monetary Economics* and the *Journal of Economic Theory*: the *Journal of Monetary Economics* cited the *Journal of Economic Theory* far more frequently than the model predicts and was cited far less frequently than predicted. This suggests a textual analysis, which we have not carried out. We can report that a major portion of this anomaly is due to counts recorded for the year 1990. Other interactions can be noted, both on the combined data and in the individual years, but they are of lesser magnitude. With the exception of the *Journal of Economic Theory/Journal of Monetary*

Table 13.14 Export Scores for the Four Central Economics Journals Alone

Journal	1987-90
Journal of Political Economy	.50
American Economic Review	.00
Quarterly Journal of Economics	-.02
Economic Journal	- 1.36

Economics anomaly, the export scores model does a fairly good job of summarizing in a compact manner all the cross-citation practices of the core journals.

The Market in References among the Four Central Economics Journals

This description of trade in references is of course incomplete; this is not a closed economy. For example, *Econometrica* plays an important role in the narrower field of econometrics and the broader field of statistics, and it imports references from both sources. It is interesting to look at a more homogeneous subset of economics journals, consisting of the four central general economics journals. This of course is not a closed economy either, but it is one that has no major well-separated exterior market (in contrast to *Econometrica*). If we refit the model for these four economics journals, the fit is remarkably good, giving $G^2 = 3.26$ with three degrees of freedom. Table 13.14 gives the estimated export scores for these journals alone, which agree quite closely with the scores they received in the previous fit.

Among these journals, there is an essentially even balance of trade between the *AER* and the *QJE*, and each of these imports references from the *JPE* in a ratio of about exp(.5) = 1.65: 1 over exports to the *JPE*. And, in turn, each of the *AER* and the *QJE* exports references to the *Economic Journal* in a ratio of about exp(1.36) = 3.9:1 over imports from the *Economic Journal*. The *JPE* exports references to the *Economic Journal* in a ratio of about exp[.50 – (–1.36)] = 6.42:1 over imports. We thus can give quantitative expression to the statement that the *JPE* is a net exporter of influence to the other three journals, the *AER* and the *QJE* are approximately equally influential, and the *Economic Journal* is a more distant net consumer of the products of the other three.

Other Comparisons

This same analysis can be applied to the data of Table 13.5 on the

Table 13.15 Export Scores for Core vs. Applied Economics Journals

Journal	Export Score
	Core vs. Agricultural Economics journals
Econometrica, AER, JPE	3.65
American Journal of Agricultural Economics	.00
Land Economics	-.37
	Core vs. Labor Economics journals
Econometrica, AER, JPE	1.60
Journal of Human Resources	.11
Industrial and Labor Relations Review	.00
Journal of Labor Economics	-.31

commerce in information between the selected applied journals and the leading general journals, and to the cross-citations between the general journals and those in finance and in economic history. The results, described in Tables 13.15-21, show a large imbalance of trade between the general and applied journals: the difference of estimated export scores between the general journals and the applied journals ranges from 1.82 to 4.02, corresponding to odds ranging from 6.2:1 to 55:1 in favor of a citation (involving a general journal and an applied journal) going from an applied journal to a general source. The major general journals are massive exporters of references and hence exporters of that type of influence measured by citations. The model fits very well except in the case of the labor economics journals. A reasonable hypothesis is that this lack of fit reflects the fact that one of the journals included was relatively new, being founded in 1983, and it had not yet settled down to a stable citation pattern by 1987. As support for this, the model does fit quite well the data for 1987 and 1990 alone (although not for 1988-89), and the trend in scores shows the increased visibility of the recently founded *Journal of Labor Economics* (Table 13.17). See Stigler (1994) for a proof that the scores are not biased by aggregating journals into a single class, as here.

The propensities for the three leading general journals to export references to the three major finance journals are highly varied, but they are accounted for by the model reasonably well (Tables 13.18 and 13.19). The trade between these same journals and two economic history journals is more balanced (and the model fits very well), but here we are dealing with two largely separate economies: There is very little acknowledged trade between these groups.

Table 13.16 Results of Fitting the Export Scores Model to the Data of Table 13.5

A. AGRICULTURAL ECONOMICS JOURNALS

	CITED JOURNAL		
CITING JOURNAL	American Journal of Agricultural Economics	Land Economics	Econometrica, AER, JPE
American Journal of Agricultural Economics:			
Observed count	1,472.0	77.0	798.0
Fitted value		76.7	798.3
Standardized residual		.313	-.010
Land Economics:			
Observed count	111.0	264.0	239.0
Fitted value	111.3		238.7
Standardized residual	-.026		.018
Econometrica, AER, JPE:			
Observed count	21.0	4.0	4,726.0
Fitted value	20.7	4.3	
Standardized residual	.060	-.132	

B. LABOR ECONOMICS JOURNALS

	CITED JOURNAL			
CITING JOURNAL	Industrial and Labor Relations	Journal of Human Resources	Journal of Labor Economics	Econometrica, AER, JPE
Industrial and Labor Relations Review:				
Observed count	393.0	74.0	52,0	284.0
Fitted value		61.1	72.8	276.2
Standardized residual		1.654	-2,434	.472
Journal of Human Res.:				
Observed count	42.0	192.0	33.0	415.0
Fitted value	54.9		32.6	402.5
Standardized residual	- 1.744		.073	.623
Journal of Labor Economics:				
Observed count	120.0	49.0	108.0	591.0
Fitted value	99.2	49.4		611.3
Standardized residual	2.085	-.059		-.823
Ecmca, AER, JPE:				
Observed count	48.0	78.0	111.0	4,726.0
Fitted value	55.8	90.5	90.6	
Standardized residual	- 1.049	- 1.315	2,137	

Note: The diagonal entries are ignored in fitting the model. For this fit, for the agricultural economics journals, $G^2 = \chi^2 = 0.02$, both with one degree of freedom (a good fit); for the labor economics journals, $G^2 = 25.06$ and $\chi^2 = 24.73$, both with three degrees of freedom.

Table 13.17 Export Scores for Core vs. Applied Economics Journals

JOURNAL	EXPORT SCORE	
	1987	1990
Econometrica, AER, JPE	1.61	1.69
Journal of Human Resources	.02	.31
Industrial and Labor Relations Review	.00	.00
Journal of Labor Economics	-.84	-.32

Note: The table demonstrates the increased visibility of the *Journal of Labor Economics* (founded in 1983). In both cases the fit is excellent, with χ^2=4.48 and χ^2=8.03, respectively, both with three degrees of freedom.

Table 13.18 Export Scores for Core vs. Finance Journals

Journal	Export Score
Econometrica, AER, JPE	.20
Journal of Financial Economics	.00
Journal of Finance	- 1.38
Journal of Financial and Quantitative Analysis	- 2.35

Comparing Segregation of the Markets

The export scores model helps analyze bilateral trade between journals, but it pays no attention to the extent of the trade. If journals A and B each cite the other 100 times, the model is indifferent whether this is 100 out of 200 or 100 out of 100,000; that is, it does not distinguish among journals that enter the same discourse relatively frequently or relatively seldom. One way to examine the extent to which two groups of journals interact is to form a simple two-way dichotomy of their cross-citations, as is done in Tables 13.22-26. Standard methods can then be employed to measure the association in the 2 × 2 tables. The most common such measures are all functions of the odds ratio θ (the ratio of the empirical odds of left vs. right column in row 1 to the same odds in row 2). Two of these, the log odds ratio $\ln(\theta)$ and Yule's $Q = (\theta - 1)/(\theta + 1)$, are given in Table 13.27 for the comparisons discussed earlier. Yule's Q is a special case (for 2 × 2 tables) of a more general measure known as Goodman and Kruskal's γ.

It is evident that the degree of segregation varies widely. If we let A denote the group consisting of the three leading core journals, then the odds ratio

Table 13.19 Results of Fitting the Export Scores Model to the Data on Finance Journals

	CITED JOURNAL			
CITING JOURNAL	*Journal of Financial Economics*	*Journal of Finance*	*Journal of Financial and Quantitative Analysis*	*Econometrica, AER, JPE*
Journal of Financial Economics:				
Observed count	884.0	317.0	38.0	247.0
Fitted value		320.8	46.0	235.2
Standardized residual		-.214	- 1.180	.772
Journal of Finance:				
Observed count	1,281.0	1,289.0	223.0	822.0
Fitted value	1,277.2		207.3	841.5
Standardized residual	.107		1.094	-.674
Journal of Financial and Quantitative Analysis:				
Observed count	492.0	532.0	201.0	286.0
Fitted value	484.0	547.7		278.4
Standardized residual	.365	-.670		.455
Econometrica, AER, JPE:				
Observed count	180.0	192.0	14.0	4,726.0
Fitted value	191.8	172.5	21.8	
Standardized residual	-.855	1,488	- 1.671	

Note: The diagonal entries are ignored in fitting the model. For this fit, $G^2 = 10.56$ and $\chi^2 = 10.17$, both with three degrees of freedom; this is a marginal fit ($.025 > P > .01$), but with no pronounced interactions.

Table 13.20 Export Scores for Core vs. Economic History Journals

Journal	Export Score
Econometrica, AER, JPE	1.43
Journal of Economic History	.01
Economic History Review	.00

$$\theta = \frac{\text{odds that a group A journal will cite in group A vs. citing in group B}}{\text{odds that a group B journal will cite in group A vs. citing in group B}}$$

varies from 1.75 (when group B is the remaining core journals) to 407 (when group B is the economic history journals). In the former case we have what is basically one market, divided on the basis of citation-measured influence; in the latter case, we have two fairly distinct groups of journals, not in frequent dialogue.

How to Fit the Export Scores Model

What we call the export scores model is known more generally in the categorical data literature as the model of quasi symmetry or the symmetric association model (Goodman, 1979; Agresti, 1990), and it is essentially equivalent to a model known in the literature on paired comparisons as the Bradley-Terry model (Fienberg and Larntz, 1976; David, 1988; McCullagh and Nelder, 1989). It can be fit easily using any program that can fit general log-linear models. One way to do this for an $n \times n$ table of cross-citation counts is simply to form a three-dimensional $n \times n \times 2$ table whose bottom layer is the original $n \times n$ table and whose top layer is the $n \times n$ table formed by reflecting the original table about its main diagonal. Treating all categories as nominal factors, fit the model of "no three-factor interactions." The estimates of the export scores are then given by the estimated two-factor interactions between the rows and the artificially constructed third-dimensional factor. If the model is fit by the program GLIM and the baseline journal counts are given in the first row and column, then the estimated export scores are given directly as the estimated interactions, the appropriate log likelihood ratio statistic G^2 is half that given by the output, and the correct number of degrees of freedom is calculated as $(n - 1)(n - 2)/2$. The standardized (Pearson) residuals are computed as:

Table 13.21 Results of Fitting the Export Scores Model to the Data on Economic History Journals

CITING JOURNALS	CITED JOURNALS		
	Economic History Review	Journal of Economic History	Econometrica, AER, JPE
Economic History Review:			
Observed count	374.0	99.0	44.0
Fitted value		103.4	39.6
Standardized residual		-.437	.706
Journal of Economic History:			
Observed count	107.0	315.0	164.0
Fitted value	102.6		168.4
Standardized residual	.439		-.342
Econometrica, AER, JPE:			
Observed count	5.0	45.0	4,726.0
Fitted value	9.4	40.6	
Standardized residual	- 1.446	.698	

Note: The diagonal entries are ignored in fitting the model. For this fit, $G^2=3.98$ and $\chi^2=3.57$, both with one degree of freedom, a reasonably close fit.

Table 13.22 Segregation Between the Three Leading Core and Six Other Core Journals

CITING JOURNALS	CITED JOURNALS	
	Six Other Core Journals	Econometrica, AER, JPE
Six other core.journals	5,065	5,663
Econometrica, AER, JPE	2,412	4,726

$$\text{standardized residual} = \frac{\text{observed count} - \text{fitted count}}{\sqrt{\text{fitted count}}}$$

if squared and summed, they give the χ^2 statistic for testing fit, and they give an indication of the cell's contribution to the lack of fit.

Table 13.23 Segregation Between the Three Leading Core and Two Agricultural Economics Journals

CITING JOURNALS	CITED JOURNALS	
	Two Agricultural Economics Journals	*Econometrica, AER, JPE*
Two Agricultural Economics Journals	1,924	1,037
Econometrica, AER, JPE	25	4,726

Table 13.24 Segregation Between the Three Leading Core and Three Labor Economics Journals

CITING JOURNALS	CITED JOURNALS	
	Three Labor Economics Journals	*Econometrica, AER, JPE*
Three Labor Economics Journals	1,065	1,290
Econometrica, AER, JPE	237	4,726

Table 13.25 Segregation Between the Three Leading Core and Three Finance Journals

CITING JOURNALS	CITED JOURNALS	
	Three Finance Journals	*Econometrica, AER, JPE*
Three Labor Economics Journals	5,257	1,355
Econometrica, AER, JPE	386	4,726

Table 13.26 Segregation Between the Three Leading Core and Two Economic History Journals

CITING JOURNALS	CITED JOURNALS	
	Two Economic History Journals	*Econometrica, AER, JPE*
Three Labor Economics Journals	895	208
Econometrica, AER, JPE	50	4,726

Table 13.27 Measures of Market Segregation Based on the Odds Ratio θ for Tables 13.22-26

	ECONOMETRICA, AER, AND JPE vs				
	Six Other Core Journals	Three Labor Journals	Three Finance Journals	Two Agricultural Economics Journals	Two Economic History Journals
θ	1.75	14.29	49.82	350.74	406.71
ln (θ)	.56	2.66	3.91	5.86	6.01
$Q = \frac{\theta-1}{\theta+1}$	.27	.87	.96	.99	1.00

Note: Large values indicate a high degree of segregation; Q measures association on a scale from −1 to 1.

In interpreting the result of these fits, one should take the standard tests as only a guide. The standard statistical model that would justify them is that of multinomial sampling, where the sending journal distributes its references (or the receiving journal distributes its citations) as a roulette wheel with unequal probabilities, producing a random array of counts in repeated independent spins. Citations, however, appear in clusters, attracted to a relatively small number of influential papers that are themselves distributed among the various journals. This increases the variability in the counts and in extreme cases can produce anomalies of the type noted in some of the analyses. The suggested procedure is nonetheless to apply this standard analysis, cautiously. If the tests reveal no pronounced lack of fit (with a fairly relaxed criterion, such as $P < .01$) and no striking anomalies in the pattern of residuals, then the fit can be accepted as capturing the major directions of the movement of information and the estimates of export scores taken seriously as indicative of citation-measured influence, relative to the collection of journals included in the study. Estimated standard errors for the scores ranged from 0.04 to 0.09 in the studies given here. If lack of fit is indicated but the preponderance is due to a few identified cells, then the score may still be used, subject to the obvious disclaimer for those situations in which such interaction (meaning departure from the additive model for log odds) is indicated. In other cases, reanalysis for a more homogeneous set of journals is suggested. In the experience reflected here, the fits have tended to be good for small sets of journals or sets of homogeneous journals, and even in the largest analysis (that of all core journals) a clear and useful set of messages emerged. It is recommended that the residuals be examined in all cases. Stigler (1994) applies this model to journals in statistics and their relationship with econometrics and economics.

NOTES

1.   As a consequence of omitting these journals, the first volume of the American Economic Association's *Index of Economic Journals* (1886-1924) is seriously inadequate.
2.   The Institute for Scientific Information, publisher of the *Social Sciences Citation Index*, has been kind enough to provide us with the cross-citation figures below their presentation threshold for the nine core journals and for most of the other journals appearing in this section; we have arbitrarily assigned a value of three in a few missing cases when the receiving journal did not appear above the threshold value.
3.   We arrived at our list of nine major, or core, journals by the following method: starting with the top 455 social science journals ranked by citations received in 1988 from all social science journals (Garfield, 1988, p. 19), we identified 52 as economics, or related, journals. From these 52 we excluded those not listed as economics journals by the AEA, as well as some extremely specialized journals (e.g., in accounting or consumer research) other than those specialized in fields we, initially, intended to analyze separately (history, finance, labor, agriculture, and law and economics; we excluded the *Journal of Legal Studies*, which receives the bulk of its citations from law journals). From the remaining 36 journals, we chose as the nine core journals those general or macroeconomics journals cited more than 700 times in 1987 and 1988 by the 36 journals combined. (Citations for 1989 and 1990 were made available to us at a later stage in our analysis.) See also Diamond (1989) on core journals. For other, earlier investigations of cross-citations involving economics journals, see Eagly (1975) and Quandt (1976).
4.   A well-known economic historian once complained to me that the *JPE* published little economic history. I asked him to go through our files of rejected articles and find a good article in economic history that we had rejected. He found none among the negligible number we had received. The specialization of journals is a matter of supply as well as demand.
5.   Of course in a field such as intellectual history there is seldom a role for empirical information.
6.   In this table we treat both simulations and classroom experiments as nonempirical. For a recent examination of the empirical content of economics journals, see Figlio (1994).

REFERENCES

Agresti, Alan (1990), *Categorical Data Analysis*, New York: Wiley.

Coats, A.W. (1960), "The First Two Decades of the American Economic Association," *American Economic Review*, **50**, 555-74.

David, Herbert A. (1988), *The Method of Paired Comparisons*, 2nd ed., London: Griffin.

Diamond, Arthur M., Jr. (1989), "The Core Journals of Economics," *Current Contents*, 3-11.

Eagly, Robert V. (1975), "Economics Journals as a Communications Network," *Journal of Economic Literature*, **13**, 878-88.

Farquhar, Arthur B., and Henry Farquhar (1891), *Economic and Industrial Delusions: A Discussion of the Case for Protection*, New York: Putnam's.

Fienberg, Stephen E., and Kinley Larntz (1976), "Log Linear Representation for Paired and Multiple Comparisons Models," *Biometrika*, **63**, 245-54.

Figlio, David (1994), "Trends in the Publication of Empirical Economics," *Journal of Economic Perspectives*, **8**, 179-87.

Garfield, Eugene (1979) *Citation Indexing: Its Theory and Application in Science, Technology, and Humanities*, New York: Wiley.

Garfield, Eugene (ed.) (1987, 1988), *Social Sciences Citation Index*, Vol.6, *SSCI Journal Citation Report,* Philadelphia: Inst. Scientific Information.

Goodman, Leo A. (1979), "Simple Models for the Analysis of Association in Cross Classifications Having Ordered Categories," *Journal of the American Statistical Association*, **74**, 537-52.

Leijonhufvud, Axel, (ed.) (1991), "The Learned Journals in the Development of Economics and the Economics Profession: Proceedings of a conference," *Economic Notes,* **20**, 1991.

McCullagh, Peter, and John A. Nelder (1989), *Generalized Linear Models,* 2d ed., London: Chapman & Hall.

National Science Foundation. (1990), *U.S. Scientists and Engineers: 1988*, Document no.90-314, Washington: Natural Science Foundation.

Quandt, Richard E. (1976), "Some Quantitative Aspects of the Economics Journal Literature," *Journal of Political Economics*, **84**, 741-55.

Stigler, George J., and Claire Friedland (1979), "The Pattern of Citation Practices in Economics," *History of Political Economics*, **11**, 1-20. Reprinted in *The Economist as Preacher, and Other Essays*, by George J. Stigler, Chicago: Univ. Chicago Press, 1982.

Stigler, Stephen M. (1994), "Citation Patterns in the Journals of Statistics and Probability," *Statistical Science*, **9**, 94-108.

14. The Scholarly Journal Literature of Economics: A Historical Profile of the *AER*, *JPE*, and *QJE**

David N. Laband and John M. Wells

INTRODUCTION

The scholarly journal literature in economics recently entered into its second century. Of the three major general journals in economics, the *Quarterly Journal of Economics* is the elder statesman, having commenced publication in 1886. The inaugural issue of the *Journal of Political Economy* was published in December 1892. Although the American Economic Association was founded in 1885, the first issue of the *American Economic Review* did not appear until 1911. These three journals are widely regarded as the major, general-interest journals in economics, a position they have occupied for decades (Laband and Piette, 1994). Most of the notable contributions to economic science during the twentieth century have been published, in part or in whole, by these journals, taken as a group.[1]

In this paper, we provide a detailed profile of the scholarly literature published in the *AER, JPE,* and *QJE* from their respective inceptions

* Reprinted with permission of the copyright holder from the *American Economist*, Vol.42, No.2, Fall 1998, pp. 47-59.

Auburn University. The data collection for this paper was accomplished while Laband was a Visiting Fellow in the Director's Section of the Research School of Social Sciences at the Australian National University during the summer of 1996. Without the financial support and scholarly hospitality provided by the RSSS, this analysis would not have been possible. Special thanks to Linda Gosnell for superb and heartwarming assistance and to James Barth, Richard Beil, and John Sophocleus for useful comments and suggestions.

through 1995. This includes an overview of the changing relative importance of articles, book reviews, and notes, comments and short papers published. We then examine the historical pattern of contributions by nonacademic authors and by female authors. Finally, we identify ebbs and flows in the topical coverage represented in this literature.

OVERVIEW

Figure 14.1 profiles the number of feature articles published (in the aggregate) in the *AER, QJE,* and *JPE.*[2]

The overall trend revealed by Figure 14.1 suggests a fairly steady increase over time in the aggregate number of articles published in these three journals. This is, however, slightly misleading. For the six year period 1886-1891, as well as for most of 1892, only the *QJE* was being published, thus the number of articles published per year is relatively small. The jump in 1893 results from this being the first full year of publication of the *JPE.* For the next 18 years the average number of articles published by both the *QJE* and *JPE* remains fairly constant. When the *AER* was introduced in 1911, the number of articles published per year (by all 3 journals combined) doubled from, in approximate numbers, 40 to 80. With acknowledged volatility, this aggregate number of articles published per year remained relatively constant for over 50 years, until 1969. In that year the *Journal of Economic Literature* began publishing book reviews for the AEA, which freed up significant page space in the *AER* for publication of additional scholarly articles. Since 1969, the number of articles published per year in the *AER* has been very stable, in the low-to-mid 50s. The *JPE*, which like the *AER*, had historically published large numbers of book reviews, also exhibits a large increase in the number of articles published per year at that time. The *QJE* exhibits a pattern of slow, steady growth over the years, excepting 1980 and 1985, when the editors responded to significant backlogs of accepted papers by publishing supplemental issues. This relatively slow growth in the number of feature articles published per year suggests that the rapid expansion of economic literature since the late 1800s noted by Lovell (1973) has occurred primarily on the extensive margin (i.e., new journals), rather than on the intensive margin (increased production by existing journals).

A profile of the total number of article-pages published per year looks very similar to the profile in Figure 14.1 of the number of articles published

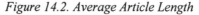

Figure 14.1 AER/JPE/QJE Articles Published per Year

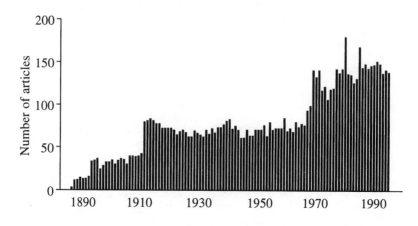

Figure 14.2. Average Article Length

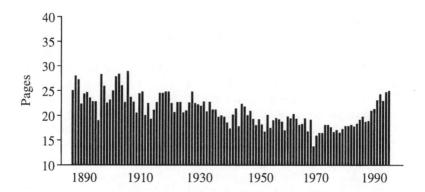

per year. While this suggests that the average length of an article has remained fairly constant over time, this is not so (Figure 14.2).

Prior to 1970, there was considerable volatility from year to year with respect to the average length of a journal article published in these three journals. This is especially evident during the late 1800s and early 1900s. From 1886 through 1969, the annual volatility notwithstanding, there was a gradual decline in the average length of an article from roughly 23 pages to approximately 17 pages. Since 1970, there has been a relatively rapid

Table 14.1 The Impact of JEL Subject Code on Article Length--OLS
Regression Results (Dependent Variable = Page Length of
Feature Articles)

Explanatory Variable	Coefficient Estimate^	Estimated Article Length
Constant	19.447[***] (0.243)	
JEL--100, Econ. Growth & Development	0.895[**] (0.390)	20.342
JEL--200, Quant. Econ. Methods & Data	1.865[***] (0.653)	21.312
JEL--300, Monetary & Fiscal Theory & Inst.	-0.09 (0.316)	19.353
JEL--400, International Economics	-1.129 (-0.349)	18.318
JEL--500, Business Administration	1.738[***] (0.631)	21.185
JEL--600, Industrial Organization	1.915[***] (0.388)	21.362
JEL--700, Agriculture, Natural Resources	0.798 (0.555)	20.245
JEL--800, Manpower, Labor, Population	1.163[***] (0.333)	20.610
JEL--900, Welfare Programs, Consumer Economics, Urban & Regional Economics	0.894[**] (0.448)	20.341

Notes: R-squared = 0.0095

F_{reg} = 9.2034[***]

N = 8667

^ standard error in parentheses

[***] t-statistic significant at 0.01 level

[**] t-statistic significant at 0.05 level

increase in the average length of an article and, simultaneously, much lower year-to-year volatility than previously. As of 1995, the average length of a feature article published in the *AER*, *JPE* and *QJE* had climbed back up to 23 pages.

In Table 14.1, we present Ordinary Least Squares (OLS) regression

Figure 14.3 Total Pages: Articles + Notes and Comments

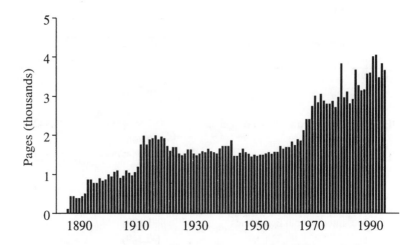

results for our estimation of the impact of JEL subject code on page-length of the feature articles in our sample. The historical mean length of a feature article published in the *AER*, *JPE*, or *QJE* is 19.45 pages. However, articles written on general economic theory (JEL subject code 000) are significantly shorter than those written in 6 of the 9 other subject codes. Only articles written on International Trade (JEL code 400) are significantly shorter (by about 6 percent) than articles on general economic theory. In contrast, papers written on Business Administration (JEL code 500) Industrial Organization, Technical Change, and Industry Studies (JEL code 600), and on Quantitative Methods and Data (JEL code 200) are nearly 10 percent longer, on average, than papers written on general economic theory.

The profile of the number of pages per year devoted to feature articles and notes, comments, and short papers (Figure 14.3) looks quite similar to the profile recorded in Figure 14.1. However, the fraction of pages devoted to notes, comments and short papers shows enormous variation over time (Figure 14.4). The historical average for this fraction is just under 0.2, but it has climbed as high as 0.5 and dipped below 0.1.

There are at least three possible, not mutually exclusive, interpretations of the variation in the fraction of page space devoted to notes and comments. First, particular editors may have played significant, albeit idiosyncratic, roles with respect to the structure of scholarly contributions published in these three top journals. Second, the increasing number of scholarly journals that "specialize" in short papers (e.g., *Economics Letters*,

Figure 14.4 Fraction of Pages Devoted to Notes/Comments

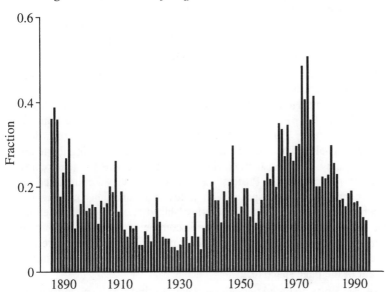

Applied Economics Letters) may have led authors of such papers to alter their submission strategies such that fewer notes and comments have been submitted in recent decades to the *AER*, *JPE*, and *QJE* than might otherwise have been the case, ceteris paribus.

Our analysis of the data provides support for both of these suppositions. In unreported empirical work we estimated the impact of specific editors on the percentage of page space in the *AER*, *JPE*, and *QJE* devoted to feature articles, notes and comments, and book reviews. For the *AER* and *JPE*, the omitted editors that the others are normalized against are the inaugural editors (D. Dewey for the *AER*, L. Laughlin for the *JPE*). The first editor of the *QJE* to be identified explicitly was Ed Chamberlin (whose tenure started July 1, 1948).[3] Thus, our analysis of the changing structure of the *QJE* began with Professor Chamberlin's editorship, on whom the estimated impacts of subsequent editors are based. Each editor's term was coded to extend one year beyond his/her nominal ending date, to account for the lag in publication of accepted papers.

We found substantial variation across journals and across editors of the same journal, with respect to the emphasis placed on publication of feature articles, notes/comments, and book reviews. For example, approximately 96 percent of the page space in the *JPE* in recent years has been devoted to feature articles. By contrast, an estimated 88 percent of the page space in the *QJE* in recent years has been allocated to feature articles, and only 73 percent of the page space in the *AER* has been so allocated. Indeed, while it is true that during the 1990s the *AER* has emphasized feature articles less than the *JPE* and *QJE*, Professor Ashenfelter has devoted a higher percentage of the *Review*'s page space to feature articles than any previous editor except the founding editor, Davis Dewey.

Professor Dewey (1911-40) devoted nearly all (95 percent) of the Review to feature articles, a structural prerogative that was changed radically by Paul Homans, who succeeded him. Shortly after assuming the editorship in 1941, Professor Homans started publishing large numbers of book reviews (e.g., 150 in 1942). This came at the expense of space devoted to feature articles, which declined to about 50 percent. During the tenure of Bernard Haley, and then John Gurley, page space devoted to feature articles fell to 46 percent. Under Professor Haley, book reviews constituted nearly 43 percent of the page space, with notes and comments making up the remaining 11 percent. Professor Gurley placed relatively greater emphasis than his predecessors on notes and comments, making this type of contribution nearly one-quarter of the total content of the Review. This came at the expense of book reviews, which he devoted just under 30 percent of the page space to.

George Borts assumed the helm in 1969, to find that he no longer needed to publish book reviews (which gave him 30 percent more page space to devote to feature articles and shorter contributions). Much of this additional space he allocated to feature articles, resulting in two-thirds of the *Review*'s total page space being devoted to feature articles and one-third devoted to shorter contributions. This distribution was followed closely by Professor Clower. Professor Ashenfelter, as noted previously, has placed an even greater emphasis on feature articles.

Traditionally, feature articles have constituted between two-thirds and three-fourths of the page space in the *JPE*, although the idiosyncrasies of specific editors are quite apparent. James Field, followed by John Clark, emphasized feature articles and de-emphasized book reviews, relative to the mix that characterized the 34-year tenure of founding editor Lawrence Laughlin. Jacob Viner (during his stint as solo editor) also tended to emphasize publication of feature articles, but this emphasis came at the expense of shorter contributions, not book reviews. More recently, Robert Mundell, followed closely by George Stigler and then Gary Becker, devoted an increasingly high fraction of the Journal's page space to feature articles. During the 1990s, less than 5 percent of the page space of the *JPE* has consisted of notes/comments and book reviews.

Of the three journals, the *QJE* has exhibited the least volatility over time with respect to the content mix, at least during the past 50 years. For most of this time, the editors have devoted at least 84 percent of the page space to feature articles and virtually no space to book reviews. Robert Mundell (1971-75) is the only exception; he significantly de-emphasized feature articles while devoting over a quarter of the *QJE*'s page space to shorter contributions.

We observed that controlling for editorial idiosyncrasies explains between 50 and 95 percent of the variation in the percent of page space in these 3 top journals devoted to feature articles, and between 50 and 90 percent of the variation in the percent of page space devoted to notes and comments.

To investigate whether the emergence of new journals that specialized in publishing short contributions led to a reduction in the percentage of page space in the *AER*, *JPE*, and *QJE* devoted to notes and comments, we searched for break dates in the times series for the percent of page space devoted to feature articles, notes/comments, and book reviews (see Bai, Lumsdaine, and Stock, 1997). We found two years with revealed regime changes that were consistent across journals: 1968 signaled an abrupt decline in the publication of book reviews in the *AER*, *JPE*, and *QJE*, while 1977 is associated with a decline in the fraction of page space devoted by all three journals to short articles, notes, comments., and replies (and a concomitant increase in page space devoted to feature articles). This corresponds closely with the inauguration of *Economics Letters* in 1978. It seems reasonable to suspect that at least some of the variation in the distribution of content between feature articles, short contributions and book reviews reflects the impact of competition in the scholarly economics journal market.

It may also be the case that occasional contributions to the corpus of economic science are of such significance as to incite a great deal of professional commentary. That is, notes and comments are lagging indicators of significant intellectual contributions. To the extent this may be true, it suggests that one might profitably scrutinize periods characterized by relatively high fractions of notes/comments in a recursive search for the "theoretical diamonds," "harvests," or "creative insights" (Vandermeulen, 1972) that birthed the commentary. It might, be argued that the sharp drop in the fraction of pages devoted to notes/comments since the mid-1970s is consistent with this interpretation, on two counts. On one hand, there may have been a relatively sharp decline in the number of truly significant contributions to economic science since the 1970s. On the other (not necessarily mutually exclusive) hand, the computer revolution since the mid-1970s dramatically lowered the cost of conducting extensive empirical tests of hypotheses. Prior to this technological revolution, notes and comments tended to provide anecdotal evidence to buttress or contradict proposed theories. As the cost of conducting (and publishing) either

Figure 14.5 Total Pages Published – All Academic Material

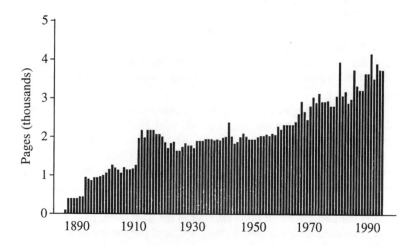

competing or complementary analyses, of power and significance in their own right, in response to a particularly provocative scholarly contribution declined, the relative importance of this type of professional contribution likely increased, with a consequent decline in notes and comments.

In Figure 14.5, the total pages of academic literature (including feature articles, notes, comments and short papers, and book reviews) published per year by the *AER*, *JPE*, and *QJE* is profiled. As in earlier years, there is a step function increase in total pages published up through and including 1911, as the *JPE* and *AER* enter the picture, so to speak. Prior to World War II the production of academic literature by these 3 journals hit its peak in the years immediately after the *AER* started publication in 1911. Production fell from 1911 through 1924. Since then, there has been a steady increase in total production of academic literature. During World War II again there was a drop in total pages published per year, but this did not change the trend line. As is clear from Figure 14.6, all three journals, but especially the *AER* and *JPE*, essentially jettisoned book reviews from the academic fare served up, once the *Journal of Economic Literature* assumed this function in 1969. While this is associated with a moderate decline in total pages published in 1969, the editors collectively filled the void, and more, by 1970 and since then. A deep trough with respect to the fraction of journal pages devoted to book reviews occurs in 1918 (the year Germany signs the armistice) and a steep decline in this fraction occurs during World War II, but is followed at war's end by an immediate rebound to the pre-war level.

Figure 14.6 Fraction of Total Pages in Book Reviews

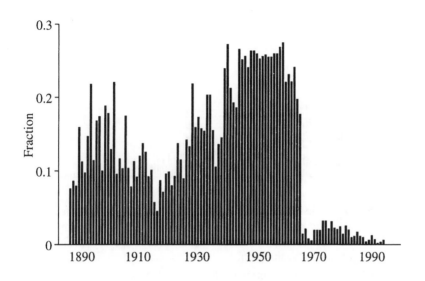

AUTHORS

One of the most obvious trends in authorship over time is the decline in contributions by nonacademic economists. This decline is chronicled in Figure 14.7.

Early contributions to the professional journal literature of economics were made, in large measure, by writers who did not list academic affiliations. However, this does not mean that these writers did not have academic affiliations, only that such affiliations were not listed. In many cases during the early years of journal publication, the author was identified along with the city (s)he lived in. Prior to, say, 1900 some articles included the author's academic affiliation while others listed the author's city of residence. Occasionally, the city listed might lead one to infer a university affiliation--e.g., Chicago, Princeton, Cambridge. Thus, it is possible, if not likely, that the high fractions of articles authored by non-academics in the late 1800s (especially) and early 1900s overstates the true fraction of articles authored by non-academic authors. However, this possible bias notwithstanding, it is clear that during this period non-academic writers contributed much more heavily to the scholarly literature of economics than

Figure 14.7 Fraction of Articles by Non-Academic Authors

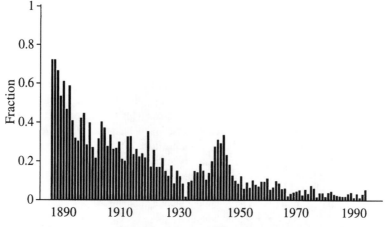

is currently the case. The decline has been steady throughout the twentieth century, with the exception of the World War II years, during which a sizable number of academic economists took temporary positions with federal agencies in Washington.

The "type" of non-academic contributor to the major economics journals also has changed considerably since the late 1800s. During the early years of these journals, non-academic contributors occasionally included individuals from private industry or trade organizations, and frequently included private individuals with no organizational affiliation whatsoever. Contributors with a public sector affiliation were very rare. In the 1990s, by contrast, virtually all of the non-academic contributors to the economic literature published in the major scholarly economics journals have public sector affiliations (e.g., federal reserve banks, Federal Trade Commission, Federal Communications Commission, U.S. Department of Justice, Securities and Exchange Commission), or affiliations with private research organizations (e.g., the RAND Corporation, Brookings Institution, Resources for the Future, American Enterprise Institute). Contributions from individuals identifying an affiliation with private industry or a trade organization or no organizational affiliation at all have essentially vanished from the professional literature of economics.

The lead article in the premiere issue of the American Economic Review was authored by Katharine Coman of Wellesley College. Although the absolute number of articles (co)authored by women in the three major general economics journals has risen over time there has been considerable ebb and flow in terms of both the fraction of feature articles published in the *AER*, *JPE*, and *QJE* and the fraction of pages published in these three journals by women.[4] There have been only three years since 1904 in which none of the feature articles published in the three major economics journals was (co)authored by a woman. However contributions by women rarely have constituted more than ten percent of the feature articles in the *AER*, *JPE*, *QJE*. Only during the 1990s have we witnessed women-authored contributions in excess of 10 percent of the feature articles published in these journals.

We estimated the impact of a trend variable, article length, and JEL subject codes on the probability that the author of an article was female; two findings are notable. First, there is no trend over time with respect to the relative incidence of scholarly contributions by women to the *AER*, *JPE*, and *QJE*. Second, relative to their contributions in the area of general economic theory, female economists have historically been much more likely to contribute scholarship in the areas of labor economics (JEL code 800) and Welfare Programs, Consumer Economics, Urban and Regional Economics (JEL code 900).

SUBJECT MATTER

In Figure 14.8, we report the fraction of articles published in the *AER*, *JPE*, and *QJE* from their respective inceptions through 1995, by *Journal of Economic Literature* subject code. For simplicity, we have followed the old 10-category code, rather than the recently adopted code that is considerably more detailed. From 1969 through 1995, the JEL codes are as reported in various issues of the JEL. Prior to 1969, the JEL code was assigned to each article by matching the title to the (most) appropriate code. Although we assigned a 3-digit JEL code to each paper, the fractions reported in the tables are based on aggregation to one-digit codes.

Not surprisingly, a large plurality of the articles (approximately 28 percent) published in the three major general economics journals over the years have addressed topics in general economic theory. Nearly twice as many articles historically have been written on subjects covered by the broad JEL 000 code than the next closest, which is Monetary and Fiscal Theory and Institutions (14.6 percent). Labor Economics (12.8 percent) and Industrial Organization (11.5 percent) are the only other subject areas in which at least 10 percent of the feature articles published in the three journals were written.

Behind this broad-brush historical perspective lie interesting trends within certain subject categories.[5] The least volatility across the decades is associated with the general economic theory category (with a larger share of the "market," this is not surprising). A couple of significant aspects of the literature in this category stand out: (1) Bohm-Bawerk's *Capital and*

Interest (1889) incited much professional discussion throughout the 1890s and, indeed, well into the twentieth century, with regard to the importance of capital; and (2) publication of Keynes' *General Theory* in 1937 was followed by a surge in papers in the general economic theory category during the 1940s and 1950s. During the first half of the twentieth century, there was increasing scholarly output of papers written about economic growth and development. This scholarly interest/production peaked in the 1950s and then declined markedly throughout the 1960s, 1970s, and 1980s. This trend reversed itself abruptly during the first half of the 1990s, with a surge in production of articles on economic growth. Feature articles written on subjects with JEL codes 200, 500, and 700 collectively comprise less than 10 percent of the papers published in the three major economics journals. The fraction of articles published that address the subject of economic statistics (JEL code 200) has remained fairly constant since the early 1900s. Feature articles on administration and business finance seem to be gaining prominence in the scholarly literature whereas articles on subjects related to agriculture have declined steadily after having enjoyed moderate prominence in the early decades of the twentieth century. For the most part, articles written in the subject code 300 (Monetary and Fiscal Theory and Institutions) during the first half of the twentieth century were about tax theory and policy. This started changing in the 1960s, as an increasing fraction of the category 300 papers addressed topics in monetary theory and policy. Starting in the 1920s and continuing into the 1930s, there were a number of industry studies published in the major economics journals, in which the authors demonstrated the impact of tariffs.[6] The fraction of articles written on industrial organization topics has declined from 15-20+ percent at the turn of the century to just under 10 percent during the 1990s. In large measure, this reflects the substantial literature on railroads (transportation is JEL code 615) and the new antitrust laws in the early 1900s, which melts away almost completely by mid-century. There was not a corresponding increase in scholarly attention paid to the development of public highways, automobiles, and air travel. In addition, a substantial portion of the early literature in this category was devoted to discussion of trusts, a discussion that has died out in recent decades. The sizable fraction of articles on labor economics during the early decades of the twentieth century reflects the considerable scholarly interest (at that time) in the role and importance of organized labor and the impact of technological progress and industrialization on labor. Writers at this time referred to the latter as "The Social Question." The increase in papers on labor economics in the 1970s and 1980s reflects scholarly interest in human capital and labor markets. Since the 1920s, there has been a more-or-less steady increase in the fraction of feature articles devoted to topics in JEL

Figure 14.8 Fraction of All Articles Published, by JEL Code

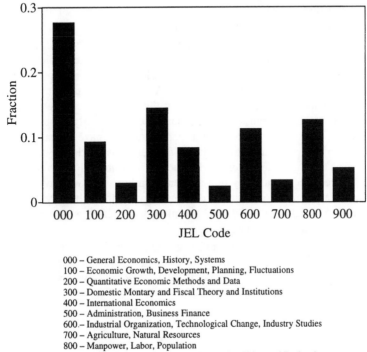

000 – General Economics, History, Systems
100 – Economic Growth, Development, Planning, Fluctuations
200 – Quantitative Economic Methods and Data
300 – Domestic Montary and Fiscal Theory and Institutions
400 – International Economics
500 – Administration, Business Finance
600.– Industrial Organization, Technological Change, Industry Studies
700 – Agriculture, Natural Resources
800 – Manpower, Labor, Population
900 – Welfare Programs, Consumer Economics, Urban and Regional
       Economics

subject code 900, which includes law and crime, education, welfare, regional, and consumer economics. By the 1990s, papers on these topics comprised approximately 13 percent of all articles published in the *AER*, *JPE*, and *QJE*.

CONCLUDING COMMENTS

More than 100 years have elapsed since the American Economic Association was constituted and since the publication of the first scholarly economics journals. In this paper, we have attempted to provide a historical profile of both the literature and the authors that have appeared in the three enduring, high-quality, general readership journals in economics: the *American Economic Review*, the *Journal of Political Economy*, and the *Quarterly Journal of Economics*. To the extent these journals are representative of scholarly economics journals generally, the trends and findings that we report may be taken as characteristic of the economics profession during the twentieth century.

We report many first-time findings. For example, it is clear that editorial prerogative is a strong determinant of the extent to which a journal emphasizes feature articles as opposed to short notes, comments, and replies (and, prior to the JEL, book reviews). A second determinant, evidently, is the existence of market competition in the form of specialty journals. We have demonstrated that the average length of a scholarly paper depends, in part, on the subject matter of the paper, and we have revealed ebbs and flows in the popularity of subjects, defined broadly during the twentieth century. We have documented the decline in contributions to the scholarly literature of economics by non-academic authors, and we have shown that female economists contribute differentially to the scholarly literature in identifiable fields (e.g., labor economics, and welfare programs, consumer economics, and law and economics).

We acknowledge that we have shed but limited light on the history of the scholarly journal literature of economics (notwithstanding the length of this paper!). Accordingly, we hope that our efforts serve as a catalyst for additional research by other scholars.

NOTES

1.   Laband (1986) argued that one of the defining features of the truly influential journals in economics was their ability to identify and "capture" for publication the lion's share of the truly influential scholarly contributions written as journal articles.
2.   This does not include eulogies, feature-length book reviews, presidential addresses, Nobel lectures, or papers published in the Papers and Proceedings issue of the *AER*. Not included also are articles published in the *AER* that were presented at the AEA conference prior to publication of the Papers and Proceedings. The profiles for each individual journal and the other analyses or statistical profiles referred to subsequently in this article are available from the authors upon request.
3.   Our efforts to obtain information from the *QJE* about the early history of the editorship were unsuccessful.
4.   There is the possibility of some mismeasurement with respect to these quantities. In these early years, authors frequently were identified by last name and initials only. Most of the time, but not always, we knew the gender of the

author. Unless we specifically knew that the author was a woman or a man, we did not assign the gender.

5. By and large, our findings (with respect to the overall relative importance of certain subjects and changes over time in the proportion of articles written on each subject) are very consistent with those of Bronfenbrenner (1966), who examined trends in the subject matter of English language economics journals over the period 1886-1963. He classified subject matter according to 23 categories so to compare ours with his requires aggregation of his categories. The time period covered by our analysis also is 32 years longer than his.

6. This corresponds with a period of significant public policy with respect to tariffs. The Emergency Tariff of 1921 was enacted under pressure from domestic industries seeking protection from the post World War I expansion of industry in Europe. The Fordney-McCumber Act was passed in 1922 and the U.S. Congress arguably birthed the Great Depression via enactment of the Smoot-Hawley Act in 1930.

REFERENCES

Bai, J., R.L. Lumsdaine, and J.H. Stock (forthcoming 1997), "Testing for and Dating Common Breaks in Multivariate Time Series," *Review of Economic Studies.*

Bronfenbrenner, M. (1966), "Trends, Cycles, and Fads in Economic Writing," *American Economic Review*, **56**, 538-52.

Laband, D.N. (1986), "Article Popularity", *Economic Inquiry*, **24**, 73-80.

Laband, D.N., and M.J. Piette (1994), "The Relative Impacts of Economics Journals: 1970-1990," *Journal of Economic Literature*, **32**, 640-66; Chapter 15 of this volume.

Lovell, M.C. (1973), "The Production of Economic Literature: An Interpretation," *Journal of Economic Literature*, **11**, 27-55.

Vandermeulen, A. (1972), "Manuscripts in the Maelstrom: A Theory of the Editorial Process," *Public Choice*, 107-11.

15. The Relative Impacts of Economics Journals: 1970-1990[*]

David N. Laband and Michael J. Piette

I. INTRODUCTION

In this paper we seek to: (1) update and backdate the paper by Stanley Liebowitz and John Palmer (L-P) that appeared in this Journal in 1984, which permits us to (2) investigate the changing "industrial organization" of the economics journal market over the period 1970 - 1990. The rationale for an update of the L-P paper is purely utilitarian: the L-P rankings are used at a number of colleges and universities to help evaluate an individual's scholarly "productivity," for purposes of allocating salary increases, as well as making promotion and tenure decisions. To the extent the relative impact of journals changes over time, and we shall see that it does, a periodic update of the index provides more accurate information for decision makers. By back-dating the L-P analysis, we are able to shed light on a number of structural issues regarding the academic journal market in economics. We examine the changing extent of the market for scientific knowledge claims in economics, in terms of both pages published and citations to the literature. We investigate the changing concentration of

---

[*] Reprinted with permission of the copyright holder from the *Journal of Economic Literature*, Vol.32, No.2, 1994, pp. 640-67.

Salisbury State University and Economic Research Services. Our data collection and database assembly efforts were assisted by John P. Sophocleus, Mark Gwartney, Michele Butler, and Scott Ralston. We received extremely valuable computer programming assistance from Jon Brunson and Edward Novak. Constructive comments were received from two anonymous reviewers. Financial support from the Faculty Development Committee at Salisbury State University is gratefully acknowledged.

citations among the premier journals and market penetration by new journals. Finally, we examine changes in the distribution of citations via Lorenz-curve analysis.

II. THE RELATIVE IMPACT OF JOURNALS: METHODOLOGY AND FINDINGS

Liebowitz and Palmer based their rankings of economics journals on the relative "impact" of the material published. Their measure of "impact" was the number of citations each journal was credited with receiving in 1980 for material published in previous years. There has been substantial discussion of the pros and cons of using citations to measure the value of a scholar's intellectual contribution (Dennis Gerrity and Richard McKenzie, 1978; Laband and Sophocleus, 1985; George Stigler and Claire Friedland, 1975). Our position is that citations are the scientific community's version of dollar voting by consumers for goods and services. Holding price constant, an individual consumer purchases goods from certain sellers because of the quality of their merchandise; however, the purchase decision may also be influenced by the buyer's friendship or family relationship with the seller and/or the buyer's hope that the seller will, in turn, patronize the buyer's establishment. Economists who study industrial organization do not make any distinctions between "good" sales and "bad" sales. Nor, we surmise, do many sellers. Sales are sales, period. All sales count towards determining each producer's market share. We do not treat the consumption of scientific literature any differently.[1]

Our methodology is the same as that employed by Liebowitz and Palmer. We collected detailed information on citations in 1970 for 50 selected economics journals indexed by the *Index of Economics Articles*. The citations referenced articles published during the period 1965-69. Thus, to be included in our sample, a journal had to have published during that entire period (it could not have started up, say, in 1967) and must have been indexed by the *IEA*.[2] The 1964-65 volume of the *IEA* indexed 127 journals. Several of these journals (e.g., *Journal of Economic Behavior* and *Journal of Economic and Business History*) were not indexed through 1969 and thus fell out of our sample. In addition, we did not include in our sample journals indexed by the *IEA* that did not bear directly on economics.[3] We also did not include most of the journals whose coverage of English articles was selective. Finally, and quite obviously, the journals included in our sample must have been indexed by the *Social Science Citation Index*. Our rankings for 1970 include all of the major journals in economics and many of the lesser ones.

In determining which journals to include in the 1990 rankings, we started with the set of journals ranked by Liebowitz and Palmer. A few journals ranked by L-P are not included in our 1990 rankings because they were not indexed by the *Social Science Citation Index* in 1990. Thus we were unable to obtain citation information for them. A small number of established journals do not appear on either the L-P list or our rankings for 1990, even though they have been published for years. Again, the omission is due to the absence of indexing of citations of these journals by the *SSCI*.[4] Entry by a number of new journals during the late 1970s and early 1980s pushed the total number of journals for which we collected citation information in 1990 to 130. The citations reference articles published in each journal during the period 1985-89.[5] The only exception in this regard is the *Journal of Economic Perspectives*, which commenced publication in the summer of 1987. Citations in 1990 for the *JEP* thus drew from a smaller pool of articles than would have been the case had it published during the entire 1985-89 period. We did not extrapolate the reported numbers for the *JEP*.

In Table 15.1 we report journal rankings in 1970, 1980, and 1990 by citations per article.[6] We included as citable literature articles, notes, comments, replies, and review articles; we did not include book reviews or advertising. Each of these counted as an "article." The reported values in Table 15.1, which range from 0 to 100, represent citations per article received by each journal in the reference year as a percentage of the citations per article received by the leading journal that year.[7]

In Table 15.2 we report journal rankings in 1970, 1980, and 1990 by impact-adjusted citations per article, using the iterative procedure developed by Liebowitz and Palmer.[8] In the initial stage of the iterative procedure citations received from journals not included in that year's rankings are assigned a weight (or value) of zero and all other citations are weighted by the percentage frequency relative to the most highly cited journal.[9] This provides a new ranking and new set of relative citation frequencies that are used in the second iteration, and so forth.[10] As in Table 15.1, the reported values, ranging from 0 to 100, represent impact-adjusted citations per article received by each journal in the reference year as a percentage of the adjusted citations per article received by the leading journal that year.

One possible shortcoming of rankings based on citations per article is that different journals have different policies regarding notes, comments, and replies. Because comments and, especially, replies tend to be end-of-discussion contributions, they attract relatively few citations. At the same time, because they are typically shorter than full articles, comments and

Table 15.1 Rankings Based on Citations per Article

	1970 Citations to Articles Published 1965-1969[a]		1980 Citations to Articles Published 1975-1979[b]		1990 Citations to Articles Published 1985-1989[c]	
1	Rev. Econ. Studies	100.0	J. Econ. Lit.	100.0	J. Econ. Lit.	100.0
2	Amer. Econ. Rev.	93.3	Yale Law J.	76.6	J. Finan. Econ.	89.4
3	Rev. Econ. Statist.	68.6	Brookings Pap. Econ. Act.	75.3	Yale Law J.	76.3
4	Quart. J. Econ.	68.2	J. Polit. Econ.	66.4	Michigan Law Rev.	76.1
5	J. Reg. Sci.	64.5	J. Finan. Econ.	61.3	J. Cons. Res.	71.3
6	Econometrica	62.2	Michigan Law Rev.	56.7	Econometrica	65.2
7	J. Polit. Econ.	59.0	Amer. Econ. Rev.	48.4	J. Acc. Econ.	61.9
8	J. Bus.	56.7	J. Legal Stud.	46.0	J. Polit. Econ.	56.0
9	Economica	55.4	Bell J. Econ. (Rand J. Econ.)	45.4	J. Amer. Statist. Assoc.	53.8
10	J. Law Econ.	51.8	J. Law Econ.	43.3	J. Legal Stud.	51.6
11	Econ. J.	47.5	Inquiry	42.1	Amer. Econ. Rev.	43.0
12	J. Finance	41.9	Econometrica	39.0	J. Monet. Econ.	37.6
13	J. Amer. Statist. Assoc.	40.7	J. Monet. Econ.	37.7	J. Bus.	37.4
14	Int. Econ. Rev.	38.5	J. Cons. Res.	33.6	J. Econ. Perspectives	37.2
15	Econ. Planning	38.0	Rev. Econ. Stud.	30.1	Bell J. Econ. (Rand J. Econ.)	36.6
16	Amer. Econ. Rev. Papers & Proc.	37.0	J. Roy. Statist. Soc. Ser. B-Meth.	28.9	Quart. J. Econ.	36.3
17	Ind. Rel.	36.2	Econ. J.	28.0	J. Roy. Statist. Soc. Set. A.-Gen.	36.3
18	Oxford Econ. Pap.	35.2	Rev. Econ. Statist.	27.8	J. Finance	36.2
19	J. Econ. Hist.	33.3	Demography	27.7	Demography	34.2
20	Lloyd's Bank Rev.	33.1	Public Pol.	27.6	J. Law Econ.	33.1

Table 15.1 continued

	1970 Citations to Articles Published 1965-1969[a]		1980 Citations to Articles Published 1975-1979[b]		1990 Citations to Articles Published 1985-1989[c]	
21	Yale Essays on Econ.	32.0	J. Urban Econ.	26.6	Rev. Econ. Stud.	31.0
22	Econ. Devel. Cult. Change	30.5	Reg. Stud.	25.5	J. Roy. Statist. Soc. Ser. B-Meth.	29.1
23	Southern Econ. J.	26.6	J. Finance	24.5	Population Devel. Rev.	28.9
24	Econ. Hist. Rev.	26.2	J. Amer. Statist. Assoc.	24.3	J. Health Econ.	25.6
25	Kyklos	25.1	J. Hum. Res.	24.0	J. Int. Bus. Stud.	25.0
26	Int. Monet. Fund Staff Pap.	23.5	Int. Econ. Rev.	23.4	Oxford Bull. Econ. Statist.	25.0
27	Public Finance	22.8	J. Math. Econ.	22.5	Brookings Pap. Econ. Act.	24.5
28	Nat. Tax J.	22.7	Quart. J. Econ.	22.4	J. Econometrics	24.5
29	J. Roy. Statist. Soc. Ser. A-Gen.	21.7	Population Stud.	22.0	Econ. J.	23.9
30	Explorations Econ. Hist.	21.0	J. Econometrics	21.4	Ind. Lab. Relat. Rev.	23.4
31	Econ. Record	19.7	J. Econ. Theory	21.0	J. Lab. Econ.	23.3
32.	Econ. Inquiry (Western Econ. J.)	18.7	J. Pub. Econ.	20.8	J. Ace. Res.	22.5
33	Land Econ.	18.7	J. Roy. Statist. Soc. Ser. A-Gen.	20.1	J. Econ. Theory	22.5
34	J. Develop. Stud.	17.5	Amer. Econ. Rev. Papers & Proc.	19.8	J. Money Credit Banking	22.1
35	Ind. Lab. Relat. Rev.	17.0	Economica	18.9	Ind. Rel.	21.9

36	J. Ind. Econ.	14.9	Ind. Lab. Relat. Rev.	18.8	Amer. Econ. Rev. Papers & Proc.	21.8
37	Bus. Hist. Rev,	14.0	J. Bus.	18.5	California Manage. Rev.	20.7
38	Manch. Sch. Econ. Soc. Stud.	13.9	J. Money Credit Banking	18.5	J. Finan. Quant. Anal.	20.0
39	Scand. J. Econ.	13.5	J. Int. Econ.	18.2	J. Int. Econ.	19.6
40	Soc. Econ. Stud.	11.5	J. Econ. Hist.	17.8	J. Hum. Res.	18.5
41	Amer. J. Agri. Econ.	10.9	J. Ace. Res.	17.8	J. Math. Econ.	17.7
42	Scottish J. Polit. Econ,	10.9	Econ. Inquiry	17.5	Econ. Geogr.	17.5
43	Quart. Rev. Econ. Bus.	9.7	Econ. Geogr.	17.4	Rev. Econ. Statist.	17.1
44	Rev. Social Econ.	8.9	Oxford Econ. Pap.	16.8	Sloan Manage. Rev.	16.5
45	Problems of Econ.	7.8	J. Ind. Econ.	16.4	J. Ind. Econ.	16.0
46	German Econ, Rev.	7.6	Urban Stud.	16.1	J. Bus. Econ. Statist.	15.9
47	South African J. Econ.	7.3	Nat. Tax J.	15.7	Econ. Hist. Rev.	15.5
48	Weltwirtsch. Arch.	6.6	Brit. J. of Ind. Rel.	15.6	J. Public Econ.	15.4
49	Economia Internazionale	3.1	J. Reg. Sci.	14.9	Economica	15.0
50	Indian Econ. J.	1.2	Amer. J. Agri. Econ.	14.5	Inquiry-J. Health Care Org.	14.7
51		-	Scand. J. Econ.	14.4	J. Reg. Sci.	14.4
52		-	Policy Analysis	14.2	J. Urban Econ.	14.1
53		-	Reg. Sci. Urban Econ.	13.9	Explorations Econ. Hist.	13.8
54		-	Ind. Rel.	13.7	Land Econ.	13.5
55		-	Sloan Manage. Rev.	13.6	Int. Econ. Rev.	13.5
56		-	Econ. Devel. Cult. Change	13.5	Reg. Stud.	13.4

Table 15.1 continued

	1970 Citations to Articles Published 1965-1969[a]	1980 Citations to Articles Published 1975-1979[b]		1990 Citations to Articles Published 1985-1989[c]	
57	-	J. Environ. Eton. Manage.	13.3	J. Environ. Econ. Manage.	13.3
58	-	Soc. Sci. Quart.	13.3	J. Forecasting	13.3
59	-	Scottish J. Polit. Econ.	13.3	Econ. Inquiry (West, Econ. J.)	13.1
60	-	World Devel.	12.5	Amer. J. Agr. Econ.	12.7
61	-	Econ. Hist. Rev.	12.5	Mon. Lab. Rev.	12.7
62	-	Manchester Sch. Econ. Soc. Stud.	12.4	Soc. Sci. Quart.	12.6
63	-	Explorations Econ. Hist.	12.3	World Devel.	12.5
64	-	European Econ. Rev.	12.2	Oxford Econ. Pap.	12.4
65	-	Canadian J. Econ.	11.8	Public Choice	12.3
66	-	J. Devel. Econ.	11.7	J. Econ. Behar. Organ.	12.3
67	-	Public Choice	11.7	J. Econ. Hist.	12.2
68	-	Land Econ.	11.2	British J. Ind. Rel.	11.6
69	-	Southern Econ. J.	11.0	Econ. Devel. Cult. Change	11.4
70	-	J. Finan. Quant. Anal.	10.8	J. Compar. Econ.	11.2
71	-	Econ. Letters	10.7	Int. J. Ind. Organ.	11.1
72	-	Labor Hist.	10.6	Reg. Sci. Urban Econ.	10.8
73	-	Lloyds Bank Rev.	10.3	J. Policy Anal. Manage.	10.6
74	-	Natural Res. J.	10.2	Soc. Res.	10.5

75	-	Weltwirtsch. Arch.	9.8	Canadian J. Econ.	10.2
76	-	Kyklos	8.6	Europ. Econ. Rev.	10.1
77	-	J. World Trade Law	8.5	Southern Econ. J.	10.0
78	-	J. Devel. Stud.	8.1	J. Econ. Dynamics & Control	10.0
79	-	Sci. Society	8.1	J. Lab. Res.	9.9
80	-	Hist. Polit. Econ.	7.7	Int. Reg. Sci. Rev.	9.9
81	-	J. Econ. Issues	7.1	Cambridge J. Econ.	9.9
82	-	Appl. Econ.	7.0	J. Devel. Stud.	9.6
83	-	Oxford Bull. Econ. Stat.	6.8	Kyklos	9.2
84	-	Soc. Res.	6.7	Sci. Society	9.0
85	-	J. Developing Areas	6.5	J. Devel. Econ.	9.0
86	-	Mon. Lab. Rev.	7.5	Nat. Tax J.	8.9
87	-	J. Transport Econ. Policy	6.4	Scand. J. Econ.	8.7
88	-	Public Finance	6.3	Manchester Sch. Econ. Soc. Stud.	8.6
89	-	J. Risk Ins.	6.3	J. Banking Finance	8.6
90	-	Int. Lab. Rev.	6.1	Soc. Choice Welfare	7.8
91	-	Int. J. Soc. Econ.	6.0	J. Finan. Res.	7.4
92	-	California Manage. Rev.	5.9	Urban Stud.	7.4
93	-	Public Finance Quart.	5.8	World Econ.	7.1
94	-	Econ. Record	5.7	J. Econ. Educ.	7.1
95	-	Int. Soc. Sci. J.	5.5	Weltwirtsch. Arch.	7.1
96	-	J. Int. Bus. Stud.	5.5	Rev. Soc. Econ.	6.5
97	-	Quart. Rev. Econ. Bus.	4.8	J. Risk Ins.	6.5
98	-	Amer. J. Econ. Sociology	4.7	Econ. Modelling	6.4

Table 15.1 continued

	1970 Citations to Articles Published 1965-1969[a]	1980 Citations to Articles Published 1975-1979[b]		1990 Citations to Articles Published 1985-1989[c]	
99	-	Rev. Social Econ.	4.4	J. Post Keynesian Econ.	6.3
100	-	Bus. Hist. Rev.	3.9	J. Econ. Issues	6.2
101	-	J. Common Market Stud.	3.9	J. Transport Econ. Policy	6.1
102	-	J. Econ. Bus.	3.6	Public Finance Quart.	6.1
103	-	Nebraska J. Econ. Bus.	2.6	Labor Hist.	5.8
104	-	J. Econ. Educ.	2.4	J. World Trade	5.8
105	-	Malayan Econ. Rev.	2.2	J. Macroecon.	5.8
106	-	J. Econ. Stud.	0.7	J. Common Market Stud.	5.7
107	-	Australian J. Agr. Econ.	0.7	Int. Lab. Rev.	5.2
108	-	Matekon	0.4	Int. J. Soc. Econ.	5.2
109	-	-		Econ. Letters	5.2
110	-	-		Natural Res. J.	5.0
111	-	-		Appl. Econ.	5.0
112	-	-		Cato J.	4.9
113	-	-		Public Finance	4.8
114	-	-		Energy Econ.	4.7
115	-	-		J. Econ. Bus.	4.4
116	-	-		J. Developing Areas	4.4
117	-	-		Econ. Record	4.3
118	-	-		Scottish J. Polit. Econ.	4.2

	Journal		
119	Hist. Polit. Econ.	–	4.2
120	Quart. Rev. Econ. Bus.	–	4.1
121	Bus. Hist. Rev.	–	4.0
122	Amer. J. Econ. Sociology	–	3.4
123	Rev. Black Polit. Econ.	–	2.8
124	Int. Soc. Sci. J.	–	2.6
125	Managerial Dec. Econ.	–	2.6
126	J. Econ. Stud.	–	2.3
127	Australian J. Agr. Econ.	–	2.0
128	Rev. Bus. Econ. Res.	–	1.5
129	Econometric Theory	–	1.4
130	Matekon	–	0.0

Sources:

a Tabulated by the authors from the 50 journals listed.

b Liebowitz and Palmer, as calculated from the *Social Science Citation Index*, vol. 6, 1980.

c Calculated from the *Social Science Citation Index*, vol. 6, 1990.

Table 15.2 Rankings Based on Impact Adjusted Citations per Article

	1970 Citations to Articles Published 1965-1969[a]		1980 Citations to Articles Published 1975-1979[b]		1990 Citations to Articles Published 1985-1989[c]	
1	Rev. Econ. Stud.	100.0	J. Econ. Lit.	100.0	J. Finan. Econ.	100.0
2	Amer. Econ. Rev.	93.3	Brookings Pap. Econ. Act.	96.9	Econometrica	78.4
3	Quart. J. Econ.	65.6	J. Finan. Econ.	62.2	J. Polit. Econ.	63.0
4	J. Polit. Econ.	63.5	J. Polit. Econ.	59.1	J. Monet. Econ.	41.9
5	Rev. of Eton. & Statist.	59.8	Bell J. of Eton. (Rand J. Econ.)	39.5	Quart. J. Eton.	41.6
6	Econometrica	46.6	Amer. Econ. Rev.	34.5	Rev. Econ. Stud.	40.7
7	J. Bus.	38.5	J. Monet. Econ.	33.0	Amer. Econ. Rev.	40.2
8	J. Finance	37.8	Economica	31.6	Bell J. Econ. (Rand J. Econ.)	40.2
9	Economica	36.7	Econometrica	31.6	J. Econ. Theory	34.9
10	Int. Econ. Rev.	35.1	Rev. Econ. Stud.	30.7	J. Finance	34.1
11	Eton. of Planning	32.8	J. Math. Econ.	24.7	J. Econ. Lit.	28.8
12	Econ. J.	32.7	J. Law Econ.	22.9	J. Acc. Econ.	25.8
13	Yale Essays on Eton.	28.3	J. Econ. Theory	22.3	J. Econ. Perspectives	23.3
14	Amer. Econ. Rev. Pap. & Proc.	26.9	J. Public Econ.	19.7	J. Bus.	21.2
15	J. Amer. Statist. Assoc.	16.8	Int. Econ. Rev.	19.0	J. Math. Econ.	20.6
16	Oxford Econ. Pap.	16.2	J. Econometrics	17.3	J. Econometrics	18.6
17	J. Royal Stat. Soc. Scr. A-Gen.	16.1	J. Ind. Econ.	16.6	Brookings Pap. Econ. Act.	15.9
18	J. Law Econ.	13.8	Quart. J. Econ.	16.2	J. Lab. Econ.	15.4

19	Econ. Rec.	13.7	Econ. J.	15.0	J. Finan. Quant. Anal.	14.3
20	J. Devel. Stud.	10.2	J. Finance	14.6	Int. Econ. Rev.	12.3
21	Southern Econ. J.	9.9	Amer. Econ. Rev. Pap. & Proc.	14.6	J. Law Econ.	11.7
22	J. Econ. Hist.	9.0	J. Int. Econ.	14.1	J. Money Credit Banking	9.0
23	Lloyd's Bank Rev.	6.3	J. Hum. Res.	13.6	Amer. Econ. Rev. Pap. & Proc.	8.8
24	Econ. Devel. Cult. Change	5.8	Rev. Econ. Statist.	12.4	J. Public Econ.	8.6
25	Econ. Inquiry (Western Econ. J.)	4.8	Public Finance	11.9	J. Amer. Statist. Assoc.	8.0
26	Weltwirtsch. Arch.	4.6	Nat. Tax Journal	9.9	J. Bus. Econ. Statist.	7.9
27	Kyklos	4.5	J. Money Credit Banking	9.9	J. Int. Econ.	7.6
28	Nat. Tax J.	4.2	Canadian J. Econ.	9.4	Econ. J.	7.5
29	J. Reg. Sci.	4.0	Manchester Sch. Econ. Soc. Stud.	9.4	Rev. Econ. Statist.	6.5
30	Int. Monet. Fund Staff Pap.	3.7	Ind. Lab. Rel. Rev.	9.0	J. Ind. Econ.	6.1
31	Quart. Rev. Econ. Bus.	3.7	J. Legal Studies	8.4	J. Banking Finance	5.5
32	Manchester Sch. Econ. Soc. Stud.	3.5	J. Bus.	8.3	Int. J. Ind. Organ.	5.2
33	Public Finance	3.5	J. Urban Econ.	8.1	J. Econ. Dynam. Control	4.9
34	Rev. Soc. Econ.	3.4	Econ. Inquiry	7.9	Demography	4.9
35	J. Ind. Econ.	3.1	Scand. J. Econ.	7.1	J. Hum. Res.	4.6
36	Economia Internazionale	3.0	J. Acc. Res.	7.0	Soc. Choice Welfare	4.6
37	Explorations Econ. Hist.	3.0	European Econ. Rev.	6.7	Ind. Lab. Rel. Rev.	4.4
38	Scand. J. Econ.	2.5	Public Finance Quart.	5.5	J. Econ. Ed.	4.3

Table 15.2 continued

	1970 Citations to Articles Published 1965-1969[a]		1980 Citations to Articles Published 1975-1979[b]		1990 Citations to Articles Published 1985-1989[c]	
39	Amer. J. Agri. Econ.	2.0	Oxford Econ. Pap.	4.9	Econ. Inquiry (West. Econ. J.)	4.1
40	Land Econ.	1.8	Southern Econ. J.	4.8	J. Roy. Statist. Soc. Ser. B-Meth.	3.1
41	Ind. Rel.	1.6	British J. Ind. Rel.	4.8	Econ. Letters	3.0
42	Problems of Econ.	1.5	Appl. Econ.	4.4	J. Econ. Hist.	3.0
43	Eton. Hist. Rev.	0.6	Kyklos	4.3	Oxford Bull. Econ. Statist.	2.9
44	Bus. Hist. Rev.	0.3	J. Environ. Econ. Manage.	4.2	J. Acc. Res.	2.7
45	Ind. Lab. Relat. Rev.	0.2	J. Roy. Statist. Soc. Ser. A-Gen.	4.1	Economica	2.6
46	Scot. J. Polit. Econ.	0.0	Public Choice	4.1	J. Finan. Res.	2.5
47	Indian Econ. J.	0.0	J. Finan. Quant. Anal.	3.4	Explorations Econ. Hist.	2.3
48	South African J. Econ.	0.0	J. Amer. Statist. Assoc.	3.0	J. Risk Ins.	2.3
49	Ger. Econ. Rev.	0.0	Inquiry	3.0	European Econ. Rev.	2.1
50	Soc. Econ. Stud.	0.0	J. Devel. Econ.	2.3	J. Econ. Behav. Organ.	2.1
51		-	Scot. J. Polit. Econ.	1.9	Scand. J. Econ.	2.1
52		-	J. Cons. Res.	1.8	Public Choice	2.0
53		-	J. Reg. Sci.	1.8	J. Compar. Econ.	1.9
54		-	Yale Law J.	1.8	Econometric Theory	1.7
55		-	Lloyds Bank Rev.	1.7	J. Legal Stud.	1.6
56		-	Econ. Letters	1.6	J. Urban Econ.	1.6

No.		Journal	Value	Journal	Value
57	–	Weltwirtsch. Arch.	1.6	J. Lab. Res.	1.5
58	–	Rev. Soc. Econ.	1.3	Public Finance	1.2
59	–	J. Econ. Issues	1.3	J. Devel. Econ.	1.2
60	–	Quart. Rev. Econ. Bus.	1.3	Southern Econ. J.	1.1
61	–	Reg. Sci. Urban Econ.	1.2	Cato J.	1.0
62	–	Ind. Rel.	1.2	Canadian J. Econ.	0.8
63	–	Nebraska J. Econ. Bus.	1.1	J. Health Econ.	0.7
64	–	Urban Stud.	1.0	Oxford Econ. Pap.	0.7
65	–	Econ. Rec.	1.0	J. Macroecon.	0.7
66	–	Oxford Bull. Econ. Statist.	1.0	Kyklos	0.7
67	–	Amer. J. Agr. Econ.	0.9	Amer. J. Agr. Econ.	0.7
68	–	Land Econ.	0.9	J. Roy. Statist. Soc. Scr. A-Gen.	0.6
69	–	J. Econ. Hist.	0.8	Ind. Rel.	0.6
70	–	Explorations Econ. Hist.	0.7	British J. Ind. Rel.	0.6
71	–	J. Econ. Bus.	0.6	Public Finance Quart.	0.6
72	–	J. Devel. Areas	0.6	Manchester Sch. Econ. Soc. Stud.	0.6
73	–	Econ. Devel. Cult. Change	0.6	Population Devel. Review	0.4
74	–	Mon. Lab. Rev.	0.6	Econ. Modelling	0.4
75	–	J. Econ. Educ.	0.5	World Econ.	0.4
76	–	Hist. Polit. Econ.	0.5	Appl. Econ.	0.4
77	–	J. Transp. Econ. Pol.	0.4	Nat. Tax J.	0.4
78	–	J. Roy. Statist. Soc. Ser. B-Meth.	0.4	J. Forecasting	0.3

Table 15.2 continued

	1970 Citations to Articles Published 1965-1969[a]	1980 Citations to Articles Published 1975-1979[b]	1980	1990 Citations to Articles Published 1985-1989[c]	1990
79	—	Public Policy	0.4	J. Int. Bus. Stud.	0.3
80	—	J. Devel. Stud.	0.4	Scot. J. Polit. Econ.	0.3
81	—	Michigan Law Rev.	0.4	Quart. Rev. Econ. Bus.	0.2
82	—	Int. J. Soc. Econ.	0.4	Reg. Sci. Urban Econ.	0.2
83	—	Int. Lab. Rev.	0.4	Cambridge J. Econ.	0.2
84	—	J. Risk Ins.	0.4	Econ. Devel. Cult. Change	0.2
85	—	Reg. Stud.	0.3	Econ. Record	0.1
86	—	Sloan Manage. Rev.	0.3	Mon. Lab. Rev.	0.1
87	—	J. Int. Bus. Stud.	0.2	Land Econ.	0.1
88	—	Malayan Econ. Rev.	0.2	Weltwirtsch. Arch.	0.1
89	—	Econ. Geogr.	0.1	J. Environ. Econ. Manage.	0.1
90	—	World Devel.	0.1	Econ. Hist. Rev.	0.1
91	—	Econ. Hist. Rev.	0.1	J. Econ. Stud.	0.1
92	—	Labor Hist.	0.1	J. Reg. Sci.	0.1
93	—	Amer. J. Econ. Sociology	0.0	Australian J. Agr. Econ.	0.1
94	—	Soc. Sci. Quart.	0.0	Bus. Hist. Rev.	0.1
95	—	Population Stud.	0.0	Energy Econ.	0.1
96	—	Policy Analysis	0.0	J. Develop. Stud.	0.1
97	—	Natural Res. J.	0.0	Int. J. Soc. Econ.	0.1
98	—	Australian J. Agr. Econ.	0.0	Yale Law J.	0.1

#		Journal		Journal	
99	-	California Manage. Rev.	0.0	J. Common Market Stud.	0.1
100	-	Demography	0.0	Rev. Soc. Econ.	0.1
101	-	Bus. Hist. Rev.	0.0	J. Transport Econ. Policy	0.1
102	-	J. World Trade Law	0.0	J. Post Keynesian Econ.	0.0
103	-	J. Common Market Stud.	0.0	J. Econ. Bus.	0.0
104	-	Sci. Society	0.0	World Devel.	0.0
105	-	Soc. Res.	0.0	J. Econ. Issues	0.0
106	-	Int. Soc. Sci. J.	0.0	Michigan Law Rev.	0.0
107	-	Matekon	0.0	Reg. Stud.	0.0
108	-	J. Econ. Stud.	0.0	J. Pol. Anal. Manage.	0.0
109	-	-		Hist. Polit. Econ.	0.0
110	-	-		Inquiry-J. Health Care Org.	0.0
111	-			Urban Stud.	0.0
112	-			Manager. Dec. Econ.	0.0
113	-			Amer. J. Econ. Soc.	0.0
114	-			California Manage. Rev.	0.0
115	-			Int. Lab. Rev.	0.0
116	-			Int. Soc. Sci. J.	0.0
117	-			Econ. Geogr.	0.0
118	-			J. Cons. Res.	0.0
119	-			J. Devel. Areas	0.0
120	-			Labor Hist.	0.0

Table 15.2 continued

	1970 Citations to Articles Published 1965-1969[a]	1980 Citations to Articles Published 1975-1979[b]	1990 Citations to Articles Published 1985-1989[c]	
121	-	-	-	J. World Trade	0.0
122	-	-	-	Sci. Society	0.0
123	-	-	-	Matekon	0.0
124	-	-	-	Natural Res. J.	0.0
125	-	-	-	Sloan Manage. Rev.	0.0
126	-	-	-	Soc. Sci. Quart.	0.0
127	-	-	-	Soc. Res.	0.0
128	-	-	-	Rev. Black Polit. Econ.	0.0
129	-	-	-	Rev. Bus. Econ. Res.	0.0
130	-	-	-	Int. Reg. Sci. Rev.	0.0

Sources:

a Tabulated by the authors from the fifty journals listed.

b S.J. Liebowitz and J.P. Palmer, as calculated from the *Social Science Citation Index*, vol. 6, 1980.

c Calculated from the *Social Science Citation Index*, vol. 6, 1990.

replies inflate the number of "articles" from which citations are drawn, which results in reduced measured impact for journals publishing notes and comments relative to journals that do not publish such fare.

In light of this possible drawback, we also report, in Appendix Tables 15.A1 and 15.A2, the relative impact of each journal with respect to both unadjusted and impact-adjusted citations per typed character space. The number of typed character spaces published by a journal was found by multiplying the number of pages devoted to the above-listed types of scholarly contributions by the estimated number of typed characters per-journal page. The latter was determined by multiplying the number of lines per page (on a representative page with no footnotes, figures, equations, or other interruptions in the prose) by the average number of typed characters per line (an average of three full lines). The citations per character measure thus controls for the volume of printed material that citations are drawn from.

III.   THE CHANGING INDUSTRIAL ORGANIZATION OF THE ECONOMICS JOURNAL MARKET

The Extent of the Market

Between 1970 and 1990, membership in the American Economic Association grew roughly 14 percent, from 18,908 to 21,578 (George Stigler, Friedland, and Stephen Stigler, 1992). However, over the same time period, the increase in the production of scholarly economic literature was much more rapid, on both the intensive and extensive margins. We are able to shed empirical light on both.

For the 41 journals that appear in both the 1970 and 1990 rankings we were able to determine the total number of articles and pages published during the relevant preceding five-year period.[11] Between 1965 and 1969, these 41 journals published 7,939 articles, notes, comments, etc., representing 86,578 pages of scholarly literature; between 1985 and 1989, these same journals published 9,790 articles, notes, comments, etc., representing 130,182 pages of scholarly literature. This represents a 23 percent increase in the number of articles published and a 50 percent increase in the number of pages published. Expansion on the external margin can be analyzed in terms of entry into the economics journal market by new journals. Between 1976 and 1985, at least 55 new economics journals commenced publication.[12] This represents a 51 percent increase over the number of journals ranked by Liebowitz and Palmer just 10 years ago. We were able to determine pages published during 1985-89 for 27 of these new entrants at 59,716. It seems clear that the market for scholarly economic literature expanded rapidly during the period of time covered by our analysis.[13]

Our findings suggest that the overall growth in citations to scholarly economics literature over the 1970-1990 period exceeded the growth in the quantity of published, scholarly economic literature. The number of pages published in scholarly economics journals, including new entrants, more than doubled between 1970 and 1990. However, we doubt that there was a tripling of pages published during this time period. In terms of citations to the previous five years' publications, the growth rate in citations between 1970 and 1990 was 484 percent. In terms of citations to all previous literature, we estimate the growth rate in citations between 1970 and 1990 to be approximately 536 percent. Total citations in 1970, 1980, and 1990 for all journals in each sample are reported in Table 15.3.

To determine whether the growth in citations occurred primarily within the set of journals that published over that entire time period or was attributable in large measure to citations appearing in new journals, we analyzed the change in citations among the group of 41 journals that appeared in both the 1970 and 1990 rankings. That is to say, we counted citations originating among the 41 journals citing papers published in the same set of 41 journals. In 1970 the total number of citations sent back and forth among these 41 journals was 2,695; in 1990 that number was 3,741. This increase of 39 percent in within-group citations is larger than the previously noted increase in the number of articles published by that set of journals during that 20-year period (23%), but smaller than the increase in the number of pages published (50%) and much smaller than the overall increase in citations over that period. It thus appears that most of the growth in citations during the period 1970-1990 is attributable to new journals citing established journals and new journals citing other new journals.

Given the fact that the growth in within-group citations to the set of 41 journals that are consistent across the 1970-1990 period is lower than the increase in the number of pages published by those journals, it seems clear that market entry must be responsible for a substantial proportion of the noted growth in citations. Some of these journals have been extremely successful, as judged by their rapid accumulation of market share vis-a-vis citations. For example, the *Journal of Accounting and Economics*, which commenced publication in 1979, ranked 7th in 1990 by citations to articles published 1985-1989 (see Table 15.1). In this regard, it outperformed numerous better-known and well-respected journals.

The performance demonstrated by the American Economic Association's

Table 15.3 Citations To Scholarly Economic Literature, 1970-1990

Number of Citations to:	1970	1980	1990
Papers published 1965-69	4,815	-	-
All papers (est.)	13,192	-	-
Papers published 1975-79	-	17,798	-
All papers	-	45,018	-
Papers published 1985-89	-	-	28,122
All papers	-	-	83,948

Journal of Economic Perspectives may be even more impressive. The inaugural volume of the *JEP* appeared in mid-1987. Thus the citation totals reported in Tables 15.1, 15.2, 15.A1, and 15.A2 are to approximately one-half the publication period of the other journals. Even with this limited publication experience to draw citations from, the *JEP* was the 26th most highly cited journal in economics in 1990 and ranked 13th that year in terms of citations per article. This powerful market penetration came within three to four years of first publication![14]

Concentration and Market Dominance

One general change that occurred over the 1970-1990 period concerns the distribution of influence across economics journals. In 1980 only six journals received more than 50 percent of the citations per article accrued by the *American Economic Review*. In 1970 and 1990 nine journals received more than 50 percent of the citations per article received by the *AER*. A simple way of measuring the competitiveness of journals, along the citations per article dimension, is to sum the scaled numbers: the higher the number, the more competitive journals are with the *AER*. The top ten journals in 1970, 1980, and 1990 had aggregate relative impact values of 679.78, 619.35, and 701.62, respectively. This suggests that the competitiveness of the economics journal market declined slightly during the 1970s but increased during the 1980s.

Table 15.4 reports summary information with respect to concentration of citations among scholarly economics journals. Let s_j be journal j's citations expressed as a fraction of all citations reported for the journals in our rankings. The Herfindahl Index, H, is then defined as $\sum_j (s_j)^2$ and ranges from zero to one. In Table 15.4 we report the Herfindahl Indexes for 1965 (derived from Michael Lovell, 1973), 1970, 1980, and 1990 for the journals included in our rankings in those years.[15]

The Influence of Economics Journals

Table 15.4   Concentration of Citations Among Economics Journals, 1965-1990

	Herfindahl Index for Entire Market			
	1965[a]	1970	1980	1990
Unadjusted Citations	0.071	0.049	0.025	0.020
Impact-Adjusted Citations		0.088	0.077	0.059

Source: a. Derived from Lovell (1973, p. 41).

The reported Herfindahl Indexes show a steady reduction in the degree of concentration in the academic journal market in economics over the 1965-1990 period and are in close agreement with values calculated by Pencavel (1992) for 320 economics journals indexed by the *Journal of Economic Literature*. The erosion is less pronounced with regard to impact-adjusted citations than unadjusted citations. Whereas the Herfindahl Indexes calculated on the basis of unadjusted citations declined much more rapidly during the 1970s than the 1980s, the Herfindahl Indexes based on impact-adjusted citations fell much more rapidly in the 1980s than the 1970s.

Table 15.5 reports the individual and joint market shares, with respect to citations, of nine "core" economics journals in 1965, 1970, 1980, and 1990.[16] Between 1970 and 1990 the share of all citations attributed to the nine core economics journals identified in Table 5 dropped by 50 percent. Indeed, the drop is probably greater than that, as the *Journal of Economic Theory* and the *Journal of Monetary Economics* were not indexed by the *Index of Economics Articles* for the entire 1965-69 period that was required to place them in the 1970 rankings; thus, we have no reported market share figures for these two journals for that year. It seems safe to say, however, that nearly half of all citations to the scholarly economics literature in 1970 went to articles published in the nine core journals. By 1990 less than 25 percent of all citations to the scholarly economies literature went to articles published in the nine core journals.

With respect to impact-adjusted citations, the concentration of citations among the core journals has been much greater and has eroded away much more slowly over time. In 1970, two-thirds of all impact-adjusted citations were to articles published in the seven core journals identified in Table 15.5. Although there was steady erosion of concentration in this regard with the passage of time, by 1990 well over 50 percent of all impact-adjusted citations were still attributed to articles published by the nine core journals.

It seems appropriate to remind the reader at this stage that over the 1970-1990 period the number of citations to scholarly economic literature

Table 15.5 Individual and Collective Market Shares of Citations for Nine "Core" Economics Journals, 1965-1990

Journal	Market Share of 9 "Core" Journals						
	Percentage of Unadjusted Citations				Percentage of Impact-Adjusted Citation		
	1965[a]	1970	1980	1990	1970	1980	1990
Amer. Econ. Rev.	11.7	13.0	7.6	6.3	19.4	16.4	11.9
J. Polit. Econ.	10.7	7.4	6.0	3.7	11.8	13.6	9.3
Quart. J. Econ.	6.2	5.6	1.4	1.8	8.0	1.6	4.7
Rev. Econ. Star.	7.9	7.1	2.8	1.7	9.3	1.9	1.4
Rev. Econ. Stud.	5.2	5.6	2.0	1.4	8.4	4.0	4.0
Econometrica	14.9	5.2	5.0	4.5	5.8	12.9	11.6
Econ. J.	5.0	3.8	1.6	1.6	3.9	1.3	1.2
J. Monet. Econ.	-	-	1.7	1.9	-	4.8	4.8
J. Econ. Theory	-	-	1.9	1.6	-	4.7	5.1
All Core Journals	61.6	47.6	30.0	24.5	66.6	61.2	54.1

Source: a. Derived from Lovell (1973, p. 41).

increased by roughly 500 percent. While the core journals participated to some degree in this expansion, collectively they lost much of their citations market share to noncore journals.

Barriers to Entry?

While it appears to be the case that new entrants have taken market share away from the top journals in economics, in some cases becoming top journals themselves, there is a certain stability among the core journals over time. Noting this asymmetry, Pencavel (1992, p.4) suggested that it is "easier for journals to enter the class of high quality journals than for journals to fall out of that class." The evidence bears out Pencavel's insight. Of the top seven most highly cited economics journals in 1965, five are ranked among the top eleven economics journals in 1990 by impact-adjusted citations per article published during 1985-1989 (see Table 15.2). The other two, the *Economic Journal* and the *Review of Economics and Statistics* are ranked 24th and 28th with respect to that measure. In terms of impact-adjusted citations per character (Table 15.A2), the stability is even more striking: four of the top five journals in 1965 (*AER, Econometrica, JPE, QJE*), were ranked in the top five a quarter-century later.

It is hardly surprising that the increasing extent of the market from 1965-1990 supported an increase in the number of high-quality economics journals. As noted, Herfindahl Indexes indicate decreasing concentration over that time period, with respect to citations. However, even though the number of high-quality journals increased over that time period, the proportion of journals attracting the lion's share of citations did not increase. Table 15.6 reports the cumulative percent of citations attracted by economics journals in 1970, 1980, and 1990 (Figure 15.1 plots the associated Lorenz Curves).

The degree of inequality in the distribution of citations diminished somewhat during the 1970s but remained virtually constant from 1980 to 1990. For all three years, the top 16 (35, 58) percent of all journals attracted 50 (75, 90) percent of all citations in each year to articles published in the preceding five years. However, in terms of impact-adjusted citations, the cumulative distribution of citations is skewed much more heavily in favor of the top journals. Approximately five (12, 21) percent of the journals attract 50 (75, 90) percent of all impact-adjusted citations. Moreover, in terms of both unadjusted and impact-adjusted citations, the inequality in the distribution of citations has remained relatively constant over the decades in question. It thus appears that expansion of the market supports greater numbers of high quality journals, but only up to a point.

Table 15.6 The Cumulative Distribution of Citations, 1970-1990

Cumulative Percent of Journals	Cumulative Share of Unadjusted Citations			Cumulative Share of Impact-Adjusted Citations		
	1970	1980	1990	1970	1980	1990
10	0.8	0.6	0.9	0.00	0.00	0.00
20	2.4	2.4	2.7	0.00	0.00	0.26
30	4.6	5.4	5.6	0.05	0.06	0.89
40	7.5	9.3	9.6	0.20	0.20	1.78
50	12.3	15.1	15.0	0.59	0.54	3.15
60	19.0	22.1	22.3	2.60	1.50	5.52
76	27.5	31.6	31.3	5.15	4.40	9.74
80	39.8	43.4	43.2	11.74	11.57	18.83
90	61.4	59.7	60.6	26.78	28.10	43.07
100	100.0	100.0	100.0	100.00	100.00	100.00
percentage of top journals with 50% of all citations	16.0	16.0	16.0	10.0	5.1	5.4
percentage of top journals with 75% of all citations	34.0	35.5	37.2	18.0	12.6	10.9
percentage of top journals with 90% of all citations	56.0	58.9	59.7	32.0	21.5	21.7

Figure 15.1 Lorenz Curves of Citations, 1970-1990

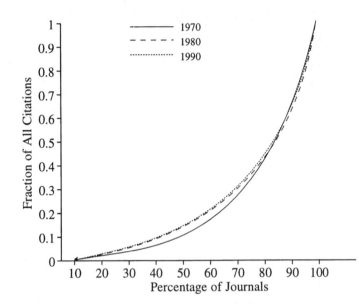

IV.   DISCUSSION

Like Liebowitz and Palmer before us, we have endeavored to rank economies journals in a manner that members of the profession find meaningful. Our rankings of economies journals in 1970 and 1990, using the methodology pioneered by L-P, in conjunction with their findings for 1980, permit us to draw a number of conclusions.

There was a steady decline in concentration of citations among the top economies journals over the period 1965-1990. In part this was due to existing journals taking market share, defined in terms of citations, from the premier journals.

New entrants into the economics journal market have also taken market share away from the long-established, premier journals. Nonetheless, the inequality in the distribution of citations in economics remained virtually constant from 1970 to 1990.

Inequality in the distribution of citations in economics is more pronounced with respect to impact-adjusted citations than unadjusted citations. That is, the citations that have the greatest impact tend to be sent from and received by a relatively small subset of economics journals.

Although the top general-interest journals in economics have more-or-less maintained their prominence over the past 20 years (in terms of rankings, not in terms of collective market share), there has been a decline in the influence of most of the "second-tier" general-interest journals. Their bad fortune in this regard apparently results from the increase in influence/importance of a number of specialty journals. The rapid entry by and success of field journals surely reflects the advantages of specialization. It has become virtually impossible to stay abreast of the scholarly literature in economics. One could probably do so in 1970 by "browsing" through the journals in the university library. The combination of budget cuts affecting library acquisitions during the 1980s and the previously documented explosion in the volume of economic journal literature, implies that the "browsing" technique of yesteryears is no longer an efficient means of identifying all relevant new contributions to the corpus of economic knowledge. The library no longer is able to subscribe to all of the journals that publish material that a scholar might find of interest. Moreover, even assuming no change in scholars' opportunity cost of time over the 1970-1990 period, the time constraint has become more binding due to the increased number of journals and articles being published. It is, however, cost-effective for scholars to browse through "field" journals that focus on topics of specific interest to them. While the scholar will not find all, or even most, of the articles published of direct and immediate relevance, the search costs of finding the relevant ones are minimized by the presence of field journals. This suggests that in the general competition among journal editors for high-quality papers (Laband and Piette, 1994), life must be getting increasingly difficult for editors of the second-tier, general-interest journals.

The relatively poor showing by economic history journals, considered as a group, in 1990 is consistent with the findings of the American Economic Association's Commission on Graduate Education in Economics (Lee Hansen, 1991). So, too, is the substantial entry by and impressive performance of numerous applied specialty journals.

The relative impact of economics journals focused on mathematics and statistics increased markedly between 1970 and 1990. In this regard our behavior as academic researchers stands in stark contrast to the fact that faculty, current graduate students and recent graduates all decry the emphasis on mathematics in the graduate economics curriculum of the late 1980s (Hansen, 1991). We cannot help but wonder whether the strong market showing (popularity) of the *Journal of Economic Perspectives*, with its emphasis on presentation of arguments and findings in essay form, reflects a widespread reaction within the profession to the mathematical/statistical emphasis of the 1970s and 1980s. If so, we would expect some fraction of new entrants, as well as current editors, in the 1990s to follow the *JEP*'s example with respect to style.

NOTES

1. It might be argued that the market for scientific knowledge claims differs from more conventional product markets. In this regard, the putative drawback to citations is that intensive citation may indicate shoddy science, if not downright fraud and that consumers would never knowingly spend their money on defective items. We have two responses. First, shoddy production is known to enhance value (and sales) occasionally in goods markets; such as when postage stamps are misprinted. Second, and more to the point, some portion of sales in goods markets occurs precisely because the buyers of that merchandise analyze it in hopes of producing an even better product than the seller from which they have just purchased.

2. A number of well-known journals started up during the 1965-69 period and thus are excluded from the 1970 rankings. Included in this set of new entrants are the *Canadian Journal of Economics, Applied Economics, Journal of Financial and Quantitative Analysis, Journal of Transport Economics and Policy, Journal of Economic Issues, Journal of Human Resources*, and the *Journal of Economic Theory*.

3. A large number of journals fell into this category and, thus, do not appear in our rankings. These include the *Accounting Review, American Historical Review, American Political Science Review, American Statistician, Foreign Affairs, Management Accounting, Michigan Academician*.

4. Included in this set of journals are the *Eastern Economic Journal* and the *Atlantic Economic Journal*. As of July 1, 1991 the Institute for Scientific Information (ISI), which compiles the *Social Sciences Citation Index* collected citation information on 155 journals classified as "Economics & Business" and 90 journals classified as "Law." By contrast, the *Journal of Economic Literature* reported publication information for 249 journals in the June 1991 issue. The *JEL* listed publication information for only four of the journals classified as law journals by ISI (*Journal of Legal Studies, Michigan Law Review, Journal of Law, Economics and Organization*, and *Yale Law Journal*). The journals classified by ISI as "Economics & Business" included 23 noneconomics journals, whereas only eight journals indexed by the *JEL* were obviously outside of the traditional sphere of economies. It thus appears that the *JEL* indexes approximately 90 economics journals that ISI does not. The 130 journals identified in our rankings for 1990 represent nearly the full set of economies journals indexed by ISI in that year, but clearly does not comprise an exhaustive set of the economics journals published during 1985-89. We are confident, however, that our rankings include all of the major economics journals published during that time.

5. Since 1977 the (ISI), which publishes both the *Social Science Citation Index* and the *Science Citation Index*, has published annually a compilation of citations for cited journals.
6. The *Journal of Economic Literature* began publishing in 1969. Hence, it is not included in the 1970 rankings. In both 1980 and 1990, however, it was the top journal in terms of unadjusted citations per article. This is undoubtedly due to the Journal's editorial policy of publishing a relatively small number of review articles that tend to be heavily cited. In addition, prior to 1969 the *American Journal of Agricultural Economics* was known as the *Journal of Farm Economics* and *Explorations in Economic History* was known as *Explorations in Entrepreneurial History*. Finally, the rankings are not affected significantly by the fact that we count citations for single years (1970, 1980, and 1990) only. Our data were sufficiently detailed to permit us to construct rankings based on two or three years' worth of citations for the 1965-69 and 1975-79 publications. The correlations between the rankings based on citations from a single year and those based on citations from two or three years are uniformly greater than .95.
7. We stress that our reliance on journals indexed by the *Index of Economics Articles* for the 1970 rankings and journals indexed by the *Social Sciences Citation Index* for all three years inevitably means that we do not have exhaustive information about citations in each year. However, the nonindexed journals probably are not cited with great frequency. Moreover, it seems unlikely that the distribution of citations in the nonindexed journals differs dramatically from the distribution in the indexed journals. Thus, we are confident that the reported rankings are fairly accurate.
8. We are happy to report that we were able to replicate the L-P results virtually perfectly (William Dewald, Jerry Thursby, and Richard Anderson 1986). We qualify the perfectly for two reasons: (1) there is at least one inconsistency in the L-P tables, where in Table 15.1, column 1 they rank *Population and Development Review* yet in columns 2 and 3 of that Table they rank *Population Studies*, and (2) we did not attempt to provide approximate values for the *Journal of Econometrics* and the *Journal of Mathematical Economics*.
9. The *American Economic Review* received the most citations in 1970, 1980, and 1990 to articles published during the five-year period preceding each of these years. Tables reporting journal rankings by total citations and total impact-adjusted citations are available upon request from the authors.
10. Like Liebowitz and Palmer, we found that convergence to a stable set of rankings occurred fairly quickly, in the neighborhood of 15-20 iterations. The rankings reported in Table 15.2 are the result of running 50 iterations.
11. Of the 50 journals ranked in 1970, the ones not ranked in 1990 are: *Economics of Planning*, *Lloyds Bank Review*, *Problems of Economics*, *IMF Staff Papers*, *Social and Economic Studies*, *South African Journal of Economics*, *German Economic Review*, *Indian Economic Journal*, and *Economia Internazionale*.
12. Since Liebowitz and Palmer's methodology was based on citations in 1980 to papers published 1975-79, journals which commenced publication in 1976 would not have appeared in their 1984 rankings. Similarly, because our methodology for 1990 was based on citations in 1990 to articles published 1985-89, with the exception of the *Journal of Economic Perspectives*, our

rankings do not include journals that started up more recently than 1985. A list of these 55 journals is available from the authors.

13. Our growth figures correspond closely with the growth rates found by Michael Lovell (1973) for output of economic articles from the late 1800s through 1965 and the number of economic journals from 1850-1969.

14. The extremely successful market penetration by the *JEP* likely has to do with its status as an AEA-sponsored journal. The AEA puts its credibility and reputational capital on the line with a new journal. This serves as an implicit guarantee of product quality to potential subscribers, thus serving to attract greater numbers of subscribers than a journal started up by an organization (such as an economics department) with less reputational capital at stake. The analogy to product markets, such as automobiles, is virtually perfect. It is easier for Ford than Laband-Piette Motors to successfully introduce a new car. That said, it is also true that brand name is no guarantee of successful market penetration with a new product, as Ford discovered with the Edsel. The strong market penetration by the *JEP* probably also is influenced by (high) caliber of authors invited to contribute papers, the timeliness, variety, and importance of the topical matter and the low marginal cost of receiving the Journal. The three AEA-sponsored journals (*AER*, *JEL*, and *JEP*) collectively attracted nearly 8.5 percent of all 1990 citations to the scholarly economics journal literature published during the preceding five years.

15. Lovell reported citations in 1965 among 108 journals, the "overwhelming majority being in economics" (p. 41).

16. These journals were identified by G. Stigler, Friedland, and S. Stigler (1992). Pencavel (1992) suggested a set of eleven "Gold Medal" journals that includes eight of Stigler's nine core journals. Arthur Diamond (1989) proposed a set of 27 core journals in economics. Our purpose is not to play favorites in this regard. Rather, our use of a set of "core" journals permits us to derive specific indices of market concentration and to observe changes in market concentration over time.

REFERENCES

American Economic Association. *Index of Economic Articles*, Vols.6-11, 1965-1969.

Dewald, William G., Jerry G. Thursby, and Richard G. Anderson (1986), "Replication in Empirical Economics: The *Journal of Money, Credit and Banking* Project," *American Economics Review,* **76**, 587-603.

Diamond, Arthur M. (1989), "The Core Journals of Economics," *Current Contents*, **1**, 4-11.

Gerrity, Dennis M., and Richard B. McKenzie (1978), "The Ranking of Southern Economics Departments: New Criterion and Further Evidence," *Southern Economics Journal*, **45**, 608-14.

Hansen, W. Lee (1991), "The Education and Training of Economics Doctorates," *Journal of Economic Literature,* **29**, 1054-87.

Institute for Scientific Information, *Social Sciences Citation Index.* Philadelphia, PA.: 1970, 1980, 1990.

Laband, David N., and John P. Sophocleus (1985), "Revealed Preference for Economics Journals: Citations as Dollar Votes," *Public Choice,* **46**, 317-24.

Laband, David N., and Michael J. Piette (1994), "Favoritism versus Search for Good Papers: Empirical Evidence On the Behavior of Journal Editors," *Journal of Political Economics,* **102**, 194-203; Chapter 8 of this volume.

Liebowitz, Stanley J., and John C. Palmer (1984), "Assessing the Relative Impacts of Economics Journals," *Journal of Economic Literature,* **22**, 77-88.

Lovell, Michael C. (1973), "The Production of Economic Literature: An Interpretation," *Journal of Economic Literature,* **11**, 27-55.

Pencavel, John (1992), "Comments on The Journals of Economics," manuscript presented at The Role of Journals in Scholarly Communication, A Centennial Conference in Memory of George J. Stigler.

Stigler, George J., and Claire Friendland (1975), "The Citation Practices of Doctoratesin Economics," *Journal of Political Economics,* **83**, 477-507.

Stigler George J., Claire Friendland, and Stephen M. Stigler (1992), "The Journals Of Economics," manuscript presented at The Role of Journals in Scholarly Communication, A Centennial Conference in Memory of George J. Stigler; Chapter 13 of this volume.

Table 15.A1 Rankings Based on Citations per Character

	1970 Citations to Articles Published 1965-1969[a]		1980 Citations to Articles Published 1975-1979[b]		1990 Citations to Articles Published 1985-1989[c]	
1	J. Polit. Econ.	100.0	J. Polit. Econ.	100.0	Amer. Econ. Rev.	100.0
2	Rev. Econ. Stud.	46.5	Amer. Econ. Rev.	93.0	J. Cons. Res.	78.0
3	Amer. Econ. Rev.	44.5	J. Econ. Lit.	81.6	J. Finan. Econ.	75.8
4	Quart. J. Econ.	38.4	J. Finan. Econ.	61.6	Econometrica	69.2
5	Rev. Econ. Statist.	37.2	Rev. Econ. Statist.	61.2	J. Polit. Econ.	65.8
6	Economica	33.8	J. Finance	58.6	J. Ace. Econ.	64.5
7	Econ. J.	32.6	Yale Law J.	58.2	Amer. Econ. Rev. Papers & Proc.	61.8
8	J. Reg. Sci.	29.9	Econometrica	57.4	J. Econ. Lit.	60.4
9	Econometrica	28.8	J. Monet. Econ.	56.7	Ind. Lab. Relat. Rev.	58.3
10	J. Bus.	27.0	Bell J. Econ. (Rand J. Econ.)	54.0	Yale Law J.	56.6
11	J. Finance	27.0	J. Amer. Statist Assoc.	48.6	J. Econ. Perspectives	55.2
12	Amer. Econ. Rev. Papers & Proc.	24.2	Brookings Pap. Econ. Act.	46.7	Quart. J. Econ.	52.6
13	Oxford Econ. Pap.	20.2	Econ. J.	43.7	J. Finance	50.6
14	Int. Econ. Rev.	17.7	J. Cons. Res.	42.1	J. Monet. Econ.	49.8
15	J. Law Econ.	16.4	J. Roy. Statist. Soc. Ser. B-Meth.	41.9	Mich. Law Rev.	47.7
16	Kyklos	16.3	J. Urban Econ.	41.8	J. Legal Stud.	46.5
17	J. Amer. Statist. Assoc.	15.7	Quart. J. Econ.	41.6	J. Bus.	44.7
18	Public Finance	15.6	Rev. Econ. Stud.	41.1	J. Urban Econ.	43.4

Rank	Journal		Journal		Journal	
19	Ind. Rel.	15.1	J. Law Econ.	40.8	J. Roy. Statist. Soc. Ser. B-Meth.	42.4
20	J. Econ. Hist.	14.9	Demography	39.4	J. Money Credit Banking	41.2
21	Southern Econ. J.	14.8	Amer. Econ. Rev. Papers & Proc.	38.1	Bell J. Econ. (Rand J. Econ.)	39.5
22	Land Econ.	14.4	J. Legal Stud.	37.3	Econ. J.	38.0
23	Econ. Devel. Cult. Change	14.1	Inquiry	37.0	Ind. Rel.	37.2
24	Lloyd's Bank Rev.	13.5	J. Human Res.	36.2	J. Health Econ.	36.3
25	Econ. Inquiry (Western Econ. J.)	13.4	J. Math. Econ.	35.3	J. Roy. Statist. Soc. Ser. A-Gen.	35.5
26	Econ. Planning	13.3	J. Econometrics	35.2	Population Devel. Rev.	35.4
27	Nat. Tax J.	13.2	Int. Econ. Rev.	34.7	Oxford Bull. Econ. Statist.	35.4
28	Econ. Record	10.2	J. Econ. Theory	33.9	Rev. Econ. Statist.	34.9
29	Econ. Hist. Rev.	9.5	Ind. Lab. Relat. Rev.	32.2	J. Amer. Statist. Assoc.	34.7
30	Amer. J. Agr. Econ.	9.1	Economica	32.1	J. Law Econ.	34.1
31	Ind. Lab. Relat. Rev.	8.5	Econ. Inquiry	32.1	Rev. Econ. Stud.	33.9
32	Explorations Econ. Hist.	7.6	Scand. J. Econ.	30.7	J. Int. Bus. Stud.	33.8
33	J. Ind. Econ.	7.4	J. Public Econ.	30.6	Demography	33.3
34	Bus. Hist. Bey.	6.0	J. Money Credit Banking	30.1	J. Econometrics	33.0
35	Manchester Sch. Econ. Soc. Stud.	6.0	J. Int. Econ.	29.4	Amer. Agr. Econ.	32.3
36	Rev. Soc. Econ.	5.9	Amer. J. Agr. Econ.	29.3	J. Econ. Theory	30.8
37	J. Roy. Statist. Soc. Ser. A-Gen.	5.8	Ind. Relat.	29.1	Sloan Manage. Rev.	29.5
38	Quart. Rev. Econ. Bus.	5.7	J. Bus.	28.2	J. Acc. Res.	29.3
39	Scot. J. Polit. Econ.	5.5	Mich. Law Rev.	27.9	J. Fin. Quant. Anal.	27.9

Table 15.A1 continued

	1970 Citations to Articles Published 1965-1969[a]		1980 Citations to Articles Published 1975-1979[b]		1990 Citations to Articles Published 1985-1989[c]	
40	Int. Monet. Fund Staff Pap.	5.3	Reg. Stud.	27.0	J. Human Res.	27.3
41	Get. Econ. Rev.	5.2	Public Pol.	26.8	Mon. Lab. Rev.	27.1
42	J. Devel. Stud.	5.1	Econ. Geogr.	25.9	Calif. Manage. Rev.	26.4
43	Scandinavian J. Econ.	4.8	Nat. Tax J.	25.5	J. Math. Econ.	26.1
44	Soc. Econ. Stud.	4.2	J. Reg. Sci.	25.4	J. Int. Econ.	26.1
45	Yale Essays Econ.	4.1	Urban Stud.	25.2	Land Econ.	24.6
46	S. African J. Econ.	3.7	Kyklos	24.8	J. Lab. Econ.	24.3
47	Prob. Econ.	3.0	Oxford Econ. Pap.	23.8	J. Bus. Econ. Statist.	23.4
48	Weltwirtsch. Arch.	2.4	Soc. Sci. Quart.	23.7	J. Ind. Econ.	23.3
49	Economia Internazionale	1.4	Pol. Anal.	23.4	Public Choice	22.5
50	Indian Econ. J.	0.6	Public Choice	22.2	Economica	22.3
51	-		Southern Econ. J.	22.0	Inquiry-J. Health Care Organ.	21.2
52	-		Brit. J. Ind. Relat.	21.8	Brookings Pap. Econ. Act.	21.0
53	-		Population Stud.	21.7	J. Environ. Econ. Manage.	20.4
54	-		Sloan Manage. Rev.	20.9	Econ. Geog.	19.6
55	-		Can. J. Econ.	20.0	J. Econ. Educ.	19.0
56	-		J. Acc. Res.	19.5	J. Reg. Sci.	18.2
57	-		Land Econ.	19.3	J. Econ. Hist.	18.2
58	-		J. Finan Quant. Anal.	19.2	J. Public Econ.	18.2
59	-		J. Environ. Econ. Manage.	18.9	J. Pol. Anal. Manage.	18.1

		Journal		Journal	
60	-	J. Econ. Hist.	18.6	J. Compar. Econ.	17.8
61	-	Labor Hist.	18.4	Econ. Inquiry (West. Econ. J.)	17.4
62	-	J. Ind. Econ.	18.1	Int. J. Ind. Organ.	17.2
63	-	Econ. Devel. Cult. Change	17.9	Int. Econ. Rev.	17.1
64	-	Manchester Sch. Econ. Soc. Stud.	17.9	Oxford Econ. Pap.	17.1
65	-	Econ. Letters	17.9	Econ. Hist. Rev.	16.5
66	-	Scot. J. Polit. Econ.	17.7	Europ. Econ. Rev.	16.1
67	-	J. Roy. Statist. Soc. Ser. A-Gen.	17.5	J. Forecasting	16.1
68	-	Lloyds Bank Rev.	17.1	J. Econ. Dynam. Control	15.6
69	-	Beg. Sci. Urban Econ.	16.9	Brit. J. Ind. Relat.	15
70	-	Econ. Hist. Rev.	16.5	Econ. Letters	1.5.3
71	-	Europ. Econ. Rev.	15.9	J. Lab. Res.	15.2
72	-	J. World Trade Law	15.7	J. Econ. Behav. Organ.	15.0
73	-	Weltwirtsch. Arch.	14.9	Southern Econ. J.	14.8
74	-	Natural Res. J.	14.4	Reg. Stud.	14.5
75	-	J. Devel. Econ.	13.5	Scand. J. Econ.	14.2
76	-	Worm Devel.	13.2	Reg. Sci. Urban Econ.	14.2
77	-	Exiplorations Econ. Hist.	13.0	Kyklos	14.1
78	-	Econ. Rec.	12.8	Nat. Tax J.	13.4
79	-	J. Devel. Stud.	11.6	Soc. Sci. Quart.	13.4
80	-	Appl. Econ.	11.4	Soc. Res.	13.3
81	-	Sci. Society	11.2	Econ. Devel. Cult. Change	13.3

Table 15.A1 continued

	1970 Citations to Articles Published 1965-1969[a]	1980 Citations to Articles Published 1975-1979[b]		1990 Citations to Articles Published 1985-1989[c]	
82	-	Public Finance Quart.	11.1	J. Post Keynesian Econ.	13.2
83	-	J. Risk Ins.	10.9	Exploration Econ. Hist.	13.1
84	-	J. Econ. Issues	10.8	Int. Reg. Sci. Rev.	12.7
85	-	Calif. Manage. Rev.	10.6	J. Devel. Econ.	12.5
86	-	Soc. Res.	10.3	Can. J. Econ.	12.4
87	-	Amer. J. Econ. Soc.	10.1	J. Devel. Stud.	12.3
88	-	Oxford Bull. Econ. Statist.	9.9	Weltwirtsch. Arch.	12.0
89	-	J. Econ. Educ.	9.9	Rev. Soc. Econ.	12.0
90	-	Mort. Lab. Rev.	9.4	Cambridge J. Econ.	11.8
91	-	J. Econ. Bus.	9.4	Manchester Sch. Econ. Soc. Stud.	11.8
92	-	Quart. Rev. Econ. Bus.	9.3	World Devel.	11.7
93	-	Int. J. Soc. Econ.	9.1	Soc. Choice Welfare	11.6
94	-	Public Finance	8.8	J. Finan. Res.	11.6
95	-	J. Transp. Econ. Pol.	8.5	J. Macroecon.	11.3
96	-	Hist. Polit. Econ.	8.5	J. Risk Ins.	10.1
97	-	Int. Lab. Rev.	7.8	Sci. Society	10.1
98	-	J. Devel. Areas	7.5	J. Econ. Issues	10.0
99	-	Rev. Soc. Econ.	7.2	World Econ.	9.8
100	-	J. Common Market Stud.	7.0	J. Banking Finance	9.7
101	-	J. Int. Bus. Stud.	6.0	Public Finance Quart.	9.5

102	-	5.4	Bus. Hist. Rev.	-	8.9	Urban Stud.
103	-	5.1	Nebraska J. Econ. Bus.	-	45.4	J. World Trade
104	-	5.0	Int. Soc. Sci. J.	-	8.2	Cato J.
105	-	2.7	Malayan Econ. Rev.	-	8.2	Public Finance
106	-	1.2	J. Econ. Stud.	-	8.0	J. Transp. Econ. Pol.
107	-	0.8	Matekon	-	7.5	Energy Econ.
108	-	0.5	Australian J. Agr. Econ.	-	7.5	Labor Hist.
109	-	-	-	-	7.3	Quart. Rev. Econ. Bus.
110	-	-	-	-	6.9	Appl. Econ.
111	-	-	-	-	6.7	Amer. J. Econ. Soc.
112	-	-	-	-	6.5	Int. Lab. Rev.
113	-	-	-	-	6.4	Econ. Rec.
114	-	-	-	-	6.1	J. Common Market Stud.
115	-	-	-	-	6.1	Hist. Polit. Econ.
116	-	-	-	-	6.0	J. Econ. Bus.
117	-	-	-	-	5.8	Scot. J. Polit. Econ.
118	-	-	-	-	5.3	Natural Res. J.
119	-	-	-	-	4.7	J. Devel. Areas
120	-	-	-	-	4.7	Rev. Black Polit. Econ.
121	-	-	-	-	4.3	Int. J. Soc. Econ.
122	-	-	-	-	4.1	Manage. Dec. Econ.
123	-	-	-	-	4.0	Bus. Hist. Rev.
124	-	-	-	-	3.9	Econ. Modelling
125	-	-	-	-	3.9	Int. Soc. Sci. J.
126	-	-	-	-	3.3	J. Econ. Stud.
127	-	-	-	-	3.3	Australian J. Agr. Econ.

Table 15.A1 continued

	1970 Citations to Articles Published 1965-1969[a]	1980 Citations to Articles Published 1975-1979[b]		1990 Citations to Articles Published 1985-1989[c]	
128	-	-	-	*Rev. Bus. Econ. Res.*	3.2
129	-	-	-	*Econometric Theory*	2.5
130	-	-	-	*Matekon*	0.0

Sources:

a Tabulated by the authors from the 50th ed.

b Liebowitz and Palmer, as calculated from the *Social Science Citation Index*, vol. 6, 1980.

c Calculated from the *Social Science Citation Index*, vol. 6, 1990.

Table 15.A2 Rankings Based on Impact Adjusted Citations per Character

	1970 Citations to Articles Published 1965-1969[a]		1980 Citations to Articles Published 1975-1979[b]		1990 Citations to Articles Published 1985-1989[c]	
1	J. Polit. Econ.	100.0	J. Polit. Econ.	100.0	Amer. Econ. Rev.	100.0
2	Rev. Econ. Stud.	43.2	J. Finan. Econ.	99.0	J. Finan. Econ.	90.7
3	Amer. Econ. Rev.	41.4	Amer. Econ. Rev.	76.6	Econometrica	89.0
4	Quart. J. Econ.	34.4	J. Monet. Econ.	61.1	J. Polit. Econ.	79.1
5	Rev. Econ. Statist.	30.2	J. Finance	60.1	Quart. J. Econ.	64.5
6	J. Finance	22.6	J. Econ. Lit.	55.0	J. Monet. Econ.	59.3
7	Econ. J.	20.9	Econometrica	47.6	J. Econ. Theory	51.1
8	Economica	20.7	Bell J. of Econ. (Rand J. Econ.)	46.4	J. Finance	51.0
9	Econometrica	20.0	Brookings Pap. Econ. Act.	37.0	Rev. Econ. Stud.	47.6
10	J. Bus.	17.0	Rev. Econ. Stud.	36.5	Bell J. Econ. (Rand J. Econ.)	46.5
11	Amer. Econ. Rev. Pap. & Proc.	16.3	Economica	36.2	J. Econ. Perspectives	37.0
12	Int. Econ. Rev.	15.0	J. Math. Econ.	35.6	J. Math. Econ.	32.4
13	Econ. Planning	10.7	Quart. J. Econ.	35.2	J. Acc. Econ.	28.7
14	Oxford Econ. Pap.	8.6	J. Econ. Theory	32.1	J. Bus.	27.1
15	Econ. Rec.	6.6	Amer. Econ. Rev. Papers & Proc.	31.4	J. Econometrics	26.8
16	J. Amer. Statist. Assoc.	6.0	Rev. Econ. Statist.	30.0	Amer. Econ. Rev. Pap. & Proc.	26.7
17	Southern Econ. J.	5.1	J. Econometrics	29.6	J. Finan. Quant. Anal.	21.3

18	J. Law Econ.	4.1	J. Inter. Econ.	29.6	J. Econ. Lit.	18.6
19	J. Roy. Statist. Soc. Ser. A--Gen.	4.0	Int. Econ. Rev.	29.3	J. Money Credit Banking	17.9
20	J. Econ. Hist.	3.7	J. Human Res.	28.1	J. Lab. Econ.	17.1
21	Yale Essays Econ.	3.4	J. Money Credit Banking	24.2	Int. Econ. Rev.	16.7
22	Econ. Inquiry (Wester Econ. J.)	3.2	J. Public Econ.	23.6	Brookings Pap. Econ. Act.	14.7
23	J. Devel. Stud.	2.7	Econ. J.	22.5	Rev. Econ. Statist.	14.0
24	Kyklos	2.7	Econ. Inquiry	22.4	J. Law Econ.	12.8
25	Econ. Devel. Cult. Change	2.5	Scand. J. Econ.	22.3	Econ. J.	12.8
26	Lloyd's Bank Rev.	2.4	J. Law Econ.	21.7	J. Bus. Econ. Statist.	12.4
27	Nat. Tax J.	2.3	J. Bus.	21.1	J. Econ. Edu.	12.2
28	Public Finance	2.2	Ind. Lab. Relat. Rev.	18.5	Ind. Lab. Relat. Rev.	11.7
29	Rev. Soc. Econ.	2.1	Can. J. Econ.	18.0	J. Public Econ.	10.8
30	Quart. Rev. Econ. Bus.	2.0	J. Finan. Quant. Anal.	13.2	J. Int. Econ.	10.8
31	J. Reg. Sci.	1.7	J. Ind. Econ.	12.6	Econ. Letters	9.6
32	Weltwirtsch. Arch.	1.6	Southern Econ. J.	12.4	J. Ind. Econ.	9.5
33	Amer. J. Agri. Econ.	1.5	J. Urban Econ.	12.2	Int. J. Ind. Organ.	8.5
34	J. Ind. Econ.	1.4	Nat. Tax J.	11.8	J. Econ. Dynam. Control	8.1
35	Manchester Sch. Econ. Soc. Stud.	1.4	J. Acc. Res.	10.6	Soc. Choice Welfare	7.3
36	Land Econ.	1.3	Kyklos	10.0	J. Human Res.	7.3
37	Economia Internazionale	1.2	Manchester Sch. Econ. Soc. Stud.	9.5	J. Banking Finance	6.7
38	Exploration Econ. Hist.	1.0	J. Amer. Statist. Assoc.	7.5	Econ. Inquiry (West. Econ. J.)	5.9
39	Scand. J. Econ.	0.8	J. Legal Stud.	7.3	J. Amer. Statist. Assoc.	5.5
40	Int. Monet. Fund Staff Pap.	0.8	Public Finance	7.2	J. Urban Econ.	5.3

Table 15.A2 continued

	1970 Citations to Articles Published 1965-1969[a]		1980 Citations to Articles Published 1975-1979[b]		1990 Citations to Articles Published 1985-1989[c]	
41	Ind. Relat.	0.6	Europ. Econ. Rev.	6.5	Demography	5.1
42	Prob. Econ.	0.5	Oxford Econ. Rev.	6.2	J. Roy. Statist. Soc. Ser. B-Meth.	4.8
43	Econ. Hist. Rev.	0.2	Public Choice	5.3	J. Econ. Hist.	4.8
44	Bus. Hist. Rev.	0.1	Public Finance Quart.	4.7	Oxford Bull. Econ. Statist.	4.4
45	Ind. Lab. Relat. Rev.	0.1	J. Reg. Sci.	4.6	J. Finan. Res.	4.2
46	Indian Econ. J.	0.0	Appl. Econ.	4.1	Economica	4.1
47	Scot. J. Polit. Econ.	0.0	J. Devel. Econ.	3.7	Public Choice	3.9
48	S. African J. Econ.	0.0	Ind. Rel.	3.5	J. Risk Ins.	3.8
49	Soc. Econ. Stud.	0.0	J. Roy. Statist. Soc. Ser. A-Gen.	3.5	J. Acc. Res.	3.7
50	Ger. Econ. Rev.	0.0	J. Econ. Educ.	3.2	Europ. Econ. Rev.	3.6
51	-		J. Environ. Econ. Manage.	3.2	Scand. J. Econ.	3.6
52	-		Brit. J. Ind. Relat.	3.1	Econometric Theory	3.3
53	-		Weltwirtsch. Arch.	3.0	J. Comp. Econ	3.1
54	-		Amer. J. Agr. Econ.	2.6	J. Econ. Behav. Organ.	2.7
55	-		Lloyds Bank Rev.	2.6	J. Lab. Res.	2.5
56	-		Econ. Letters	2.5	Explorations Econ. Hist.	2.4
57	-		J. Cons. Res.	2.4	Public Finance	2.2
58	-		Reg. Sci. Urban Econ.	2.2	Cato J.	1.8
59	-		Scot. J. Polit. Econ.	2.1	J. Devel. Econ.	1.8
60	-		Land Econ.	2.0	Amer. J. Agr. Econ.	1.8

No.		Journal	Value	Journal	Value
61	-	Urban Stud.	1.9	Southern Econ. J.	16.5
62	-	J. Econ. Bus.	1.8	J. Legal Stud.	1.6
63	-	Oxford Bull. Econ. Statist.	1.7	J. Macroecon.	1.4
64	-	J. Econ. Issues	1.5	Ind. Relat.	1.1
65	-	Inquiry	1.5	Kyklos	1.1
66	-	Quart. Rev. Econ. Bus.	1.3	J. Health Econ.	1.1
67	-	Econ. Rec.	1.3	Can. J. Econ.	1.1
68	-	Explorations Econ. Hist.	1.1	Oxford Econ. Pap.	1.0
69	-	J. Econ. Hist.	1.1	Public Finance Quart.	1.0
70	-	Econ. Devel. Cult. Change	1.1	Brit. J. Ind. Relat.	1.0
71	-	J. Develop. Areas	1.0	Manchester. Sch. Econ. Soc. Stud.	0.8
72	-	Yale Law J.	1.0	J. Royal Stat. Soc. Set. A-Gen.	0.7
73	-	Nebr. J. Econ. Bus.	0.9	World Econ.	0.6
74	-	J. Roy. Statist. Soc. Ser. B-Meth.	0.9	Population Devel. Rev.	0.6
75	-	Sloan Manage. Rev.	0.9	Nat. Tax J.	0.6
76	-	Rev. Soc. Econ.	0.9	Appl. Econ.	0.5
77	-	Mon. Lab. Rev.	0.8	Quart. Rev. Econ. Bus.	0.4
78	-	Hist. Polit. Econ.	0.7	J. Int. Bus. Stud.	0.4
79	-	J. Risk Ins.	0.7	J. Forecasting	0.4
80	-	J. Devel. Stud.	0.6	Scot. J. Polit. Econ.	0.4
81	-	Int. Lab. Rev.	0.5	Reg. Sci. Urban Econ.	0.3
82	-	Int. J. Soc. Econ.	0.5	Mon. Lab. Rev.	0.3
83	-	J. Transp. Econ. Pol.	0.4	Econ. Model.	0.3
84	-	Reg. Stud.	0.4	Cambridge J. Econ.	0.3

Table 15.A2 continued

	1970 Citations to Articles Published 1965-1969[a]	1980 Citations to Articles Published 1975-1979[b]		1990 Citations to Articles Published 1985-1989[c]	
85	-	Public Pol.	0.3	Econ. Devel. Chlt. Change	0.2
86	-	Econ. Geogr.	0.3	Land Econ.	0.2
87	-	Malayan Econ. Rev.	0.3	Weltwirtsch. Arch.	0.2
88	-	J. Int. Bus. Stud.	0.2	Econ. Rec.	0.2
89	-	Lab. Hist.	0.2	J. Environ. Econ. Manage.	0.2
90	-	World Devel.	0.1	J. Econ. Stud.	0.2
91	-	Econ. Hist. Rev.	0.1	Australian J. Agr. Econ.	0.1
92	-	Amer. J. Econ. Sociology	0.1	J. Reg. Sci	0.1
93	-	Mich. Law Rev.	0.1	Econ. Hist. Rev.	0.1
94	-	Soc. Sci. Quart.	0.0	Energy Econ.	0.1
95	-	Natural Res. J.	0.0	Rev. Soc. Econ.	0.1
96	-	Calif. Manage. Rev.	0.0	J. Devel. Stud.	0.1
97	-	Population Stud.	0.0	J. Post Keynesian Econ.	0.1
98	-	Australian J. Agr. Econ.	0.0	Bus. Hist. Rev.^	0.1
99	-	Pol. Anal.	0.0	J. Transp. Econ. Pol. 0.1	
100	-	Bus. Hist. Rev.	0.0	Int. J. Soc. Econ.	0.1
101	-	Demography	0.0	J. Common Market Stud.	0.1
102	-	J. World Trade Law	0.0	J. Econ. Bus.	0.1
103	-	J. Common Market Stud.	0.0	Yale Law J.	0.1
104	-	Sci. Society	0.0	J. Econ. Issues	0.1
105	-	Soc. Res.	0.0	J. Pol. Anal. Manage,	0.0
106	-	Matekon	0.0	World Devel.	0.0

No.					
107	-	Int. Soc. Sci. J.	0.0	Reg. Stud.	0.0
108	-	J. Econ. Stud.	0.0	Hist. Polit. Econ.	0.0
109	-	-	-	Inquiry-J. Health Care Org.	0.0
110	-	-	-	Urban Stud.	0.0
111	-	-	-	Manag. Dec. Econ.	0.0
112	-	-	-	Mich. Law Rev.	0.0
113	-	-	-	Amer. J. Econ. SocioLogy	0.0
114	-	-	-	Calif. Manage. Rev.	0.0
115	-	-	-	Int. Lab. Rev.	0.0
116	-	-	-	Int. Soc. Sci. J.	0.0
117	-	-	-	Econ. Geogr.	0.0
118	-	-	-	J. Cons. Res.	0.0
119	-	-	-	J. Devel. Areas	0.0
120	-	-	-	Lab. Hist.	0.0
121	-	-	-	J. World Trade	0.0
122	-	-	-	Sci. Society	0.0
123	-	-	-	Matekon	0.0
124	-	-	-	Nat. Res. J.	0.0
125	-	-	-	Int. Reg. Sci. Rev.	0.0
126	-	-	-	Rev. Bus. Econ. Res.	0.0
127	-	-	-	Rev. Black Polit. Econ.	0.0
128	-	-	-	Soc. Res.	0.0
129	-	-	-	Soc. Sci. Quart.	0.0
130	-	-	-	Sloan Manage. Rev.	0.0

Sources: a Tabulated by the authors from the 50 journals listed. b Liebowitz and Palmer, as calculated from the Social Science Citation Index, vol. 6, 1980. c Calculated from the Social Science Citation Index, vol. 6, 1990.

Index